CU00746117

PagePlus 11
Resource Guide

Second Edition
January 2006

This book has been created and output in entirety using Serif PagePlus

This document, and the software described in it, is furnished under an end user License Agreement, which is included with the product. The agreement specifies the permitted and prohibited uses.

© 2005 Serif (Europe) Ltd. All rights reserved. No part of this publication may be reproduced in any form without the express written permission of Serif (Europe) Ltd.

All Serif product names are trademarks of Serif (Europe) Ltd. Microsoft, Windows and the Windows logo are registered trademarks of Microsoft Corporation. All other trademarks acknowledged.

Serif PagePlus 11.0 © 2005 Serif (Europe) Ltd.

Companies and names used in samples are fictitious.

Clipart samples from Serif ArtPacks © Serif (Europe) Ltd. & Paul Harris

Portions images © 1997-2002 Nova Development Corporation; © 1995 Expressions Computer Software; © 1996-98 CreatiCom, In.; 1996 Cliptoart; © 1996-99 Hemera; © 1997 Multimedia Agency Corporation; © 1997-98 Seattle Support Group. Rights of all parties reserved.

Digital image content© 2005 JupiterImages Corporation. All Rights Reserved.

Portions TrueType Font content © 2002 Arts & Letters Corporation. All Rights Reserved.

Bitstream Font content © 1981-2005 Bitstream Inc. All rights reserved.

Portions graphics import/export technology © AccuSoft Corp. & Eastman Kodak Company & LEAD Technologies, Inc.

THE PROXIMITY HYPHENATION SYSTEM © 1989 Proximity Technology Inc. All rights reserved.

THE PROXIMITY/COLLINS DATABASE® © 1990 William Collins Sons & Co. Ltd.; © 1990 Proximity Technology Inc. All rights reserved.

THE PROXIMITY/MERRIAM-WEBSTER DATABASE® © 1990 Merriam-Webster Inc.; © 1990 Proximity Technology Inc. All rights reserved.

The Sentry Spelling-Checker Engine © 2000 Wintertree Software Inc.

The ThesDB Thesaurus Engine © 1993-97 Wintertree Software Inc.

WGrammar Grammar-Checker Engine © 1998 Wintertree Software Inc.

PANTONE® Colours displayed in the software application or in the user documentation may not match PANTONE-identified standards. Consult current PANTONE Colour Publications for accurate colour. PANTONE® and other Pantone, Inc. trademarks are the property of Pantone, Inc. © Pantone Inc., 2001.

Pantone, Inc. is the copyright owner of colour data and/or software which are licensed to Serif (Europe) Ltd. to distribute for use only in combination with PagePlus. PANTONE Colour Data and/or Software shall not be copied onto another disk or into memory unless as part of the execution of PagePlus.

How to contact us

Our main office (UK, Europe):

The Software Centre, PO Box 2000, Nottingham, NG11 7GW, UK

Main	(0115) 914 2000
Registration (UK only)	(0800) 376 1989
Sales (UK only)	(0800) 376 7070
Technical Support (UK only)	(0845) 345 6770
Customer Service (UK only)	(0845) 345 6770
Customer Service/	
Technical Support (International)	+44 115 914 9090
General Fax	(0115) 914 2020
Technical Support E-mail	**support@serif.co.uk**

American office (USA, Canada):

The Software Center, 13 Columbia Drive, Suite 5, Amherst, NH 03031

Main	(603) 889-8650
Registration	(800) 794-6876
Sales	(800) 55-SERIF or 557-3743
Technical Support	(603) 886-6642
Customer Service	(800) 489-6720
General Fax	(603) 889-1127
Technical Support E-mail	**support@serif.com**

Online

Visit us on the Web at	**http://www.serif.com**
Serif newsgroups	**news://news.serif.com/**
	SerifPagePlus

International

Please contact your local distributor/dealer. For further details please contact us at one of our phone numbers above.

Comments or other feedback

We want to hear from you! E-mail **feedback@serif.com** with your ideas and comments.

Contents

Introduction

Welcome to the PagePlus 11.0 Resource Guide—whether you are new to PagePlus 11 or a seasoned professional publisher, the *Resource* Guide offers content to help you get the best out of PagePlus. From a range of novice and professional tutorials to get you started or to help accomplish a complex project, to full-colour previews of PagePlus's Design Templates, Schemes, Object Styles and more, the Resource Guide is something we hope you can return to time and time again.

About the Guide

The *Resource Guide* is your key to getting even more out of PagePlus and is organized into the following chapters.

- **Tutorials** Step-by-step training covering the basics of using PagePlus and how to tackle some interesting projects.
- **Templates** A useful gallery of all the Design Templates available with PagePlus 11 and its Resource CD.
- **Colour Schemes** Attractive previews of PagePlus 11's Schemes.
- **Object Styles** Full-colour previews of the "instant effect" Object Styles.
- **Image Gallery** An at-a-glance guide to all the images included with the PagePlus 11 Design Templates and on the Resource CD.
- **Fonts** Never be without a typeface again—preview of all available fonts.

How the Resource Guide was made

This full-colour *Resource Guide* was created and output using PagePlus, employing many of PagePlus's features. These include BookPlus to unify separate publications with a common page numbering system, Mail and Photo Merge with Repeating Areas to automatically create pages with picture content based on a folder of images, and the comprehensive Find and Replace functionality to apply text styles consistently (and quickly) throughout.

Finally, each chapter has been incorporated into a PagePlus Book comprised of multiple publication "chapters" and has been published as a press-ready PDF, accurately maintaining all text, fonts, images, and native colouring, all in a suitable CMYK colour format for professional printing. Be sure to read the Tutorials chapter for more information about PagePlus's powerful new features!

Tutorials

1

Welcome to the Serif PagePlus 11 Tutorials

These tutorials include material for beginners as well as more experienced PagePlus users.

If you're new to the PagePlus Desktop Publishing (DTP) environment, following the **Learning Lab** sequence will give you an opportunity to experiment with creative tools and techniques. To begin, you'll produce a basic publication using a variety of PagePlus objects. Subsequent tutorials develop this publication cumulatively, guiding you to explore each object's possibilities. You can start right in with Learning Lab 1, or jump forward at any point. We've provided versions of the Lab publication at each stage of completion as part of your PagePlus installation.

In addition to the **Learning Lab** structured tutorials, we also offer two other sections:

- **Beyond the Basics**—Intermediate-level coverage of topics like PDF publishing and PagePlus productivity.

- **PagePlus Projects**—Step-by-step guidance to boost your mastery of PagePlus capabilities.

To access files needed by the tutorials, browse to the **Workspace** folder in your PagePlus installation. Usually, you'll find this folder in the following location: **C:\Program Files\Serif\PagePlus\11.0\Tutorials\Workspace**

We hope you enjoy working through these exercises!

Learning Lab 1: Creation Tools

Welcome to the PagePlus Learning Lab—you'll be a desktop publishing expert in no time! This tutorial introduces you to the objects that serve as the building blocks of PagePlus publications. The goal is to make sure you've encountered these basic creation tools prior to tackling other tutorials. You'll produce a collection of simple objects that you can use later on in the Learning Lab sequence.

1 To get started, run PagePlus (or choose **File/New/New from Startup Wizard...**), and from the Startup Wizard click **Start from Scratch.** Choose the **Regular/Normal** category, select a Portrait, Letter or A4 **(illustrated) page size,** and then click **Finish** to create a new blank publication. Your working view should be set so you can see the whole page; click the **Full Page** button on the top **View** toolbar if necessary.

A4

The creation tools are available on the left toolbar—the Tools toolbar. To select any tool, you simply click its button. We'll try them out, one by one.

> It's always a good idea to save your work as you proceed. To continue working with this file in future tutorials, we suggest you save it as **My Lab.ppp** in a convenient folder.

Text frames are the basic containers for text in PagePlus. They work equally well for single words, standalone paragraphs, multi-page articles, or chapter text.

2 To create a rectangular frame, click the  **Text Frame Tool** button. Move the cursor back over the page area and observe the horizontal and vertical rulers as you move around. The moving lines on each ruler let you see exactly where the cursor is located on the page at all times.

3 Move the cursor so the lines are at the 1 inch/2 cm mark on each ruler, then click and drag out a rectangle to the 4 in/10 cm mark horizontally and to 3 in/8 cm vertically. Release the mouse button and the new frame appears.

Notice that the active tool has reverted to the ▶ Pointer and that there's a flashing cursor inside the frame, waiting for you to type something.

4 Type the words 'Standard text frame.' The text will be small, but that's fine for now.

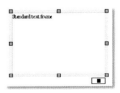

5 Click somewhere on the page outside the frame and you'll deselect the frame. Now click once in the frame and the flashing cursor reappears.

Creation Tools

Notice that the frame object itself has a light grey bounding box with eight darker handles (see previous illustration). The colour of these handles represents the layer to which the object is assigned and so can appear to be different, but we'll leave them as they are for now and investigate layers later on.

6 Click the frame's bounding box to select the whole frame as an object. The flashing cursor has disappeared.

7 Try moving and resizing the frame object using the bounding box and handles. When resizing via one of the corner handles, hold down the **Shift** key to preserve the frame's proportions. As you drag, notice that the **Transform** tab, HintLine, and rulers provide feedback on the selected object's current size and position. As you put together a publication, that feedback will be valuable regardless of the kind of object you're working with.

Once you've selected any PagePlus object in this way, you can drag the bounding box to move the object around, or drag the handles to resize the object.

8 Further down the Tools toolbar, click the 🔲 **Shaped Frame** button. This opens a flyout with a number of choices for irregularly shaped frames. Select the icon at the lower left (**Hourglass**). Locate the cursor at the 1 in/2 cm (H) and 3.5 in/9 cm (V) ruler marks, but instead of dragging, just click the mouse to produce an hourglass frame at a default square size.

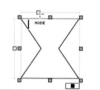

9 Click inside the frame for an insertion point and type 'Shaped frame.' Type some more text and see how the text magically fits to the frame's contours.

10 Notice that the flyout button now shows the icon of the most recently used tool (in this case for the **Hourglass** frame), so to select that particular tool again you'd only need to click the icon, not the down arrow.

Notice that this frame has two adjustment handles that let you fine-tune its proportions. Every shaped text frame is so equipped, for an incredible variety of typographic effects.

11 Click the 🔲 **Table tool**, located below the two frame tools, and then click on the page at the 1 in/2 cm (H), 6 in/16 cm (V) mark. The **Create Table** dialog opens with a selection of preset layouts.

12 You can step through the list to preview them, but for now choose the plain **Default** layout and set the **Table Size** values to 4 rows and 3 columns. Click **OK** to produce the table at a standard size on your page. (As with frame creation, you could also have dragged out a region to specify the table dimensions.)

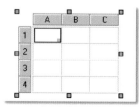

13 Click for an insertion point in the top left cell and type "Table." (For more on tables, see the "**Tables**" tutorial.)

Creation Tools

Besides placing text in a frame or table, you can create free-standing artistic text elements.

14 Click the **A** **Artistic Text Tool** button. On the page, click at the 1 in/2 cm (H), 8.5 in/22 cm (V) point and drag down about 3/4 inch (1.5 cm) to set the size of the text. When you release the button, a flashing cursor appears. Type 'Artistic,' press the **Enter** key, and then type 'text.'

15 Click the text object's grey bounding box to select the whole object, then click the ☰ **Align centre** button on the Context bar. There's nothing especially "artistic"about the text at this point, but all that will change in the "Gradient and Bitmap Fills" tutorial.

16 Take a moment to adjust the placement of your four sample objects so they fit neatly along the left half of the page **(Illustrated right)**. To move an object, click its bounding box, then drag from an edge when you see the ⬧ cursor.

Now it's time to try your hand at drawing. Don't worry—no special skill is required!

17 Just below the **Artistic Text** tool you'll see the **Line Tools** button. Click its down arrow to view the three Line Tool buttons on the flyout and select the first one, ✎ **Freehand Line**. In the blank region at the upper right of the page, draw a wavy line from left to right, a few inches long.

18 Now select the ╲ **Straight Line** tool, second on the flyout, and this time produce a straight line segment below the freehand sample.

19 Select the third ∿ **Curved Line** tool. This lets you construct a line in a series of segments, while changing the segment type "on the fly" with the aid of the **Curve** tools on the Context bar. The default ⌒ **Smart Corner** segment type provides automatic curve-smoothing... but for now, select ⌒ **Symmetric Corner**. This will entail two click-and-drag steps.

20 Below your other two lines, click once on the page and drag a very short distance, then release to create a starting node. Click again a couple of inches to the right of the starting node and drag around a bit before releasing (notice you can "pull" the curve into various shapes). Your second click defines the curved line segment.

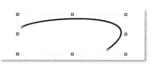

21 Select the **Pointer** tool—the **Curve** tools appear in the Context bar.

We'll return to your three line samples in the "Lines and Shapes" tutorial.

Creation Tools

Last but not least, let's introduce QuickShapes. These are stored on another flyout, just below lines.

22 Click the down arrow on the  **Quick Shape** button and move the cursor around the menagerie of icons, noting the various tooltips. Pick the one at the top left (Rectangle) and draw a box below your line samples, about 2 inches (5 cm) wide, 1 inch (2.5 cm) high. Notice that the QuickShape (like the shaped frame you created earlier) has an adjustment handle. Drag this up and down to create concave and convex corners; finish with convex corners on the shape.

23 Add another QuickShape, this time the Wave (third row down, to the right of centre). Adjust the left handle up and the right handle down, to widen the band. We'll turn this into a tricolour flag in the "Gradient and Bitmap Fills" tutorial.

Artistic text

24 Arrange the objects on the right side so the lower third of that side remains empty **(illustrated right)**.

25 To continue working with this file in future tutorials, save it as **My Lab.ppp** in the Workspace folder, normally found at **C:\Program Files\Serif\PagePlus\11.0\Tutorials\ Workspace**.

Congratulations—you've now met nine of the ten basic PagePlus elements. We'll be adding the tenth element in the next tutorial, "Importing Images."

Learning Lab 2: Importing Images

Introduces you to the basics of importing images into PagePlus publications.
As the Learning Lab sequence continues, we'll import a couple of sample pictures and touch on a variety of options you should know about in order to get the best image quality, whether on paper or in a Web publication.

1   Open the **My Lab.ppp** file you edited in the previous tutorial, or (if you skipped that one) open **Lab01.ppp** in the **Workspace** folder (normally **C:\Program Files\Serif\ PagePlus\11.0\Tutorials\Workspace**). This starts as a one-page publication in Paper Publishing mode, with an assortment of basic object types and some empty space at the lower right.

2   Click the 🖾 **Actual Size** button on the View toolbar and scroll or pan so you're centred on the blank area.

3   Click the 🖾 **Import Picture** button on the left Tools toolbar. In the dialog, locate the **Workspace** folder and select the file named **motorcycle 32.jpg**. Keep the dialog open as we take a brief detour.

4   Notice the options at the lower right of the dialog box (right). The **Preview** setting simply facilitates browsing by showing a thumbnail of the selected file—a motorcycle, in this case. There are also options for the dots-per-inch (dpi) settings of the image imported. In most cases, leaving the **Place at native dpi** default setting is best, but **Place at 96 dpi** is often useful when working in **Web Publishing** mode.

The **Embed** and **Link** choices are more significant. Embedded images become part of the publication file; linking images places a reference copy of the image on the page and preserves a connection to the original file. For more information, see online Help.

💡 As a shortcut to embed a picture from a file, you can simply drag its file icon into the PagePlus workspace. Another method is to use **Copy** and **Paste** (or **Paste Special**) commands via the Windows Clipboard; in this case the resulting picture format depends on the specific data available on the Clipboard.

5   Select **Embed**, and then click **Open**. On the page, you'll notice a special cursor. To set the size of the imported image, drag out a rectangle from left to right, just below the **QuickWave** object. Release the mouse and the picture appears. Notice that it's got a bounding box and handles to allow moving and resizing.

Note also that the Picture tools display in the Context bar.

Importing Images

6 Click on the lower-right corner handle and drag out slightly to enlarge the image proportionately. If you press the **Shift** key as you drag a corner, you can distort the image freely. Click the **Transform** tab and notice the values showing the current horizontal and vertical percentages. Generally, you'll want to leave pictures—especially photos—at their original aspect ratio.

At the bottom of the workspace, the **HintLine** offers "keyboard modifiers"—keypresses that alter the behaviour of your mouse for speedy tool switches and fast formatting changes. Note that the picture name is now visible in the HintLine.

7 Now choose **Picture** from the **Insert** menu. On the submenu, notice the choices for importing Photo CDs, TWAIN (scanned or digital camera) and Empty Frame images. For now, select **From File**, which leads to the same dialog we've just used.

> Empty Frames allow pictures to be replaced more easily, which is useful when performing a MailMerge. We'll revisit this in the "Auction Catalogue" tutorial.

8 In the **Workspace** folder, select **Frame.gif** and click **Open**. This time, instead of dragging, just click in the space below and left of the motorcycle picture to embed the new image at its actual size.

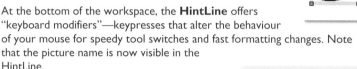

Frames.gif

We've chosen these two sample pictures for good reason. Both GIFs and JPGs are widely used on the Web because (unlike other bitmap formats like BMP or WMF) they can significantly compress picture data for faster image loading.

GIFs have an additional property: they can store animation sequences by packing multiple images into a single file. Let's switch to Web Publishing mode and take a look.

> Each format has its advantages. GIFs are limited to 256 colours and preserve all the original picture detail, whereas JPGs can handle millions of colours and there's generally some tradeoff of detail related to the degree of compression used. Photos generally look fine as JPGs, especially when scaled-down like this motorcycle example, while the GIF format is best for low-colour, sharp-edged images such as the Frames.gif image.

9 Choose **Switch to Web Publishing** from the **File** menu. This doesn't alter your document, only the PagePlus window.

10 Choose **Web Object** from the **Insert** menu and select **Animated GIF** from the submenu. The **Import Animated GIF** dialog opens.

Importing Images

11 Browse to the tutorials' **Workspace** folder (as mentioned at the start of the tutorial) and select **RockRoll.gif**. Note that the preview is always animated when inserting animated GIFs so you know what image you will be importing.

When you're done browsing, click **Cancel**. We'll revisit animated GIFs in the "Web Publishing" tutorial.

12 Choose **Switch to Paper Publishing** from the **File** menu. Let's round out the tutorial with some additional image options.

13 Double-click the motorcycle picture and you'll see the familiar **Import Picture** dialog. That's how easy it is to replace one existing image with another. (You can also click **Replace Picture** on the Context bar.) For now though, click **Cancel**.

14 Click the motorcycle image, click the **Swatches** tab, and choose a red sample. In the lower right corner of the **Swatches** tab, click the arrow next to the **Tint** box, and then drag the slider until a tint value of 50% is displayed. You'll see the photo bathed in pink, as the original hues have been replaced with a 50/50 mix of red and white. Keep this in mind as a great effect for backgrounds! For now, click **Edit/Undo** (**Ctrl+Z**) to undo the change.

15 Choose **Picture** from the **Format** menu. Using the **Colour Mapper**, you can make extensive colour changes to draw-type (vector) images and objects. The **Photo Optimizer Wizard** helps you to improve the print quality of a selected bitmap picture on a specific printer, while **Picture Transparency** lets you specify a single colour as a transparent or 'dropout' colour.

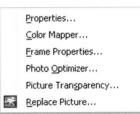

The Context bar also provides a selection of tools that you can use to enhance and manipulate your imported images. Click **Image Adjustments,** click **Add Adjustment**, and then explore the various options in the drop-down list.

Images are an essential part of many paper and Web publications and now you know how to incorporate them in your PagePlus projects. You've also got a complete set of basic PagePlus objects to experiment with as you proceed through the Learning Lab sequence. PagePlus online Help has lots more information—just look up "images" in the Index.

It's time to save the publication and move on to the next tutorial.

Learning Lab 3: Layout Tools

Introduces you to layout tools that enable you to make the most of the PagePlus environment.

Whether you're designing a greeting card, a poster, a newsletter, or a Web site, page layout involves arranging text and graphics into pleasing compositions. In the "Creation Tools" and "Importing Images" tutorials, you've seen how easy it is to move and resize objects in PagePlus, but effective layouts depend on careful planning and precise execution.

1 Open the **My Lab.ppp** file you edited in the previous tutorial, or (if you skipped that one) open **Lab02.ppp** in the **Workspace** folder. This starts as a one-page publication in Paper Publishing mode, with an assortment of basic object types.

Artistic
text

Let's start by explaining the **master page** level—the background of your publication, where you can place objects you'd like to appear on every page, such as headers and footers, page numbers, or a border design. Every publication has a master page level and can include any number of different master pages. Master pages are shared between pages.

2 On the right of the workspace, click the **Pages** tab and notice the upper (Master Pages) and lower (Pages) panes, each with ✚ and ━ buttons for adding and deleting pages on that level and a button for access to the **Page Manager** or **Master Page Manager** dialogs.

Note: To display or hide a PagePlus tab, click **View/Studio tabs**, and then select from the list of tabs.

3 In the Master Pages panel (click the arrow to expand the pane), double-click the **Master A** page, which switches you to the master page editing level. It's blank at this point... we're going to add a simple footer.

4 Choose the 🅰 **Artistic Text** tool and click just inside the blue-line page margins at the lower left corner.

Type 'PagePlus Learning Lab - ' (note the hyphen and spaces). Then choose **Page Number** from the **Insert** menu.

Select the text object (click its bounding box) and choose a font you like from the Context bar; we've used Balloonist. Adjust the object's position so it fits neatly in the corner.

5 Click the box that says "Master A" at the left of the lower HintLine toolbar—a shortcut to switch between the two levels. Back on page 1, you'll see the footer in the corner... and as you'll see, it will be present on every page you add that uses this "Master A" master page.

PagePlus offers additional "page levels" with its Layers functionality. Like the background Master Page and the foreground Page in your publication, Layers are also combined in a stack to form your overall design. We'll pass on Layers for now, though and keep our document single-layer and simple! To learn more, see the PagePlus online Help (press **F1** on your keyboard any time).

The page number field will update automatically on each page. Note that if you try to select the footer text now, you can't; for editing purposes, the two levels are completely separate.

6 Next, click the 1 in/2 cm mark on the horizontal ruler. A red line appears—you've just created a **ruler guide**. These are non-printing lines you can use to help visualise the main lines of your layout and to align headlines, pictures and other layout elements. It's easy to move the lines around as needed.

7 Click and drag the guide line a little from side to side.

PagePlus supplies a number of other layout visualisation aids... you just need to know where to find them.

The **Margin Guide** settings correspond to the blue-line box around your page area, while the **Row** and **Column Guides** let you further subdivide the page. If you specify more than one row or column, you'll see dashed blue lines on the page. Like the red ruler guides, these blue lines are only for layout purposes—they don't constitute objects in the publication and they don't print out.

8 Choose **Layout Guides...** from the **File** menu. Select the **Guides** tab and you'll see that it lists the vertical guide line you just placed. If you want to reset it to precisely 1.000 inch, select the text in the Vertical box, type '1' and click **Change**.

9 Switch back to the **Margins** tab.

10 **Cancel** the dialog and choose **Dot Grid** from the View menu. Now if you look very closely at your page, you'll see little points spaced exactly one ruler unit apart. A special-purpose tool for precision placement, it's initially left invisible—but it's good to know it's there when you need it. You can customise the colour, spacing, and style in **Tools/Options** (for example, a grey-line grid as shown).

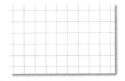

Snapping serves as an alignment aid in conjunction with all the guide elements we've just explored. You can even specify which particular guides should be snapped to.

Switch the grid off again before proceeding.

Layout Tools

11 Click the 🔳 **Snapping** button at the right side of the lower HintLine toolbar. The button should be down, to turn on the snapping feature.

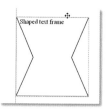

12 Select each of the objects on the left side of the page in turn and drag each one slightly toward the ruler guide. You'll see the "snap" as each object's left edge fits into alignment.

13 Before proceeding, remove the ruler guide by dragging it off the page and turn Snapping off.

14 Choose **Options** from the **Tools** menu and select the dialog's **Layout** tab.

Notice that you can adjust the grid dot spacing, style and colour. Below that, you can select which layout elements to hide or lock (to prevent accidental changes) and which elements should function like "magnets" when Snapping is turned on.

15 **Cancel** the dialog, then draw a selection bounding box around the three graphic line objects at the upper right, creating a multiple selection that includes all three. Then choose **Align Objects** from the **Arrange** menu.

Left

16 In the **Align Objects** dialog, take a moment to inspect the illustrations of the various alignment options. In the **Horizontally** section, choose **Left** and click **OK**.

In one step, you've just achieved what it took four steps to accomplish (with ruler guide and snapping) for the left-hand objects! But we think you'll agree that either method beats trying to position the objects by eye alone.

17 While the three graphics are still selected, click the 🔳 **Ungrouped** button.

18 Now you've created a single, temporary object that you can manipulate in a variety of ways. For example, drag out slightly from the group object's lower right corner. All three objects inside the group respond. Now choose the **Rotate** tool and drag the upper right corner slightly.

19 Before proceeding, click the 🔳 **Grouped** button to separate the three graphics as independent objects, as before.

💡 This was a rather simple example, but grouping can be invaluable when you're combining various pieces of text and images—for example to create a logo.

So far, we've just looked at ways of placing elements horizontally and vertically. But objects often need to overlap, whether to avoid a "floating islands" appearance that can weaken a composition, or for impressive visual effects such as montage. So how does PagePlus deal with the depth dimension?

20 Drag the motorcycle image over so it covers the "Artistic Text" sample **(illustrated)**.

Why does the image go in front of the text, instead of behind it? Think of a hand of playing cards, where one card is in front, one is at the back and the rest are arranged in between. In PagePlus publications, objects are added one by one to the front of a comparable "stack", normally called the **z-order** (x and y refer to horizontal and vertical positions or dimensions). In this case, the image was added after the text, so it's relatively toward the front or top of the z-order.

It's quite simple to rearrange the z-order, but first... let's assume your motorcycle completely obscures the text object. How can you get at the text?

21 Hold the **Alt** key down and click the image. **Alt**-click again. Notice the bounding box and handles changing as the selection switches between the two objects. It's a great shortcut to know about!

22 With the image selected, click the ⬚ **Send to Back** button on the top Arrange

toolbar. Click the ⬚ **Bring to Front** button for the opposite effect. For more precise adjustments in multiple-overlap situations, the Arrange menu also includes **Back One** and **Forward One** items.

23 Move the motorcycle image back to its location on the right—we'll be using it again—then save the publication and move on to the next tutorial!

Learning Lab 4: Text Frames

An overview of the "mechanics" of using text frames. We'll assume you're already familiar with creating text frames, as covered in the "Creation Tools" tutorial. For tips on page make-up and layout aesthetics, see the "Create a Newsletter" and "Create a Business Card" Projects.

1 Open the **My Lab.ppp** file you edited in the previous tutorial, or (if you skipped that one) open **Lab03.ppp** in the Workspace folder. This starts as a one-page publication in Paper Publishing mode, with an assortment of basic object types.

2 Click the **Pages** tab, then click the + button to create a new page "2 of 2." Click the **Multipage** button on the **View** toolbar. Drag on the array flyout to select a "2 x 1 Pages" view so you can see both pages side by side. So that the footer you added to the master page in the previous tutorial appears on the new page, drag Master A on top of page 2 of 2 on the Pages tab.

3 On page 1, draw a selection box around both text frames. Then drag the multiple selection over to page 2. Click elsewhere to deselect them, then click in the top frame and select/delete the words "Standard text frame." Do the same for the shaped frame so that no text remains in either object.

4 Select the top frame's bounding box, then enlarge it by dragging a corner so that it occupies roughly the top third of the page.

5 While holding down the Ctrl key, click and drag the standard frame's bounding box to create a copy, then position the new frame on the lower third of the page.

6 Select the shaped frame (**Alt**-click if the other frame is in the way) and move it down to the centre of the page. Your page should look as shown, right.

7 Right-click on the upper frame and choose **Text File**.

In the Workspace folder, select **Text frames.stt** (a formatted WritePlus file). With the **Retain Format** option checked, click **Open**. Click **No** to decline the AutoFlow option (although in other situations this might be applicable). The frame fills with text—overflows with it, in fact, as indicated by the "+" sign in the two ⊞ ⊞ buttons below the frame.

The left button provides the AutoFlow ability we declined when importing the text file a moment ago; the right one lets us link the frame. Our goal is to link several frames together so the story flows through them. We'll be working exclusively on page 2 from here on, so let's move in for a closer look.

8   Click the ⊞ **Multipage** button on the top **View** toolbar and select the I x I option.
    Then display page 2 by double-clicking 2 of 2 on the **Pages** tab, or clicking the **Next
    Page** button. If the red-underlined text marked by AutoSpell proves distracting, you can
    turn off the feature on the **Tools/Options/General** tab.

> 💡 There are several ways of dealing with overflowing text. You can enlarge the frame
> itself, edit the story text (or reduce its point size or spacing) to fit the current frame, or
> create one or more additional frames to contain the overflow. In practice, you might
> combine all three approaches to achieve a perfect balance of content and composition.

9   Click the top frame's right-hand **Link** button. Move the
    pointer over the middle hourglass frame and click when
    you see the cursor change from 🖑 to 🖑. Now the
    shaped frame fills with text, continuing the story from the
    top frame (where the button has changed to ⊡). The
    arrow denotes an intermediate frame; the red colour tells
    us an overflow condition exists. If you now select the
    hourglass frame, you'll see it now has acquired the two "+"
    buttons denoting a final frame
    with an overflow condition.

10 Repeat step 9 with the
    shaped frame selected,
    clicking its right-hand **Link**
    button and then "pouring"
    text into the lower standard
    frame. The ⊡ button on
    the final frame indicates
    we've reached the end of
    the story and there's no
    overflow.

    Here's a quick detour to
    demonstrate a useful
    alignment option...

> 💡 We have created frames manually and made
> text flow between them by manually linking them.
> At any time (not just when importing) you can use
> AutoFlow to create and link new frames
> automatically. Just click the final frame's left
> AutoFlow button. You will be asked if you want to
> AutoFlow your text with new pages containing
> frames the same size as the first or new pages with
> frames the size of the page.

11 Right-click the hourglass frame and choose **Text Format**,
    then **Vertical Alignment**, then Bottom. The text in the
    frame won't change, but it will jump to the bottom of the
    hourglass. It's a layout effect that might come in handy!

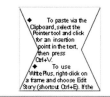

12 You've seen the **Link Frame** button in action; let's take a
    moment to examine the various Frame tool buttons.

Text Frames

13 Click the ▣ **Previous Frame** and ▣ **Next Frame** buttons and you'll see the cursor jump from one frame to another. This proves especially useful when stories span frames across several pages, as for example in a newsletter, as the display will also switch to the correct page for you.

Next to the ▣ **Link Frame** button (the equivalent of clicking the button on the frame) is the ▣ **Unlink Frame** button, which lets you remove a frame from a linked sequence, leaving the story intact in the remaining frames.

The next several buttons facilitate fitting story text into the available frames and they affect all the text in a given story, not just selected characters.

> Each frame can contain multiple columns and each frame has left and right column guides as well as top and bottom column blinds which bound the flow of text. You can drag directly or use a dialog to adjust these boundaries.

The ▣ **AutoFit** button scales story text exactly to the selected frame(s) by adjusting its point size and (if necessary) other properties.

Adjacent on the Context bar, the ▣ **Enlarge Story Text** and ▣ **Shrink Story Text** buttons give you manual control by letting you alter the text size incrementally.

14 Select the top text frame, then click the ▣ **Frame Setup** button to bring up a dialog that lets you set the frame's column and margin properties. Type "2" as the number of columns, then click **OK**.

15 Move the pointer to the top of the left column and when it changes to ↕, drag down a small amount. You'll see the top **column blind** (a dashed line) move down and the story text along with it. Repeat this at the left and bottom of the column, bringing the boundaries in slightly.

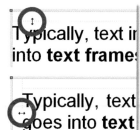

Text frames may look like simple boxes or shapes, but their ability to link together and control text flow turn them into powerful layout tools. You may not immediately use all the available adjustments, but it's good to know they exist.

We'll come back to frame text in the "Text Wrapping" tutorial, and touch on other frame properties elsewhere.

Learning Lab 5: Lines and Shapes

Covers line properties, turning lines into closed shapes and techniques of line-editing.

Because so many objects have line and shape properties, you'll find this tutorial especially valuable. We'll assume you're already familiar with creating lines and QuickShapes, as covered in the "Creation Tools" tutorial.

1 Open the **My Lab.ppp** file you edited in the previous tutorial, or (if you skipped that one) open **Lab04.ppp** in the **Workspace** folder.

This starts as a two-page publication in Paper Publishing mode, with an assortment of basic object types and several experimental text frames. On the **View** menu, select **Normal** and on the toolbar click the 🖿 **Full Page** button.

Lines can be either straight or curved. They have line properties like colour and weight (thickness). When you draw a new line, it takes on the current default line properties; initially the default settings are for a solid black line with a weight of 1.0 point.

2 With the ↖ **Pointer** tool, select the freehand line at the upper right of page 1.

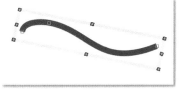

3 Click the **Line** tab. In the weight list, select '5.0 pt' to widen the line. Notice that you can use other controls to set the line type, start and end attributes.

4 With the line still selected, click the (**Colour** or **Swatches** tab). Click the ⌐ **Line** button, and then click a blue sample. The line's colour changes.

5 Switch to page 2 and click the shaped (hourglass) frame sample. Click the (**Swatches** tab), click the **Text** button, and click a colour to apply to the text in the frame.

🕯 You can use the Line tab, or the Line dialog (click Line and Border on the Format or right-click menu) to set the line properties of many objects, including shapes, text frames, artistic text and tables.

But frame objects have line properties, too.

6 Click the tab's **Line** button and then click a red colour. Now you've got a red hourglass. If you wish, you might go even further and change it to a thick dashed line using the **Line** tab!

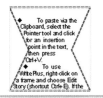

Lines and Shapes

7   Return to page 1. With the **Pointer** tool, click the
    straight line sample to select it. Now choose the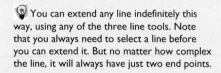
    Freehand Line tool and move it over the node at the
    right end of the line.

The $^+_\lambda$ cursor signals that you can click and drag at this
point to extend the line. Try this now—just add a short
curve to the straight line

Now let's see what happens when
we connect the line's two end
points.

> You can extend any line indefinitely this
> way, using any of the three line tools. Note
> that you always need to select a line before
> you can extend it. But no matter how complex
> the line, it will always have just two end points.

8   Drag from one of the line's end
    nodes to the other. Release the
    mouse button when you see the
    cursor change to $^+_\lambda$.

Completing the circuit creates a closed shape. Because
shapes have an interior region that can be filled, they
have fill properties as well as line properties. The
interior region takes on the default fill as soon as a line
is closed to become a shape.

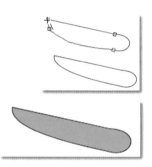

9   Click the **Pointer** tool and select the new shape. On
    the **Colour** tab, click the ⊒ **Fill** button and then a
    green colour sample. We'll look at more imaginative
    uses of fills in the "Gradient and Bitmap Fills" tutorial.

> To change the default properties for a given type of object, use the "by example"
> method: Format a sample object the way you want it, then right-click it and choose
> **Update Object Default** from the **Format** flyout. Default settings are local to the
> publication, unless you choose **Tools/Save Defaults** to record them as global.

By now, you may be realizing that all lines in PagePlus, whether they stand alone or
surround a shape, are composed of one or more curved line segments, each with nodes
at its end points. A straight line is just a special case of a curved line, so our third line
sample—the curved line—is really the most "typical" of the three.

10 Select the curved line sample and move the pointer along it. At the end points, you'll
    see a -¦- cursor, while along the length of the segment a ▶∿ appears. Try dragging the
    middle of the segment a short distance. Now select the closed shape you just filled and
    drag one of its curved segments in the same manner.

Lines and Shapes

So now you know that the **Pointer** tool serves as an editing tool for lines and you can drag from the middle of any curved segment to reshape it. How about nodes?

11 Select the curved line sample and click its left-hand node. The node turns orange to show it's selected and you can see control handles attached to the node and its neighbour.

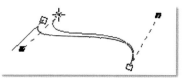

Together, the control handles define the profile of the adjacent line segments (specifically the slope and depth of the segments leading off from each node). Try dragging the handles a bit to see how easily you can reshape the curve.

12 Now select the filled shape above and click its top right node. Locate the Curve tools on the Context bar and move the pointer across its buttons.

We'll briefly summarize the various buttons and leave you to experiment with them on your own.

- The ⊥ **Add Node** and ☲ **Delete Node** buttons let you do just that; the more detailed a line (or outline) is, the more nodes it will need.

- You've seen how to close a curve by connecting line ends; ⊬ **Close Curve** and ⊬ **Break Curve** provide reversible control over this joinery.

- There are several different node types, which determine the degree to which a given corner is sharp, smooth, symmetric or Smart (for an auto-fit); you can switch a node from one type to another for fine control. See the online help topic "Drawing and editing lines" for details.

- ◇ **Straighten All Lines** and ○ **Fit Curves** substitute straight line or curved line segments, respectively, throughout the existing line.

- Finally, ↹ **Reverse Curves** switches the ordering of nodes, so that the start of the curve becomes its end (without changing the shape of the curve). It's handy when you have path text along the curve and want to flip the text from the "inside" to the "outside" of the curve or vice versa.

The Curve tools will come into play again in our next tutorial, "Wrapping Text."

Learning Lab 6: Wrapping Text

Teaches you how to make frame text flow around page objects.

We'll assume you're already familiar with text frames, as covered in the "Creation Tools" and "Text Frames" tutorials. Experience with line editing (covered in the previous "Lines and Shapes tutorial") will also serve you well.

1   Open the **My Lab.ppp** file you edited in the previous tutorial, or (if you skipped that one) open **Lab05.ppp** in the **Workspace** folder. This starts as a two-page publication in Paper Publishing mode. Select the **Multipage** button and highlight the 2 x 1 configuration from the flyout so that you're viewing the entire document.

Your Learning Lab publication includes a selection of all the basic PagePlus object types, along with several experimental text frames. As you've seen, text frames are containers with text flowing through them and shaped frames are one way of making text follow the contours of the container. Frame text can also flow around (or even inside) other objects in a variety of ways—an effect called wrapping. When an object overlaps text in a frame, whether the text wraps—and if so, how—depend on two settings: one for the frame, one for the object.

2   Right-click the frame lowest on page 2 and choose **Frame Setup**. In the dialog, just note in passing that the **Text Will Wrap** box is checked. That means the frame's text will wrap to any overlapping objects, according to each object's settings. Clearing the box would switch off wrapping for this frame, regardless of object settings. Leaving it checked for now, click **Cancel**.

3   Drag the GIF image at the lower right of page 1 over and drop it near the lower left corner of the bottom page 2 frame. Click the 🖾 **Actual Size** button for a closer look. Nothing yet has happened to the text flow.

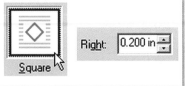

4   Select the graphic (you may need to **Alt**-click if the frame is in the way), then click the 🔲 **Wrap Settings** button on the top Arrange toolbar. Note the various icons that illustrate the wrap effects available.

The distance value is also known as the **standoff** and is an important part of fine-tuning the wrap for best effect

5 In the **Wrapping** section, select **Square**. In the **Distance from text** section, type a **Right** value of .2 in/.5 cm. Click **OK.**

6 Drag the graphic around to different positions on the page. You'll see that the frame text now avoids the graphic on all sides—more so on the right, where the standoff is greater. Finish by placing the image to the left of the last paragraph (the one that starts with "The illustration..."). Depending on prior work you've done in the publication, you may need to adjust the size of one or more text frames on your page to line up the story text with the image.

To edit frame properties directly, Alt-click to select only the tra aries of the column.

Select · Select · Selec The illustra frame, th · frame, th · Frame, you're (1) o the curs the curs watch t umn bound 1 2 3 slightly. Not the margin

PAGEPLUS LEARNING LAB - 2

💡 You can set text wrap properties for any object that overlaps a frame—a picture, artistic text, even another frame—for a variety of creative possibilities. Note that any overlapping objects are still quite separate from the text they overlap. For example, if we inserted an extra paragraph earlier in this page 2 story, the illustration would no longer line up with its descriptive paragraph and some repositioning would be needed. When text changes are minimal, you can often retain a particular effect by adjusting the standoff value or by switching to a different wrap style.

The **Top & Bottom** and **Square** wrap settings make sense for rectangular objects. But what if you want to flow text around a curved or irregular contour, for example, the outline of a motorcycle?

7 Switch to page 1 and zoom in on the motorcycle image. Right-click it and choose **Wrap Settings**.

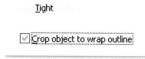

Tight

Set a **Tight** wrap and select the **Crop object to wrap outline** box. Click **OK.**

☑ Crop object to wrap outline

An object's wrap outline dictates how text flows around the object. If you've worked with the Crop tools, you know about another perimeter, the crop outline—an object's boundary after portions of its edges have been cropped away. Using "crop to wrap" (per the Wrap Settings you've just specified) is a convenient way to achieve both results.

Let's see how it works.

💡 Editing the wrap outline is just like editing a closed curve (if the terminology isn't familiar to you, see the "Lines and Shapes" tutorial) and any changes you make here will also crop the image.

Wrapping Text

8 With the motorcycle image selected, click the  **Edit Wrap** button. A dashed outline with four corner nodes appears around the object and the Curve tools display in the Context bar.

We want to end up with a shape that fits the motorcycle's profile.

9 The ⟳ **Fit Curves** button is a good first step: it converts the box to an ellipse. Then, for easier editing, it's a good idea to set all four of the nodes as **Sharp**, rather than **Smooth**.

You'll need to add a couple of nodes where the motorcycle's shape is concave, i.e., either side of the wing-mirror. Then it's simply a matter of moving certain nodes around and carefully adjusting their control handles, as illustrated.

10 At any point, you can drag the image across to page 2 and place it over the top text frame—straddling the two columns, if you like. Even if your outline isn't precise, you'll get a good idea of the final result. And by the way... you can still scale the photo up or down in place and the wrap/crop outline will scale accordingly.

Time to save the publication and move on.

Learning Lab 7: Schemes

Shows you how to switch schemes, modify existing schemes, and create your own. A **scheme** in PagePlus is a cluster of five complementary colours that you can apply to specific elements in one or more publications. Whether you're working with design templates, with sample designs in the Gallery, or with from-scratch publications, use the **Schemes** tab to choose from over 50 preset schemes.

1 Open the **My Lab.ppp** file you edited in the previous tutorial, or (if you skipped that one) open **Lab06.ppp** in the **Workspace** folder. This starts as a two-page publication in Paper Publishing mode. Adjust your view so that you can see all of page 1.

   Let's begin with a simple demonstration of schemes in action.

2 Click on the **Schemes** tab and drag it to the left to detach it. Once it's free-floating, resize it vertically so it takes up less space and position it where it won't obscure the workspace. Ours shows the **Abacus** scheme; select this if you want the examples to match.

3 Now click the **Gallery** tab and select the **Samples** category of objects. Click **Art** and drag from its thumbnail onto the blank region at the upper left of page 1.

4 Click the **Swatches** tab. Notice the five numbered colour samples in the lower left corner—you'll want to keep an eye on them!

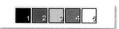

5 On the **Schemes** tab, click a scheme sample other than the one currently highlighted. Instantly you'll see the logo's colours update with those of the new scheme. Press the down arrow on the keyboard a few times to step through the list of scheme names.

As you switch schemes, notice how the five numbered samples on the **Swatches** tab take on the five scheme colours.

Compare the five colours with the colours used in the logo. Can you tell which number corresponds to each element of the logo design? Don't forget to set the scheme back to the **Abacus** scheme before continuing these steps.

Colour schemes in PagePlus are essentially a "paint by numbers" system with five numbers. Each named scheme swaps its own five specific colours into those five slots. For example, if an element has been marked with scheme colour 1, it takes on whichever colour happens to occupy slot 1 in the current scheme.

Each publication can have just one colour scheme at a time. The current scheme is highlighted on the Schemes tab and its five colours also appear on the (Swatches tab). Marking elements with scheme colours is as easy as applying line and fill colours.

Schemes

6 Select the lozenge-shaped **QuickBox** on the right side of page 1 and drag a corner to scale it down so it's exactly 1 in/2.5 cm wide. If you have Snapping enabled you may need to enter values on the **Transform** tab to achieve an accurate size. Drag it across to the left side of the page.

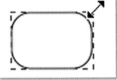

7 Choose **Replicate...** from the **Edit** menu and choose the following dialog settings: Create line, Line length 5, Offset, Horizontal 1.2 in (3 cm), Vertical 0. Click OK and you'll have a row of identical QuickBoxes. Click elsewhere to deselect them.

8 Now we'll fill the five boxes with five different scheme colours. On the **Swatches** tab, drag from the **Scheme Colour 1** box (here shown using the **Abacus** scheme) to the first box to give it a solid fill. Repeat this with the next three scheme colours, assigning each one to a different box. Just to be different, give the fifth box a fixed, sky blue fill (from the second row of the colour gallery).

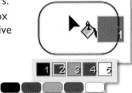

As with fixed colours, any shading or tinting you apply to scheme colours is preserved if a new set of scheme colours is swapped in. Using shades and tints in this way lets your publications employ many more than just the five base scheme colours.

9 Select the first box and on the **Swatches** tab, adjust the **Shade/Tint** value to about +40%. Select another scheme (**Island**, for example) and notice how the first box now takes a lighter value than the base scheme colour 1.

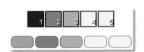

In PagePlus, the named schemes as listed on the **Schemes** tab are all defined globally, so they're available for use in any PagePlus publication. All the schemes use **CMYK** colours suitable for professional printing (except for the Web schemes which use monitor-friendly **RGB** colour values). Each publication is associated with one of these named schemes, whether or not it actually employs any scheme colours. If the dozens of preset schemes—combined with shades, tints and gradients—still aren't enough for you, it's easy enough to modify one or more colours within a scheme, or create a brand-new scheme.

You can use scheme colours not just for solid fills and lines, but for gradient fills that blend multiple colours. For hands-on practice with gradient fills, see the next tutorial, "Gradient and Bitmap Fills."

Schemes

10 Click **Tools/Scheme Manager...**, on the dialog's **Schemes** tab, the list lets you pick any of the named schemes as a starting point for customisation. We'll leave it set for the current scheme, Island, which is already highlighted. Click the **Edit** tab.

We won't actually modify a scheme at this point, but the procedure is straightforward. In the **Scheme Manager** you'd simply choose a different value for one or more of the listed scheme colours, then use the **Save Scheme...** button to record the changes. You can overwrite existing schemes, but unless you're sure that's what you want, make a habit of saving revised schemes under a different name.

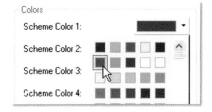

11 That concludes our tour of schemes. Cancel the Scheme Manager, then drag the **Schemes** tab back over to the tab group on the right to dock it.

It's time to save the publication and move on.

Learning Lab 8: Gradient and Bitmap Fills

Takes you beyond simple solid colour fills into the realm of multi-colour fill effects.
In several of the earlier Learning Lab tutorials, we've applied solid colours to lines and fills.
Now it's time to take things a step or two further.

1 Open the **My Lab.ppp** file you edited in the previous
"Colour Schemes" tutorial, or (if you skipped that one)
open **Lab07.ppp** in the **Workspace** folder. This starts
as a two-page publication in Paper Publishing mode.
Adjust your view so that you can see all of page 1.

2 Click the **Swatches** tab, click the down-arrow next to
the 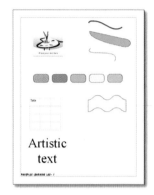 **Gradient** button.

The submenu lists three types of fills collectively known
as **gradient fills**, because they provide a gradation or
spectrum of colours between two or more
"key"colours. The three types are named **Linear**,
Elliptical, and **Conical**.

3 Click each of the three gradient fill types to get a quick impression of the fills in their
respective sample galleries. Click the **Bitmap** button.

Unlike gradient fills, bitmap fills apply bitmapped images or patterns to the object. The
gallery is subdivided into categories, with a drop-down list to switch between thumbnail
galleries. We'll return to these later.

4 For now, switch back to the **Linear** fill gallery. Locate "Linear Fill 8" (watch the popup
text) and drag from its sample (illustrated right) over to the QuickWave shape on page
1. Drop the fill onto the object.

If you examine the applied fill, you'll see it's made up of just two colours, grading from a
solid blue at one end to a solid yellow at the other. Let's take a closer look.

5 Choose the **Fill** tool on the left Tools toolbar. You'll see the object's **fill path**
displayed as a horizontal line across the middle, with a node at either end. Try using the
Fill tool cursor to drag the nodes slightly. As you drag, the fill changes position across
the object.

> Experiment with the **Fill** tool to discover new effects! For example, you can widen
> or narrow the gradient's extent, even drag either node completely outside the
> object. You can even click and drag with the Fill tool to redraw the gradient.

Each gradient fill type has a characteristic path. Ellipse fills begin at the centre, with a two-line path so you can adjust the fill's extent in either direction away from the centre. Conical fills have an arc-shaped path around a central focus. In this exercise, we're going to stick with the linear fill, but feel free to create a couple of new QuickShapes and play with the other types. Besides adjusting the fill's path on an object, you can edit the fill itself for endless variety and complexity.

6   On the **Swatches** tab, click the **Palette** button, and then click the white solid colour sample and drag it onto the yellow node of the linear gradient (shown right). That's all it takes to redefine any of the key colours in a gradient fill.

7   Now drag from the red solid colour sample to the middle of the gradient. Drop the colour when you see a small "+" sign appear in the cursor. You've just added another key colour. Repeat this step, adding a second red node near the first one. Then drag the two red nodes apart for a wider red band, yielding a "tricolour" banner effect.

💡 Starting with any preset gradient fill, you can substitute your own colours and add or delete key colours as needed, simply by manipulating the gradient nodes. Or if you prefer a dialog-based approach, right-click the object and choose **Fill...** from the **Format** flyout. And gradient transparency effects, extremely useful in montage work and illustration, basically lay a "visibility spectrum" across an object instead of the "colour spectrum" used in gradient fills. You'll find detailed coverage in online Help.

Now for a bitmap fill...

8   Select the sample of artistic text at the lower left of page 1. Retype it as "Greenery," then select the whole object and choose a heavy but flowing font (we've used **Seabird Heavy SF**).

9   Increase the point size so there will be something visible to fill! Switch to the **Bitmap** Fill type and select the "Foliage" category. Click any one of the green thumbnails (we've used Bitmap Fill 7).

10 Choose the **Fill** tool and you'll see the fill path displayed as two lines joined at a centre point. Nodes mark the fill's centre and edges.

To reposition the fill's centre, drag the centre node. To create a skewed or tilted fill region, drag one or both edge nodes sideways.

Unlike gradient fills, bitmap fills don't simply "end" at the edges of their fill paths. Rather, they tile (repeat) so you can fill indefinitely large regions at any scale. By dragging the edge nodes in or out with the **Fill** tool, you can "zoom" in or out on the fill pattern.

It's time to save your file and move on.

Learning Lab 9: Tables

Formatting tables and their text, applying effects, using QuickFill and QuickClear.

If you've been following the tutorial sequence, you've had a chance to play with all the sample objects in your Learning Lab publication, save one: the table. Now its time has come!

1 Open the My **Lab.ppp** file you edited in the previous tutorial, or (if you skipped that one) open **Lab08.ppp** in the Workspace folder. This starts as a two-page publication in Paper Publishing mode. Adjust your view of page 1 to **Actual Size** and locate the sample table object.

When originally creating the table, we intentionally left it plain. Let's go back to the format gallery, which will provide an overview of table styling options.

2 Right-click the table and choose **Table/AutoFormat...** alternatively, you can choose table commands from the **Table** menu.

The dialog presents a list of sample tables, which differ in their use of **Lines** (inner and outer cell borders), **Cell Fill** (cell colour), **Font** (bold, italic, etc.) and **Alignment** (left, centre, etc.). You can pick any sample and use the checkboxes to specify which of the sample's attribute(s) to apply to your actual table. This lets you "mix and match", for example by applying (in two passes) the Colour from one sample and the Font from another.

3 Click or scroll through the list and notice how the attributes vary from one sample to another. This will give you a good idea of the styles you can apply by hand to any table. For now, **Cancel** the dialog to leave the table unchanged.

4 Right-click the table again and take a quick survey of the **Table** submenu.

There are commands to insert, select, or delete rows and columns; to merge or separate cells; and to set cell properties. We'll come back to that last item in a moment.

5 Click away from the menu to dismiss it, then select the table's bounding box. Drag the table's right edge further right to expand it slightly.

The table as a whole is a distinct object and once you've selected it, you can move, resize, delete and copy it along with its contents. You can also select one or more cells, rows, or columns within the table.

Tables

6 Click in any cell to select it, then drag from the middle of one cell to the middle of another to select a range of cells (you'll see the range highlighted in blue). Try clicking the grey control button over a column to select the column. Finally, drag from the middle of one row button to the middle of another to select a range.

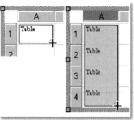

Now let's try adding some text to the table... quickly!

7 Select the upper left cell (it should already contain the word "Table"). Click the small square at the cell's lower right corner and drag it down to the bottom of the table. The **QuickFill** feature instantly propagates the text from the initial cell.

8 Type 'I' into the top cell of the second column and repeat the QuickFill drag down the second column. This time, QuickFill extends the numeric sequence '1, 2, 3...'. Finally, type 'Feb' into the top right cell and apply QuickFill to continue the month series.

> 🐭 QuickFill is great for setting up tables quickly. It can also extend the alphabetic sequence and any numeric progression (a series of numbers with a common difference).

9 Select the first column and then select '14 pt' in the **Point Size** list on the Context bar.

Within each cell, you can click for an insertion point or drag to select a range of text. Selecting a cell or range effectively selects all the text in that region. Each cell within a table behaves like a mini-frame, although table text doesn't flow or wrap like frame text. Otherwise, you can vary character and paragraph properties, apply named text styles and treat the contents of any cell much like regular text.

10 Select the whole table (click the bounding box), then click the ☰ **Align Centre** button on the Context bar to re-align all the table text. On the **Format** menu, choose **Vertical Text Alignment**, then select **Centre** from the submenu.

11 Select just the top row, then set its text to '14 pt Bold' on the Context bar.

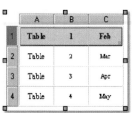

12 With the top row still selected, right-click and choose **Table/Cell Properties...**.

13 On the **Border** tab, inspect the set of cell border choices and click the second preset in the top row. The Edge Selection preview shows (with arrows) which edge lines will be affected by your line style choices; leave them all selected for now and click the **Line Style...** button.

Tables

14 Type '2' into the **Weight** list to widen the line, then choose the red sample in the **Colour** drop-down gallery. Click **OK**. The Edge Selection preview updates to show how the border will appear.

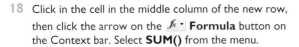

15 Select the **Fill** tab and choose 'Solid' from the list. Click the red sample and choose '+30%'from the **Shade/Tint** list. Click **OK** to apply your settings to the selected range of cells. The colour will look weird until you deselect the cells; then you'll see a light red header row with a solid red border.

16 Select the three cells below the header in the right-hand column; remember to drag between the middle of the cells rather than from their edges. You'll see a QuickFill handle at the lower right of the range. Click it (you'll see a "+" cursor) and drag up and left to the opposite (top left) corner of the selected range. If you've executed this **QuickClear** function precisely, the cells' contents will vanish. If not, just undo the result and try again.

17 Right-click in the cell containing the number 4, click **Table**, click **Insert**, and then click **Rows**. Leave the number of rows to insert as 1, select **After selected cells**, click **OK**.

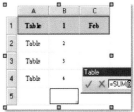

18 Click in the cell in the middle column of the new row, then click the arrow on the f_x ▾ **Formula** button on the Context bar. Select **SUM()** from the menu.

PagePlus has auto-completed a formula for you, summing the contents of column B. Press **Enter** on your keyboard to apply the formula. The figure 10 should appear in cell B5—the result of the formula =SUM(B1:B4). To break it down, **=** denotes a formula, **SUM** is the function and **(B1:B4)** is the range of cells in the calculation.

> **Note:** There are a wide range of auto-formatting features to complement the spreadsheet functionality of the PagePlus Table tool. For further information, we recommend you take a look in the Help file's "How to Work with Tables" section. Armed with this knowledge, you can confidently create and customise tables in your PagePlus publications.

To see a powerful implementation of tables in action, click the 🗓 **Insert Calendar** button on the **Table** flyout of the Tools toolbar.

The Calendar Wizard steps you through a series of choices, culminating in a table-based calendar. You can apply what you've learned here to fine-tune the table design.

Learning Lab 10: Adding Graphic Flair

Introduces you to techniques like filter effects and transparency to raise your publications above the ordinary.

Throughout this Learning Lab sequence, the emphasis has been on experimentation, not on graphic design principles. But in fact, much great graphic design is adventurous—it gets noticed because it bends the rules without necessarily breaking them. So although our focus here on "graphic flair" is really an excuse to play with more tools, bear in mind that the notion of "flair" isn't incompatible with good taste.

1 Open the **My Lab.ppp** file you edited in the previous **Tables** tutorial, or (if you skipped that one) open **Lab09.ppp** in the Workspace folder. This starts as a two-page publication in Paper Publishing mode. Adjust your view of page 1 to **Fit Page**.

2 Choose the  **Rotate** tool from the Tools toolbar. Select the artistic text object ("Greenery") and rotate it about 15 degrees counter-clockwise (watch the **Transform** tab readout). Then reduce its size approximately 75% before holding the **Ctrl** key down, then click the object and drag a copy to the right of the original.

3 Choose the 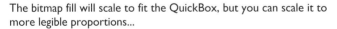 **Pointer** tool and click for an insertion point in the copy. Replace the text with the word "Galleries." Adjust the position of the two text objects so they balance each other on the page.

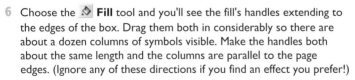

4 Now choose the **QuickBox**—first on the QuickShapes flyout—and draw one big rectangle extending out to the blue page margins (you can leave the page footer text exposed). If your defaults are set so the shape has a line border, click the **Line** tab, and select "None" from the centre drop-down list to remove it.

5 On the **Swatches** tab, click the **Bitmap** button. In the fill gallery, select the "Miscellaneous" category and click the last thumbnail, showing dollar and pound signs. Set the **Shade/Tint** slider to '+30%.'

The bitmap fill will scale to fit the QuickBox, but you can scale it to more legible proportions...

6 Choose the **Fill** tool and you'll see the fill's handles extending to the edges of the box. Drag them both in considerably so there are about a dozen columns of symbols visible. Make the handles both about the same length and the columns are parallel to the page edges. (Ignore any of these directions if you find an effect you prefer!)

7 Once you've got the fill adjusted, switch back to the **Pointer** tool, then click the **Send to Back** button to place the box behind the rest of the page contents.

Adding Graphic Flair

The graphic effect of a lightened pictorial background behind other elements, less subtle than watermarking, is sometimes called 'ghosting.' It's especially useful with photographs, where you can achieve the effect by applying a transparency (see below) to an image.

8 Return to the **Pointer** tool and with the box selected, choose the _fx_ **Filter Effects** tool. Select **Colour Fill,** then click the **Colour** button and choose the bright green sample in the first row (or a close match: your colour table may differ, depending which palette the publication is using).

9 Set the **Opacity** slider to about 12. Watch the preview window or click **Apply** to see the effect on the actual object. Click **OK** to return to the page.

Let's now look at a filter effect that's especially well-suited to text.

10 Drag a marquee around the 'Greenery Galleries' sample (you can group them for convenience) and choose _fx_ **Filter Effects** again. This time, select **Drop Shadow**. Set the **Opacity** slider to about 65 and other settings as follows: **Blur** 12, **Distance** 5, **Intensity** 5. Then click **OK**.

11 The resulting drop shadow not only adds 'flair,' but helps the text rise above an otherwise very busy background. And there are lots more effects to explore... several shown to the right.

Time to try one more graphic technique: **transparency**.

Transparency effects are great for montage effects, highlights, shading and shadows and for simulating rendered realism. Applying transparency to an object gives the effect of variable erasure, while leaving the original object intact: you can remove or alter the transparency at any time. Transparencies work like fills that use 'disappearing ink' instead of colour. A gradient transparency varies from more 'disappearing' to less, as shown right. It makes a differenc which object is in front (here, the pentagon); where there's more transparency, more of the object(s) behind will show through.

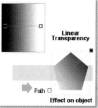

12 Switch your view to page 2 of the publication and select the motorcycle image. Click the **Opacity** tab and select the **Gradient** type. The Gradient gallery groups together **Linear**, **Ellipse**, and **Conical** transparency samples.

Adding Graphic Flair

The lighter portions of the samples represent more transparency. We want to apply a 'vignette' effect to the motorcycle so that it fades away around the edges. An Ellipse transparency roughly approximates the shape of the cropped image.

13 Locate and click **Ellipse Transparency 82**.

We'll need to make a couple of adjustments to the transparency path. For one thing, we can't see enough of the motorcycle because the transparency path doesn't extend out far enough.

14 Choose the 🔲 **Transparency** tool and drag the centre of the transparency up towards the indicator on the side of the motorcycle. Drag the outer nodes away somewhat to make the transparency more circular and rotate it for better placement.

We can see most of the motorcycle, but the transparency gradient falls off too gradually from its centre. Ideally, we'd like much sharper falloff fairly close to the motorcycle's edges. We can achieve this by adding a couple of extra **key values** to the gradient.

15 Right-click and choose **Format/Transparency**. In the dialog, click the **Edit** button. Below the Properties gradient, notice the two key value indicators that look like tiny houses—a black one (denoting zero transparency) at the left and a white one (full transparency) at the right.

16 Click in (or just below) the gradient sample, about a third of the way along and then again about two-thirds of the way. This will add two more key value indicators—both black to start with—and now the gradient falls off quite sharply on the right side.

17 With the third indicator (the newest one) selected—you can tell because its 'roof' is black, unlike the others—click the lightest sample below the **Properties** box. This sets the transparency value at that point to 'full' and moves the sharp falloff to the middle part of the gradient.

Now click **OK** twice and inspect your results.

Most of the motorcycle should now be fully visible. The two new nodes are represented on one axis (remember, because it's an elliptical fill, they affect the whole fill symmetrically). Drag any of the nodes to adjust the transparency for best appearance. Since the motorcycle was irregularly shaped to start with, the results won't be perfect, but you can see what a difference modifying the gradient has made.

Now that we've introduced transparency, we'll conclude this tutorial by inviting you to go on and take a look at the collection of **Photo Edge Effects** in the Bitmap Transparency Gallery. They're sure to spark your imagination!

Learning Lab 11: Web Publishing

Deconstructs a Web page design template to highlight what's unique about Web publications.

We'll assume you've followed the Learning Lab sequence (Tutorials 1 through 10) up to this point and are fairly comfortable with PagePlus fundamentals. This tutorial will proceed through a sample Web publication, pausing along the way to point out the new objects and options that are available.

You can convert any paper publication into a Web site with the **File/Switch to Web Publishing...** command. For example, we could convert the Learning Lab publication into a Web site. However, let's begin instead with a design template intentionally designed as a Web publication. Deconstructing its various elements will provide the knowledge you need to customise a design template publication, or start your own site from scratch in the future.

1   To get started, run PagePlus (or choose **File/New/New from Startup Wizard...**) and from the Startup Wizard click **use a design template**.

In the **Web Sites** category, select the 'Business' sample, then click **Finish**.

The publication appears in the PagePlus edit window, in Web Publishing mode, with the **User Details** dialog open to let you customise text details.

We should mention that text details in design template publications are stored in ordinary text frames, but these frames contain special **answer text fields** linked to the template. As long as you update the details via the **User Details** dialog, you preserve the link—but if you type into one of the frames by hand, you'll erase the link and from that point on you'll have ordinary frame text. If you start a Web publication from scratch, you'll be dealing with ordinary text at all times. For more information, see online Help.

Altering detail text is easy—just type and click—so we'll move on to the colour scheme option.

2   Click the **Schemes** tab to choose the colours to be used in your Web site.

Note that the scheme samples have the same names as in Paper Publishing mode, but here they are more complex—they also include colour definitions for Hyperlinks, Followed Hyperlinks, and page Background. You can modify any of these scheme colours using the Scheme Manager, as covered in the "Colour Schemes" tutorial.

One more thing: the Web scheme's Background can use a tiled bitmap instead of a solid colour—if it does, you'll see a 📋 icon in the scheme sample.

Web Publishing

3 For an example of a picture background, switch to the 'WWW 7' scheme. You'll see the various page elements that use scheme colours take on the new definitions.

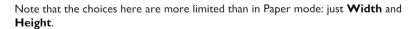

Also note the subtle repeating bitmap in the page background. The actual bitmap is shown, right.

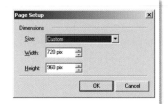

Now let's explore how the Web site is put together, starting with the setup of the pages themselves.

4 Choose **Page Setup...** from the **File** menu.

Note that the choices here are more limited than in Paper mode: just **Width** and **Height**.

You can select starting VGA or SVGA dimensions, or enter custom settings **(see right)**. Since Web pages scroll downward, extra height gives your layout room to grow. Any left-over space at the bottom won't show up on your final Web pages, because PagePlus automatically trims it away when exporting. It's a good idea to set up a taller page initially than you think you'll need, but you can always return to the setup dialog to add height as needed.

5 Cancel the setup dialog, then click the ▶ **Next Page** button to step through the site's five pages.

Web site content extends not only downward on each page, but outward (or wherever cyberspace is located) into linked page sequences. Here, the design template provides a starting series of five pages "in a row," i.e., without any complex branching. Note that certain elements change from page to page; these are stored on the publication's page level. The shared, invariant items are located on the background or master page (as covered in the "Layout Tools" tutorial).

6 Click the ◄ **First Page** button, then click the **Current Page** ('1 of 5') box next to it to switch to the master pages.

Click some of the elements on the page, then drag—you can see that some of the background elements are grouped, while other text frames remain separate and how important layering elements is to create eye-catching layouts **(see right)**. Press **Ctrl+Z** to restore the original placement.

In paper publications, using the master page was optional. In Web mode it's essential, if only to keep all these background elements lined up from page to page!

If your site has more than one page, **hyperlinking** is essential—it's what enables visitors to navigate through your site—and it's easily accomplished. Let's see how it's been used here.

At the right of the master page, notice the set of text frames containing the names of the various pages in the site. The underlining lets you know that these are hyperlinks which together comprise a navigation bar ("navbar"), another key feature of any Web site.

7 Ungroup the navbar elements and double-click the text for "About Us." Both words highlight because, as explained above, this is User Details answer text so it behaves as a unit. Then choose **Hyperlink** from the **Insert** menu.

The dialog shows the hyperlink target that's already installed for this text. You'll see that the target is a page in your current site, namely "2 - Page 2," which is in fact the one set up for About Us content. You could re-link the text at this point simply by choosing a different target—including any Internet Uniform Resource Locator (URL), or e-mail address, or a local file.

To create a new hyperlink in existing text, you would first select the range of text you wanted to link, then choose **Hyperlink** and complete the link. You can hyperlink in the same way from graphic objects, too!

Hoping that the concept is firmly established, we won't experiment any further right now.

The Hyperlink Manager gives you an overview of all the object and text hyperlinks in your publication, listed in "from/to" format by page number. From this convenient command centre, you can display, modify, or remove any of the links. You're sure to come back here as your publication grows in complexity and includes more links from pages, not just the master page.

8 **Cancel** the dialog and then choose **Hyperlink Manager...** from the **Tools** menu.

9 Switch back to the page level (on page 1) and click the body text starting with "Here's the place."

No answer text here... this is a standard text frame containing placeholder text in a story, which should be quite familiar to you at this point Just in passing, body text in Web design template publications is customarily marked with "Scheme Colour 1," so it takes on whichever colour has been defined as Scheme Colour

1 in the current scheme. Of course, you can use any colour you like when designing a Web site from scratch. Also, it's a good idea to run the **Layout Checker** (located on the **Tools** menu) to trap errors where text might not all fit in the given frame.

10 Click the picture below the body text (you may need to **Alt**+click as it is underneath the text frame in z-order).

Web Publishing

The HintLine shows you this is a linked bitmap image; again, it's just a placeholder. You can move or resize it and double-clicking will bring up the **Import Picture** dialog. Manipulating images in Web mode is exactly as you've practiced it in Paper mode throughout the tutorial sequence.

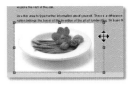

When you export a publication as a Web site, PagePlus exports each picture as a separate bitmap file, using the original file name if it's still known. Pictures other than GIFs, JPEGs or PNGs are converted to PNGs by default, but you have wide control over the export settings. Let's take a quick look at a dialog that lets you control not only picture settings but other key page and site properties.

11 Choose Web Site Properties... from the **File** menu.

On the **Page** tab, you can set the title of the current page, which will appear in the title bar of the visitor's Web browser. Note that the current page has no title at present. You can alter a page's file name and/or file extension if necessary and even whether or not to centre the page in the browser.

12 Click the **Background** tab, where you can add a sound file to your site that will play in the background while your site is being viewed. The bottom of this tab is used to add a background image where one is not currently set. If you are using a Master page (as we have done) then this option is not available as the attributes of the assigned Master page will be used.

13 Click the **Search** tab, where you can enter search engine descriptors to increase the likelihood that your Web site will be "noticed" by major Web search services.

14 Finally, click the **Graphics** tab. Here's where the global export settings for Web pictures are stored. In a separate dialog, you can set exceptions for particular images on a case-by-case basis.

15 Click **Cancel**, then (with the placeholder picture still selected), choose **Web Picture Manager** from the **Tools** menu (illustrated right). The initial settings determine the range of images inspected: any or all of those in the publication. For now, leave it set for **Selected Object Only** and click **Finish**.

For each image you're checking, a dialog opens to let you adjust the export settings. It also provides a way of entering alternate text for Web site visitors to read while an image is downloading. Each "tag line" you provide will appear inside the image frame during the time the image is being loaded into the visitor's Web browser. You'll find full details on all these image settings in the online Help topic "Setting Web picture display options."

16 For now, click **Close**.

Web Publishing

We've had a chance to inspect essentially all of the Web Page template components. Here are some additional Web elements that you can use to enrich your Web site, using online Help as your guide:

- **Sound and video files:** Sounds can include either background sounds (step 13) or linked sounds triggered by a mouse click, for example on an icon or hyperlinked object.

- **Animated marquees and animated GIFs:** Lively scrolling text, cartoons, and logos, as you previewed in the tutorial.

- **Rollovers:** Multi-state buttons that respond to mouse events by displaying different images, for example an "up" or "down" graphic.

- **Hotspots:** Transparent, hyperlinked regions drawn over parts of a page. Usually placed on top of bitmap pictures, they act like buttons that respond when clicked in a Web browser.

- **HTML and Java code fragments:** PagePlus inserts a marker into your publication at the site where the code will run.

Just as a Paper publication isn't much use unless it's printed, a Web publication can't show up in a browser until it's been converted into HTML pages and image files. PagePlus lets you "preview" the site as temporary files that appear in your own browser or "publish" it to either a specific local folder or a file transfer protocol (FTP) address. There are a few details you'll need to work out with your Internet Service Provider, so we'll let you read up on these options in online Help.

Let's now conclude this tutorial with a quick publishing demo.

17 Assuming you do have a Web browser installed, choose **Preview Web Site in Browser** from the **File** menu. In the dialog, click the **Select All** button and click **OK**.

Behind the scenes, the PagePlus publication is exported to a temporary folder and your Web browser launches, displaying the site's Home page. Simple as that!

Well, that concludes the Learning Lab sequence. Where to go next? It's up to you. From here, of course you can return to the start of the chapter and hand-pick some additional tutorials from the list. Add a dash of inspiration and in no time you'll be creating your own publications from scratch with confidence!

Beyond the Basics: Hands-on Efficiency

A useful guide to the use of keypresses to modify mouse actions.

This simple guide covers some lesser-known productivity enhancements: keyboard and mouse combinations that modify how some tools behave or provide shortcuts to speed up your work. We've modified the PagePlus HintLine to provide tool and object-sensitive tips like these throughout your design process—but you can browse this handy guide for an overview of tips that are sure to improve your workflow.

Alt-key selection

When you are using your mouse to click over a stack of objects that includes text, holding down the **Alt** key on your keyboard lets you easily toggle which object is selected. Normally, when you click over a text object, further clicks move the text edit cursor around. If you have an object behind your text and cannot select it because of this text behaviour, holding down the **Alt** key will ensure that your clicks continue to "drill down" through the stack, selecting other objects under your cursor.

Alt-key rotation

A handy time-saver: when using your **Pointer** tool for moving, selecting, or resizing objects, holding down the **Alt** key will temporarily switch to the **Rotate** tool.

Alt-key snapping toggle

Whether you have **Snapping** switched on or off, there are times when you want the benefit of freeform or constrained positioning of your objects. Normally, of course, you would switch Snapping on or off accordingly, but if you hold **Alt** while you are dragging an object you will temporarily toggle the Snapping behaviour, saving you the trouble!

Ctrl-key selection

In earlier versions of PagePlus, when you had objects enclosed as a group, you could not modify individual elements without first ungrouping. This meant that even though individual objects in a group could (in theory) have their own attributes such as fills and effects, you had to ungroup in order to modify a single object... which dissolved any group-wide effects. Problem solved! You can simply use the **Ctrl** key while selecting to individually edit elements in a group (for example, one component of a complex group object)... no more need to ungroup. Not only that, holding **Ctrl** while you double-click an object will select all objects of that type (on your current page).

Shift-key selection

Multiple selections are useful when you need to edit several objects that either aren't adjacent to each other, or have nearby objects that you want to avoid editing. It's now easier to draw a marquee selection boundary (drag with the Pointer tool) around objects to select them. Previously, when drawing a marquee selection boundary around a few objects, if the initial click was over another object, that object would be selected and moved. Now, if you hold down the **Shift** key, the initial click does not select and move underlying objects, making it easier to create multiple selections on a busy page. Also, repeated **Shift**-drags will add enclosed objects to existing selections.

Hands-on Efficiency

Shift-clicks on individual objects, unlike **Shift**-drag-selections, will toggle objects on and off in a multiple selection. **Shift**-clicks are extremely useful for selecting multiple objects that are not adjacent to each other, or have objects nearby that you do not wish to include in a multiple selection.

Ctrl-key copying

A firm favourite! Holding **Ctrl** on your keyboard while dragging an object will create a copy of it. Release the **Ctrl** key after you've released your mouse button and PagePlus will have dropped a copy of the selected object(s) at your cursor position. Even quicker than Copy and Paste! Hold **Shift** after you've Ctrl+dragged to constrain the movement of your new object before you let go of the mouse.

Shift-key resizing

When you draw something with PagePlus—whether it's a QuickShape, a custom shape, a line, or a text frame—you are likely to have to resize it at some point during the design process. Holding down the **Shift** key while you resize using a corner handle of your object will keep the object to its original aspect ratio, i.e. the width and height will grow proportionally. Very handy for making sure that your shape isn't distorted when you resize it, and useful for ensuring that your QuickEllipse draws as a circle and your QuickRectangle draws as a square. An exception to this rule is imported pictures: they can be freely resized when holding **Shift** and maintain their aspect ratio when resized without any additional keypresses.

Shift-key constraining

A handy tip when drawing fills and transparencies: try holding down the **Shift** key while you are moving the "end" nodes of the fill or transparency path. Their position will be snapped to coincide with 15° rotation steps. If you are working on a fill and want it to be perfectly horizontal, vertical, or at any 15° stepped angle in between, this method is invaluable. You can also use **Shift**-key constraining when editing your lines, especially useful for straight lines. End-nodes snap to 15° rotational values as described above, but line joins behave slightly differently—holding **Shift** will constrain movement of the node (or a whole object) to horizontal and vertical planes as well as extending the line in existing directions. Have a go, it's as easy to get used to and could save you time, effort, or worry when designing in the future

Wheel mouse modifiers

The wheel of your wheel mouse has grown into a very useful design aid. Normal behaviour for wheel rotation is to move the page view up and down—vertical scrolling. Holding **Ctrl** will switch the wheel to zoom mode. Holding **Shift** will switch the wheel to horizontal scrolling mode and holding **Alt** will switch the wheel to vertical scrolling mode! But that's not the end of the wheel's usefulness... click and hold the mouse wheel, then move your mouse around for an added extra; **panning**.

We hope you find these shortcuts useful!

Beyond the Basics: Publishing PDFs

The ins and outs of publishing Portable Document Format (PDF) files get detailed coverage in the online Help file, so this tutorial provides a run-through with some important "dos and don'ts" along the way.

> **Note:** Before proceeding, if you do not already have Adobe® Reader® or Adobe Acrobat® Reader installed, run **AcroSetup.exe** from the AcroReader folder of your PagePlus CD-ROM.

1 To get started, open **PDF Publishing.ppp** in the **Workspace** folder of your PagePlus installation (normally **C:\Program Files\Serif\PagePlus\11.0\ Tutorials\Workspace**).

We've set up this document specifically to demonstrate a few of the potential pitfalls of PDF publishing. While this guide will focus on PDF output, you'll find some of the principles involved are also relevant to printing.

2 On the **File** menu, select **Publish as PDF**.

In the **Publish PDF** dialog, on the **General** tab, set the output **Compatibility** to your particular version of Adobe (Acrobat) Reader, for example 'Acrobat 5.0' and select **Preview PDF file in Acrobat**.

3 Click the **Compression** tab.

Under **Colour Images**:

- Select 'Downsample Image,'
- Choose '96' in the adjacent resolution list.
- Set the **Compression** to 'JPEG,'
- Set the **Quality** to 'Low.'

This low resolution setting will make it easier to spot areas of the publication that have been converted to images on output.

For the purposes of this tutorial, we'll skip the **Prepress** tab (with settings for professional publishing) and **Security** tab (which offers password protection for electronic document distribution). Both are detailed in online Help.

Publishing PDFs

4 On the **Advanced** tab, set your **Transparent Area DPI** to '96' and clear the following options:

- **Embed Fonts**
- **Mask Images**
- **Strip Images**
- **Render Complex Fills as Bitmaps**

5 Click **OK** and then click **Save**. This saves the file with the same name as your PagePlus publication—**PDF Publishing.pdf**. Leave PagePlus open for use later in the tutorial.

The PDF file opens in your installed Adobe Reader with Page 1 on view.

6 As you scroll down the document, note that the images and text appear much as they looked in the original PagePlus document!

We've chosen these settings specifically for this tutorial. Review the details in online Help to determine the correct settings for a particular "real-world" publishing task.

7 Click the **Next Page** button or continue to scroll down to Page 2.

Internal Filter Effects

Note that the title at the top of Page 2 has been converted to a graphic.

We know this because it appears of lower quality than in the original PagePlus document and the text is no longer selectable. This has happened on Page 2 because the text uses an internal filter effect (in this case, **Inner Shadow**). Other internal filter effects include Bevels and Inner Glow.

Because internal filter effects change the interior of the object, it turns into a bitmap graphic in the PDF rather than remaining as text (as did the similar object without an internal filter effect on Page 1). If you find this conversion objectionable, use external filter effects (like Outer Glow and Drop Shadow), or no filter effect at all.

8 Continue scrolling downwards. Pause your scrolling at the red starburst, which on this page has a **Bevel** filter effect and has been output as an image in the PDF file.

Text Behind Rasterized Area

Examine the text to the right of the **QuickStar**. Note that it's darker and more jagged than regular text. In fact, it's also been converted to a graphic. But why?

For a PDF, as for a printout, the starburst with its pixel-based bevel effect needs to be **rasterized**—converted to a bitmap—on output. Bitmaps are always rectangles, so any text within that rectangle will also be converted to bitmap form.

Publishing PDFs

Compare this result to Page 1's unfiltered QuickStar, which remains a vector shape in the PDF because it has no internal filter effect or applied transparency. Here, the text remains unaffected.

To avoid accidental text-to-graphic conversion in PDF publishing, make sure vulnerable text sits *in front of* any problematic shapes in your PagePlus document—select the text object, then click the 🔳 **Bring to Front** button. QuickShapes with these filter effects will still be reproduced as graphics, but text in front will be intact.

9 Scroll down Page 2 to the image of the castle. Note that on Page 1 the text was unaffected around this image but here some of the text has also been converted to a graphic and loses quality in the process.

Text Behind Image Transparency

This pitfall follows from the same general principle we've just covered. Again, text behind part of an image's outlying region has been rasterized. The image in question is a PNG bitmap graphic that contains its own transparency. PagePlus itself detects this transparent region if you apply a **Tight Wrap** for the text to flow around. But as you might expect, if the text is behind the transparency when you publish to PDF, it will merge with the bitmap image. You can avoid this by bringing the text to the front of the stack of objects in PagePlus, as described above, or by using a different method of outputting transparency as discussed later.

10 Scroll to the bottom of the page and examine the graphic and text at the lower left. Note that the text near the lion image has not been converted to a graphic.

Crop Outlines

An image is cropped using the ⬚ **Irregular Crop Tool**. Here, we switched from straight-line cropping to curved lines using the Curve tools. Cropped objects remain properly cropped when published as PDF. Although all images are rectangular, close cropping tells the PDF to snip the image using the outline created in PagePlus—the image 'ends' before it touches any part of the text, leaving the text unaffected. This is an efficient way to constrain the area affected by the image. Where possible, PagePlus will always use these clipping paths to limit the effect of images on their surrounding area—PDFs fully support clipping paths.

11 Close Adobe Reader and return to the PagePlus document **PDF Publishing.ppp**.

12 On the **File** menu, click **Publish as PDF**, click the **Advanced** tab and select the **Strip Images** box. Set the **Strip Size** to 5 pt (5 points equals almost 2 mm) and click **OK**. Save the PDF file as **PDF Publishing 2.pdf**.

13 Examine the two output pages in Adobe Reader again. You'll note that there are fewer differences between pages 1 and 2 this time; Page 2 contains far less rasterized text.

Complexity

Using the **Strip Images** option rebuilds the publication's images using lots of thin strips, rather than one rectangular picture. Each strip can be of differing length, so less area in total is converted to a picture and there's less chance of other objects near graphics being converted to pictures.

This is a more accurate way of faking transparent regions in PDFs, but It does produce more complex PDF files that can be slower to draw and print (or may not open at all in older versions of Acrobat Reader).

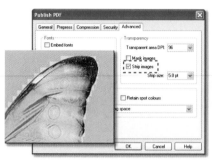

To reduce the complexity, publish with this option cleared, or increase the strip size. (If you clear the option, you'll find our previous tips useful to avoid large areas of rasterization.)

Finally, let's look at some of the other options we've encountered on the **Advanced** tab—these will be invaluable if **file size** is ever important to you.

14 Close Adobe Reader. In your PagePlus document, click **File/Publish as PDF**.

15 On the **Advanced** tab, select the **Embed Fonts** box and clear **Exclude common fonts** and **Subset Fonts**. Set your **Transparent area DPI** to '300.'

16 On the **Compression** tab, change the (Colour) **Downsample Image** setting to '300' dpi and set **Compression** to 'None.' This combination of settings will produce higher-quality graphics and accurate representations of your text. Click **OK** and save the file with the name **PDF Publishing 3.pdf**.

File Size

The first file we made with graphics settings of 96 dpi and no font embedding resulted in a 121 KB file. The final file with high-resolution graphics settings and embedded fonts made a 2.16 MB file—almost 18 times larger! The file size may differ between operating systems as different font files are used. Much of this increase is a byproduct of having chosen font embedding, which includes font files as part of the PDF file to ensure they're available on each host machine for accurate display. To conserve file size, skip embedding fonts like Arial and Times New Roman, which all Windows users will have (select the **Exclude common fonts** option). Select the **Subset fonts** option to embed only those font characters used in your file, rather than entire fonts.

The remainder of the file size increase is due to higher-quality graphics settings. If your PDF is intended for sharing by e-mail or the Web for viewing on-screen, you should downsample images to 96 dpi, with an equivalent transparent region. Consider image compression for even smaller files—a lower-quality setting will result in smaller files. If you are sharing the PDF file for a friend to print on their desktop printer, you might like to use higher-quality graphics settings, but note that this will increase the file size if your publication contains graphics, special graphic effects, or areas of transparency.

Beyond the Basics: PDF Links

Being able to publish your PagePlus creations as Portable Document Format (PDF) files is a real advantage. This tutorial further expands the possibilities by showing you how to add and manage bookmarks and hyperlinks.

Bookmarks made for PDF publishing are only visible when the document is viewed on-screen using Adobe® Reader, Adobe® Acrobat®, or the older Adobe® Acrobat® Reader— they display in a pane at the left of the screen and provide **hotlinks** to parts of your document. **Hyperlinks** provide a shortcut to Web pages, e-mail addresses and more. Both bookmarks and hyperlinks are included when publishing for on-screen viewing.

1 From the PagePlus Startup Wizard, select **use a design template**. In the **Brochures** category, in the **Side Tri Fold A4** previews, select 'Hotels' and click **Open**.

You can take this opportunity to complete the **User Details** dialog questions, which will be saved by PagePlus for future use, or continue with the next tutorial step.

2 Select the images in the centre of page 1, then on the **Insert** menu, click **Bookmark** (or press **Ctrl+R**).

In the **Insert Bookmark** dialog, in the **Text** field, type "Title Page." This is the text that will appear in the docked Bookmark pane when you view the document later as a PDF in Adobe® Reader or Adobe® Acrobat® Reader. Click **OK**.

3 When prompted, type a name for this anchor (the anchor is the destination-point for a bookmark). We've called ours 'Title Logo.'

Click **OK**. Your readers won't see the anchor names, but they're handy so that you as author can tell them apart. You can even have more than one bookmark pointing to the same anchor!

You've just created a hot link for readers of your publication, available while they have your PDF open in Acrobat Reader. We'll be switching to a second method for adding the next bookmark and there's a third type covered later, too.

4 Select the text frame at the bottom of the page and select **Bookmark Manager** from the **Tools** menu. The Title Page bookmark should be the only one listed and it should be highlighted in blue. Check the **Create as Sub-Entry** box, then click **Create**.

This opens the **Insert Bookmark** dialog that we've seen before.

5 In the **Insert Bookmark** dialog, type the name "Title Image," click **OK**, and then click **OK** again to apply the same name to the anchor at this location. Clear the **Create as Sub-entry** box, then click the publication name at the top of the bookmarks list (to set the top level as the next one to create bookmarks in). Click **Close**.

We used the Bookmark Manager to add this second bookmark because it allowed us to create the bookmark as a second-level link, hanging off of our first bookmark—making a sub-entry as denoted in the dialog. This is a useful method for creating bookmarked tables of contents or to draw attention to specific parts of the document that don't deserve a top-level bookmark. Further information and design advice about bookmarked documents is available in the Help topic "Creating a PDF Bookmark List."

So far we've tackled two types of bookmark—a **top-level bookmark** anchored on a small graphic object and a **sub-entry bookmark** anchored on an image of note. Both have used anchors, which PagePlus creates automatically during the bookmark creation. But bookmarks do not necessarily need to anchor to specific objects. We'll proceed to more typical use of bookmarks now by creating entries for each page of the publication.

6 Ignoring whether an object is selected or not, press **Ctrl+R** to add the next top-level bookmark.

In the **Insert Bookmark** dialog, in the **Text** box, type "At Your Service," then click **A page in your site**. In the **Page Number** drop-down list, select **Inside Leaf** and click **OK**.

7 Repeat this procedure to bookmark the inside pages and the back of the brochure. Name the bookmarks **Reservations, Restaurant, Special Deals**, and **Contact Us**.

Before we publish our bookmarked document, there's another important step to undertake.

8 Select the text above the image on Page 1 of your publication. It is grouped, so use the Ctrl key to select the centre frame on its own. This text answers the **Company** question of the **User Details** dialog we are using. When the text is selected (shown right), press **Ctrl+K** to add a hyperlink. Type a Web address to link to—we've used http://www.serif.com. Click **OK**.

9 On the **File** menu, click **Publish as PDF**. In the **Publish PDF** dialog:

- On the General tab, select the **Include hyperlinks, Include bookmarks, Include PageHints**, and **Impose pages** options.
- On the **Compression** tab, in the **Colour Images** section, select **Downsample images** and set the adjacent value to 96.
- On the **Advanced** tab, set the **Transparent area DPI** to 96. Click **OK**.

These settings will prevent the PDF we're about to make from being unnecessarily large as we're designing for on-screen viewing at the moment.

10 Click **Save** to give the PDF the same name as your
PagePlus publication. The PDF should open in Acrobat
Reader and display a Bookmark Pane to the left of the
screen. This can be undocked or closed, but is best used
as intended, to give quick, structured access to notable
parts of the document!

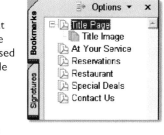

We've now completed the main tutorial steps.
However, there's some additional information you
should be aware of. This concerns our **Impose Pages**
choice in step 9, and a tip concerning auto-creation of PDF Bookmarks.

Even in PagePlus there can be (on purpose) vast differences between what's on screen
and what's printed. This brochure is a prime example—there are six thin pages in the
publication but these would traditionally be resequenced and positioned for printing on
just two sides of regular paper to make a tri-fold brochure. PDF Publishing with
PagePlus allows you to choose whether your publication is laid out as it is on screen,
or (imposed) as it would be when
printed. There are exceptions to this
rule: PDF publishing will not include
imposition for small publications
destined to be printed many times on
one piece of paper, or tiled output
where your publication is spread
across multiple pieces of paper. The
PDF itself is not a piece of paper (of
course) so different rules apply!

For pages that are resequenced after the
PDF is published, note that bookmarks,
hyperlinks and PageHints are ignored as
these are useful on-screen features that
do not transfer to a printed medium.
These electronic publishing options are
therefore tied to whether or not you
select **Impose Pages**.

11 Try republishing this PagePlus
document as a PDF imposed for
printing to quickly determine the difference.

12 Oh, don't forget... we also added a hyperlink to this
PDF. Hover the cursor over it in Acrobat Reader to
check the address we've pointed to.

Congratulations, all done!

If you're designing a long document and using text styles to offer a consistent look to your
chapter titles, section headings, topic headings, subheadings, etc, you'll be able to automatically
create a set of structured bookmarks based on your use of text styles. Click the
Automatic... button in the Bookmark Manager and specify which styles you wish to be used
as 1st, 2nd, 3rd, etc. level of PDF bookmark. This is much like creating a Table of Contents
with PagePlus and is discussed in the "Building a Table of Contents" tutorial.

Beyond the Basics: Building a Book

Demonstrates the use of **BookPlus**, the book management tool built into PagePlus. With BookPlus, you can create a book from a set of separate PagePlus (*.PPP) publication files. These separate files become book chapters, which you can then arrange in any order. BookPlus takes care of page numbering and lets you unify styles through the whole book. You can create a **Table of Contents** and/or **Index** (see appropriate tutorials for more on these features) that encompasses the entire volume.

In this tutorial, you'll have a chance to take BookPlus for a test drive, using an old science text to build a sample book.

1 On the **File** menu, click **New**, then **New Book**.

For future reference, note that you would use the **File/Open...** command to open .PPB book files you had already created.

BookPlus opens a new book file with the default name "Book1." The big blank region in the centre, reserved for the chapter list, is calling out to us to add some chapters.

2 On the **Chapter** menu, click **Add,** and then use the dialog to browse to your Workspace folder.

In a typical installation, you'll find this at **C:\Program Files\ Serif\PagePlus\11.0\Tutorials\Workspace.**

You'll see eight .PPP files starting with the prefix 'MMS.' Select them all and click **Open**.

Check that BookPlus is now listing the correct files in its **Chapter** column. The five files with "Ch" in their title are the book's main body text, chapters 1 through 5; the three additional files consist of introductory "front matter." From now on we'll be using the word "chapter" as BookPlus uses it... and as far as BookPlus is concerned, there are eight chapters here. Each separate file constitutes a separate chapter, whether it's a single-page title file or a ten-page block of body text.

Currently, these chapters are listed alphabetically, which isn't how we want them arranged in the book—but that's easily corrected.

3 One by one, drag each of the lower three files up and drop it into the proper position as shown, right.

> BookPlus saves its settings as a compact .PPB book file, separate from the source publication files. As soon as you've created a new book file, you can begin adding chapter files to it.

#	Chapter
1	MMS Ch 1.ppp
2	MMS Ch 2.ppp
3	MMS Ch 3.ppp
4	MMS Ch 4.ppp
5	MMS Ch 5.ppp
6	MMS Contents.ppp
7	MMS Intro.ppp
8	MMS Title.ppp

#	Chapter
1	MMS Title.ppp
2	MMS Intro.ppp
3	MMS Contents.ppp
4	MMS Ch 1.ppp
5	MMS Ch 2.ppp
6	MMS Ch 3.ppp
7	MMS Ch 4.ppp
8	MMS Ch 5.ppp

Building a Book

At this point you're probably curious to see just what you're working with... so let's take a closer look in PagePlus.

Note that BookPlus renumbers its **Pages** column automatically when you reorder chapters. It instantly updates the actual numbers in any open chapter files, or takes care of it the next time you open a chapter file from BookPlus. You can force updates in closed chapter files using the **Renumber Pages** command on the **File** menu.

4 **Shift**- or **Ctrl**-click to select the first four chapters, then choose **Open** from the **Chapter** menu. You can also double-click an individual chapter name to open it. Take a few moments to peruse each of the publication windows.

You should see a title page (illustrated right) for Marvels of Modern Science (1910); a one-page introduction; a table of contents with brief chapter summaries; and the first chapter ("Flying Machines"). With the exception of some centring and point size tweaks to the front matter, the entire text has been left plain, exactly as it was when imported from a public domain text file.

5 Switch to the **MMS Ch1.ppp** window and click the ▶ **Next Page** button.

As you can see, we're using a **facing page** layout. The page number display indicates we're looking at pages '5,6' of '4-15,' reflecting that the publication contains pages 4 through 15 of the book. Footers at the bottom of each page include a page number field. We intentionally didn't insert footers in the front matter chapters, so as not to have page numbers appearing there.

By design, the chapters have been set up to use the same dimensions and layout and we've chosen a single (rather than dual) master page to keep things simple. Note that BookPlus can't alter the basic structure of your publications, so when producing a book of your own it will be up to you to keep the setup consistent from one chapter to the next. Let's now to take a look at some of the tasks where BookPlus really shines, such as managing page numbering and styles.

6 Switch back to the BookPlus window. Note that the **Status** column now lists the four open chapters as 'Open.' Choose **Save** from the BookPlus **File** menu and call the book file **Marvels.ppb**. Saving the book file doesn't have any effect on the publication files.

Traditional book design dictates that chapters should start on a right-hand (odd-numbered) page and that goes for front matter as well: we'd like our Introduction and Table of Contents to appear on the right.

Before

Pages
1 - 1
2 - 2
3 - 3
4 - 15
16 - 23
24 - 34
35 - 40
41 - 51

However, if you glance at the chapter list, you'll see that four of the chapters currently start on an even page (illustrated right). That's because BookPlus by default has imposed consecutive page numbering. It's easy to override that setting and ensure correct placement.

7 Choose **Book Page Number Options** from the BookPlus **File** menu and select **Continue on next odd page. Insert blank page when necessary** should already be checked. Click **OK**.

After

Pages
1 - 1
3 - 3
5 - 5
7 - 18
19 - 26
27 - 37
39 - 44
45 - 55

You'll see the page numbers update instantly and now all the chapters begin (literally) on the right side. Any pages "added" won't be seen until you print or export, (illustrated right). You can confirm the changes in the PagePlus workspace, where the **MMS Ch 1** window will show that what used to be pages 5 and 6 have been renumbered as 8 and 9.

If you've had some experience developing publications with PagePlus, you know that it lets you define custom **text styles**, **object styles**, **colour palettes**, and **colour schemes** and that these custom settings are saved along with each publication file. If you haven't worked with these features, see the Learning Lab series of tutorials and online Help. If you have, you'll appreciate the ease with which BookPlus can "synchronize" these settings throughout all the chapters in a book. Simply designate one chapter as the style source and use it as the model for the rest of the book.

Traditional book design also observes various conventions for page numbering. We've suppressed page numbers in the front matter chapters of our sample book by not including page number fields. But suppose we wanted the first page of body text to appear as page 1, rather than bearing the number 7 as it does at present? We could use the **Chapter Page Number Options...** command from the **Chapter** menu to force page numbering for any chapter to start from any specific value. The same dialog lets you employ Roman numerals, letters, or other schemes in a chapter's numbering—for example, in a Foreword or Appendix.

After defining attributes in the style source chapter, you can select which attributes in other chapters should use the same settings. Let's try this with something as fundamental as the "Normal" text style.

8 Notice in the BookPlus window that the "Ch1.ppp" chapter is listed (in the **Synchronized** column) as the style source; all others are shown as "unsynchronized."

Chapter	Synchronized
Title.ppp	unsynchronized
Intro.ppp	unsynchronized
Contents.ppp	unsynchronized
Ch 1.ppp	style source
Ch 2.ppp	unsynchronized
Ch 3.ppp	unsynchronized
Ch 4.ppp	unsynchronized
Ch 5.ppp	unsynchronized

This is because "Ch1" was the first file imported into the book, before we rearranged chapters. You can designate any other file as the style source by selecting it and choosing **Set Style Source** on the **Chapter** menu. For present purposes, we'll leave things as they are.

9 Switch to the **MMS Ch1.ppp** window and select any word in the text. On the Context bar, you'll see that it's marked with the Normal style, using 12.0 pt Times New Roman. Now suppose we want to update the Normal style and propagate that change through the entire book.

Building a Book

10 Choose 'Accord Light SF' from the fonts list on the Context bar and '11.0' as the point size. Choose **Update Text Style** from the **Format** menu and answer **Yes** at the prompt. This takes care of changing the text in the current publication which (as noted) is the style source for the rest of the book.

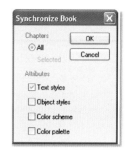

11 Switch back to BookPlus and choose **Synchronize**... from the **File** menu. In the dialog, select All chapters (noting that you might also update chapters selectively). In the **Attributes** section, select **Text styles** and clear the rest. Click **OK**.

12 In the **Synchronized** column, all the formerly "unsynchronized" chapters now have time stamps confirming the operation. For closed chapter files, BookPlus makes the modification and saves changes behind the scenes; note that the Modified date matches the synchronized date for these files. All open chapter files are updated, but changes won't be officially saved until you close the files.

Chapter	Synchronized
Title.ppp	9/12/2004 2:12:50
Intro.ppp	9/12/2004 2:12:50
Contents.ppp	9/12/2004 2:12:50
Ch 1.ppp	style source
Ch 2.ppp	9/12/2004 2:12:50
Ch 3.ppp	9/12/2004 2:12:51
Ch 4.ppp	9/12/2004 2:12:52
Ch 5.ppp	9/12/2004 2:12:52

13 Switch to PagePlus and inspect one of the "front matter" windows, for example MMS Contents. As expected, its Normal text is now defined as using the Accord 11 pt font.

Finally, BookPlus lets you output your entire book (or portions of it) via printing, PostScript®, or PDF. You'll find details in online Help. Again, the procedures are almost identical to those you've used for single files. As proof of the pudding, let's go for it and export our book as a PDF.

14 In PagePlus, first make sure all your publication files are closed and changes saved. Assuming you haven't strayed from the tutorial instructions, everything should now be synchronized with numbering options set correctly.

If you're trying to pull a diverse set of publication files into a consistent whole, you're sure to appreciate the ease with which BookPlus imposes design conformity. The longer the book, the more time you'll save!

Another asset when producing multi-chapter output is the ability to create a **Table of Contents** and/or **Index** from BookPlus (using the **Insert** command on the **Chapter** menu) that spans the entire set of publication files. Operationally, it's just as straightforward as building these elements for a single document.

For more information, see the "Building a Table of Contents" and "Building an Index" tutorials, which use sample files to step you through the basics.

15 In BookPlus, on the **File** menu, choose **Publish as PDF**. In the **Publish as PDF** dialog, there's no need to change anything. On the **General** tab, you should see the **Print Range** set by default to output the **Entire book**. Click **OK**.

You'll be prompted for a title and a few moments after clicking **Save**, Adobe Reader will open and display your brand new 55-page book!

In its present state, the book is exceedingly plain—no italics, no illustrations, no index. But there's no doubt it's a book and it came together in remarkably little time. Now that you've seen how BookPlus simplifies the process, feel free to use these chapter files to gain more practice with various aspects of desktop publishing. If you're interested in exploring other copyright-free texts, we suggest you visit the massive archives of the **Project Gutenberg**—http://promo.net/pg (note that international copyright laws vary and restrictions may apply).

Good luck with your book-building adventures!

Beyond the Basics: Building a Table of Contents

A table of contents is a useful addition to any long document with a hierarchical structure—i.e. sections, subsections, perhaps sub-subsections, and more. The PagePlus Table of Contents Wizard can automatically extract a TOC (up to six levels deep) from your publication's existing structure. In this tutorial, with the aid of a sample document, you'll see not only the Wizard but the powerful **Find & Replace** command in action.

The Table of Contents Wizard figures out what's "important" and "less important" in your publication by looking at its typography—taking advantage of the fact that the formatting used for titles, headlines, and subheadings denotes their relative prominence. Quite simply: bigger and bolder means more important. It's standard practice (and highly advisable) to define and apply named text styles to these elements, especially in a long document. PagePlus includes several built-in styles (illustrated, right) designed for just this purpose. You can use them in any publication "as is," redefine their attributes, or invent styles of your own. See online Help if you need to review the basics of text styles.

> **Heading**
>
> **Heading 1**
>
> *Heading 2*
>
> Heading 3

1 Open the sample file **TOC.ppp**—a specially prepared chapter from *Marvels of Modern Science* (used in the "Building a Book" tutorial). The publication should be in your **Workspace** folder (normally **C:\Program Files\Serif\ PagePlus\11.0\Tutorials\Workspace**).

> CHAPTER I: FLYING MACHINES
>
> ¶Early Attempts at Flight
>
> It is hard to determine when men first
> myth, legend and tradition we find all
> from the very dawn of authentic histor
> writers have made allusion to the subje
> must have early taken root in the restle

A quick glance at the content shows it's a simple 13-page layout with one story in a connected frame sequence.

Unlike indexing, preparing a Table of Contents requires very little intellectual effort. The only prerequisite, as we've said, is that the structural elements be marked consistently with named styles. At the moment this chapter consists entirely of plain text using the Normal style; we've left the style-marking task for you. First, let's mark the chapter title itself.

2 Click for an insertion point anywhere in the top (chapter) line. On the Context bar, expand the **Styles** drop-down list and select the **Heading** style.

Because the "Heading" style definition calls for 24 pt text, the resulting title is too wide for the page. Let's update the style directly from the text.

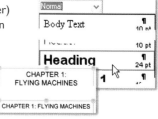

3 Select the entire title paragraph—triple-click in the text.—and choose **20.0 pt** from the **Point Size** drop-down on the Context bar.

Building a Table of Contents

This updates the selected text, which now should fit on one line.

4   To update the style definition, choose the **Heading** style from the **Styles** drop-down list. PagePlus knows that the selected text is already marked as "Heading" and asks whether you want to update the named style from the text, or reapply the style to the text. Select **Update the style to reflect recent changes** and click **OK**.

5   As a test, now try applying the **Heading** style to another paragraph on the page (select in the paragraph, then select the style). Notice the text turns to 20 pt, not 24 pt. Be sure to undo the change so it's back to **Normal**.

With the chapter title marked, we can now proceed to the headings and subheadings, using **Find & Replace** to speed the job. You've no doubt noticed the peculiar "#" and "@" symbols on the page. To make things easier we've pre-marked the headings and subheadings with these delimiters throughout the chapter. You can use Find & Replace from the main workspace or from WritePlus; in order to see the whole story at a glance, let's use WritePlus.

6   To open WritePlus, right-click in the text and choose **Edit Story**. On the **Edit** menu, click **Find & Replace**.

Using the **regular expression** search feature, we can find each of the headlines that start with the "#" character. This entails using a set of special symbols to tell PagePlus what to look for.

Optional step: To review all the possible symbols, click the small button to the right of the Find box, choose **Regular Expression** and browse the submenu. For complete instructions on constructing regular expressions, see online Help.

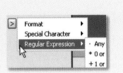

7   Under **Options**, check **Regular expressions**. PagePlus will now interpret what you type into the **Find** box as an expression, rather than as literal text to be searched for.

8   Type exactly this into the Find box: **#.+^.**

It looks strange, but PagePlus will interpret this as an instruction to "Find the next string that consists of these..."

#	the character "#"
.	any single character
V	one or more of the preceding (i.e. of *any character*)
^.	an end-of-paragraph mark

In other words, PagePlus should select all the characters in the next paragraph that starts with "#". And in this case, that will be a headline! (If you've any doubts, click **Find Next**.)

Building a Table of Contents

9   We want to apply the "Heading 1" style to all found lines. Click the arrow button to the right of the **Replace** box and choose **Format**, then **Style**. Choose **Heading 1** from the list of styles.

10 If your **Find** and **Replace** boxes look like the illustration to the right, you're ready to proceed. Click **Replace All**. PagePlus should report that 7 occurrences were replaced. Click **OK** to cancel the message, but keep the **Find & Replace** dialog open.

11 Next, we'll look for subheads—lines that start with '@'—so in the **Find** box, type @ over the #, leaving the rest of the expression intact.

12 Click the arrow button for the **Replace** box and select the **Heading 2** style. If your dialog entries look like our illustration, click **Replace All**. This time, 5 occurrences will be replaced.

Let's remove the delimiters now, again using a regular expression to save time.

13 Type exactly this into the **Find** box: [@#] This expression will locate any single character in the string between the two brackets.

14 Click the arrow button for the **Replace** box, choose **Format**, then choose **Clear Format** to remove the style specification, leaving just an empty **Replace** box. Now click **Replace All**. All 12 delimiter characters will be deleted. Close the **Find & Replace** dialog and click the ✓ **Finish** button to close WritePlus.

Now that the publication's main elements have been marked with styles, we're ready to build the Table of Contents. Note that the chapter consists of 13 pages at the moment.

15 On the **Insert** menu, choose **Table of Contents** and click **Next** at the first Wizard screen. When asked where you'd like to place the TOC, leave the selection **On a blank page at the start of your publication** and click **Next**.

16 At the next step, you have the option of adding a title (such as "Contents") and displaying page numbers. Select both options and click **Next** again.

17 The tab leader serves to connect each entry with its page number. Select one of the dotted-line options and click **Next**.

The next screen lets you tell PagePlus which text to pull out of the publication and plug into the table of contents. The check boxes let you assign a particular text style (as listed down the left) to a specific level of the TOC (as listed across the top).

18 We used the Heading style for the chapter title, the most important element of the TOC. Select the box in the first column next to **Heading**. Headlines—one level less important—are using the Heading 1 style, so select the box in the second column in the **Heading 1** row. Subheads, using Heading 2, should go at the third level. If your assignments look like our example to the right, click **Next** and then click **Finish**.

Style	1st	2...	3...
Footer	☐	☐	☐
Header	☐	☐	☐
Heading	☒	☐	☐
Heading 1	☐	☒	☐
Heading 2	☐	☐	☒

Building a Table of Contents

Your new TOC appears on the first page. Note that PagePlus has pushed the original page content onto an additional page and correctly numbered the resulting pages.

19 Click for an insertion point in the first line ("Contents") and note that the style "Contents-Title" appears in the **Styles** list. Click on lower lines and you'll see that PagePlus is using built-in text styles to format each level of the TOC, from "Contents-1st" on down. The styles for each level differ only as to the amount of indent.

If you want to change the table's appearance—for example, use a different font or add some extra space before or after a level—you can simply update the Contents styles just as we did with the Heading style in step 4. You can also use the **Text Style Palette**, accessible through the **Format** menu.

If your publication's content changes—for example, you add some sub-subheads at an even lower level—you can run the Wizard again with the option of replacing the existing TOC.

TOC in a PDF: If you're exporting a publication as a PDF file, you can take advantage of bookmarks—links that appear in a separate pane of the Adobe Reader® when the PDF is displayed. Using a wizard very much like the Table of Contents Wizard, PagePlus can automatically generate a nested bookmark list up to six levels deep, similarly derived from named styles in your publication. For more, see the "PDF Links" tutorial.

Book-length TOC: You can use **BookPlus** to create a Table of Contents for a multi-chapter book just as easily as for a single publication! In each case, you'll need to begin by designating a specific chapter where the resulting pages should be added. Otherwise the steps are identical to those you've practiced here. To try your hand at producing a book using sample files, see the "Building a Book" tutorial.

In sum, building a Table of Contents takes a great deal less time and effort than constructing an index and, because it's usually right up front, it's a conspicuous and useful feature to add to any longer publication. Just get into the habit of using named styles—the rest is easy!

Beyond the Basics: Building an Index

In a long document such as a report, manual, or non-fiction book, an index is an essential aid to the reader. The PagePlus **Index Wizard** helps you create an index with main entries and subentries, based on **index entry marks** you insert using WritePlus. We'll lay out the basic steps and let you practice on a writing sample.

1 Open Chapter 4 of our classic text *Marvels of Modern Science*, MMS Ch4.ppp. This should be in your Workspace folder (normally C:\Program Files\Serif\PagePlus\11.0\Tutorials\Workspace).

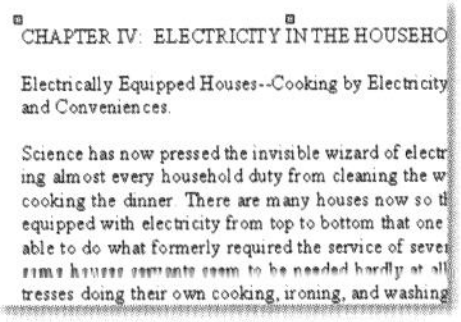

> CHAPTER IV: ELECTRICITY IN THE HOUSEHO
>
> Electrically Equipped Houses--Cooking by Electricity and Conveniences.
>
> Science has now pressed the invisible wizard of electricing almost every household duty from cleaning the w cooking the dinner. There are many houses now so th equipped with electricity from top to bottom that one able to do what formerly required the service of sever arms houses servants seem to be needed hardly at all tresses doing their own cooking, ironing, and washing

You may recognise this chapter ("Electricity in the Household") from the "Building a Book" tutorial. We suggest you save the file under a different name, so as not to get it confused with the original chapter.

2 Take as much time as you like to peruse this short chapter and think about how you might index it, without actually starting to list index terms. At this point you're interested in developing a mental filter— your own set of criteria for the

> As a general rule, you'll begin indexing by jotting down or typing up a separate list of possible entries, using key vocabulary terms and concepts. If it's your own writing you're working with, you'll have the advantage of being a "content expert"... but in this case the material is unfamiliar. No problem there, because it's always a good idea to put yourself in the place of a non-expert approaching the content for the first time.

kind of words that will qualify as index terms, given the material and your sense of who will be reading it.

Indexing is anything but a mechanical process. It takes skill and insight, to understand:

- **What an index is for**—obviously, for looking up a specific thing: the reader will want to know whether a topic occurs in the book. Equally, for showing at a glance the disparate places where a topic is covered and the weight the author has given to it. A skilled reader knows that scanning a good index provides a unique glimpse into a book's content. So aim for an index that provides that kind of richness.

- **What's not on the printed page**—it's important to scan literally, of course, looking for key terms that occur frequently or are simply more important. Just as useful is a more abstract approach: coming up with entries that may not literally occur in the text, such as **synonyms** for words that are used, or **superordinates**—main entries that will serve to cluster related subentries, shown to the right. In other words, don't miss the forest for the trees.

> devices
> = machines
> = appliances
>
> devices
>   annunciator
>   dumbwaiter, electric
>   plate rack manipulator
>   potato-peeling machine

Building an Index

- **Where to stop**—How detailed does your index need to be? How "deep" do you need to go in digging for descriptors? It's useful to know where to draw the line, or there'll be no end to your labours!

Finished with your chapter review? A casual browse has revealed that it's basically an inventory of the "house of tomorrow" (circa 1910)—a catalog of gadgets associated with various household places and functions.

3 For this chapter, start by making a list of all (or most) of these futuristic devices. It's a great idea to put these into a separate list of "candidate" terms, as in our example, right. Note that we've simply listed terms in the order they occur in the text. The idea at this stage is to extract and cluster, rather than alphabetise. For a useful index, we'd want to go beyond the single terms and plan ways of enhancing the list—for example, creating groups of **two-level entries** where multiple terms appear as subheads under a common main head. You'll get a glimpse of this as we move on to mechanics and begin marking entries.

4 Right-click the text and choose **Edit Story** to display WritePlus. Locate the first device term ("annunciator") in the text and click for an insertion point just before it. (You can also select the whole word or insert anywhere within it.)

annunciator
phonograph
telephone
door mat
automatic brush
escalator
dumbwaiter
oven
broiler
vegetable cooker
saucepan
dishes
incandescent lamp
clock
dishwasher
dryer
plate rack manipulator
plate warmer
gridiron
broiler
diskstove
waffle iron
potato peeling machine
floor-scrubber
dish-washer
coffee-grinder
meat chopper
dough-mixer
cutlery-polisher
water-heater
tea kettle
tub
wringer
flat iron
fireplace
fountain
pad

5 Click the  **Mark Index** button. The **Mark Index Entry** dialog displays the adjacent (or selected) word or phrase as the **Main entry**. Click the **Mark** button, which adds the entry to the index and closes the dialog.

The new index entry appears as a blue field, between curly brackets. You can edit an existing index entry by selecting between the entry and its word, then clicking **Mark Index**. Remove an entry field directly by selecting it and pressing **Delete**.

{annunciator}

6 Move on to the next term ("phonograph"), which you'll find a couple of lines down. Again, click to insert before the word, then click the **Mark Index** button.

With the dialog open, let's take a brief look around. You can use an entry as it is, or type new text for the main entry and sub-entry (if any)—but you must include a main entry for each sub-entry. At the upper right, you'll see the beginnings of an index list in a scrolling field that displays entries and sub-entries alphabetically. To reuse any entry, simply click it in the list.

7 Select the word "phonograph" in the **Main entry** field and use **Ctrl+X** to cut it, then **Ctrl+V** to paste it into the **Subentry** field. Type the word "devices" as the main entry and click **Mark**.

This time, we inserted a two-level entry.

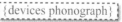

{devices phonograph}

8   Proceed on through the text, repeating the mark entry process for as many device terms as you can find—at least another dozen or so. Some can have one level, some two. For phrases like "door mat", select the phrase before clicking **Mark Entry**.

You might want to edit some entries, for example inserting "saucepan, electric" instead of just "saucepan." Make sure to insert some entries toward the end of the chapter, to add variety to the page references.

Inserting **cross-references** (directing users who look up one term to "See:" entries listed under another term) is an efficient way to enhance your index. The marks can be placed anywhere in the actual text—often the best place is at the start or end of a story, where they're easy to review and alter.

Let's try one.

9   Click to insert before the chapter title, then click the **Mark Index** button. In the dialog, select **Cross-reference**. The field already contains the word "See: " and for this example, type the word "devices" after that. In the main entry field, type "machines," then click **Mark**.

Index	
Main entry:	machines
Subentry:	
Options	
● Cross-reference:	See: devices
○ Current page	
Page number format	

10   When you're ready to build the actual index, click ✓ **Finish** to switch back to the main PagePlus screen. Notice that your index entries aren't visible here.

11   Choose **Index** from the **Insert** menu to run the Index Wizard. Click **Next** to step through the screens. The Wizard lets you pick where the index should be placed—for example, in the selected frame sequence, on a blank page, or to replace an existing index. In this case, we suggest you go for a blank page at the end of the chapter. As for formatting, you can uncheck **Include Index separators**; there aren't enough entries to warrant alphabetical dividers! Select a dotted line as a **Tab leader**.

12   Complete the Wizard sequence and take a look at your first index, which should look like our example, right. The various parts of the index (Title, Main entry, Sub entry, Separator) each use one of the built-in **text styles**.

You can easily modify the appearance of the index simply by altering one or more of these style definitions (see online Help for details). And you can keep on adding or editing index entries, then run the Wizard again to update the information.

Index

annunciator	1
brush, automatic	2
devices	
phonograph	1
telephone	1
door mat, electric	2
dumbwaiter, electric	2
escalator	2
fireplace, electric	5
flat iron, electric	5
fountain, electric	5
incandescent lamp	2
machines	See: devices
pad, electric	6

We've covered the mechanics of index-making. Before tackling a real indexing job, however, be sure to have a glance at the additional advice on the following page...

Indexing Tips

Experience is the best teacher and you'll undoubtedly discover your own indexing tricks. Here are some to get you started:

- **Use a pasteboard list:** We've pointed out how important it is to compile a preliminary list of "candidate" index terms before forging ahead with indexing. You can create a narrow text field on the pasteboard (using a white background fill) and type or paste your candidate terms there. Because the field is on the pasteboard, it's accessible no matter what page you're viewing—even from WritePlus!

- **Use markup, with Find & Replace:** You may find it helpful to use the main window to apply a colour like Cyan or Magenta to candidate index terms in the text. Then in WritePlus, you can use Find & Replace to locate the coloured terms and insert index marks. The Find & Replace dialog stays open while you work. If you prefer, you can apply underlining to candidate terms (providing the rest of the text doesn't use underlining). Be sure to restore the text to black (or non-underlined) when you're done.

- **Copy and paste:** When you know an index term will recur frequently through the text, here's a time-saver: Insert an initial index mark for the term, then select and copy the resulting index field. Use Find & Replace to locate subsequent occurrences of the term and simply paste the mark wherever it's needed.

- **Make multiple passes:** Be prepared to cycle through the basic steps repeatedly. You can either move systematically down your original list of candidate terms or work your way through the publication—or a bit of both. Pause from time to time and build an index from the marked text, each time replacing the previous index. This will let you maintain a current, top-level view of how the index is developing. You can print out the index pages or export them to rework the list and then use it as a plan for the next revision.

- **Proofread carefully:** Watch out for misspelled or redundant entries in the index, such as a term used in both its singular and plural forms and make corrections as needed.

- **Indexing a book:** Plan to spend additional time "up front" reviewing the content of the entire book before forging ahead. Working out your indexing criteria in advance will really pay off with a longer publication! And budget for more mechanical labour as well: you'll need to place index marks in each chapter and proofread closely to keep terminology consistent. The good news is that you can build an index for a book (a set of multiple chapters) just as easily as for a single publication—see online Help for details.

Indexing can be a real intellectual workout... but it's a rewarding opportunity to apply your unique knowledge of the material at hand. Once you've built an index you feel proud of, you'll have a new respect for people who do this for a living!

Beyond the Basics: Search Engine Optimisation

You've spent time, money, and effort developing a Web site. But how do you attract visitors to it? Improving your site's ranking in **search engine** results will definitely get you noticed. This tutorial offers a range of basic and advanced tips—mainly focusing on choosing effective **keywords**, then building on them to apply other search engine optimisation strategies.

Web site keywords can be individual words or whole phrases. They can appear almost anywhere, even hidden in the HTML code as a keyword "tag." We'll start with this **meta tag** and then progress to more significant design considerations.

1 To start, simply create a new, blank Web site—either click **use a design template** from the Startup Wizard and pick a site from the Web sites category, or create a new paper publication and choose **Switch to Web Publishing** from the **File** menu.

2 In Web Publishing mode, click **File/Web Site Properties...** and click the **Search** tab.

3 The **Search** tab displays two text boxes:

- In the upper text box, type a brief description of the content on *this page* of your Web site. This text will display when a search engine finds the page. The description can be any length, but the first ten words or so are the most important.

  💡 Aim to have a clear, concise description containing many of your chosen keywords and keyword phrases. If you have a multi-page site and certain pages offer unique content, you can improve the wording of your visible text to improve your site's chances of an even higher search engine ranking.

- In the lower text box, type the keywords and key phrases that categorise this page. Separate keywords and keyword phrases with commas, e.g., **sculpture, stainless steel sculpture, dragon sculpture, stainless-steel**. The site-wide keywords will be included in the HTML code of each page in the site and can be used by search engines to help determine a rank for your site amongst search results.

4 On the **File** menu, click **Preview Web Site in Browser**, make sure all pages are selected for preview and click **OK**. In your Web browser, choose the **View Source** command (usually available via the browser's **View** menu). Notice where your keywords have been added in the HTML code.

Search Engine Optimisation

What keywords might potential visitors enter if they were searching for what your site has to offer? You might be competing with millions of other sites if your searched-for keyword is "sculpture"but only a couple of thousand other sites if your searched-for keyword is "stainless steel sculpture." For example, if you offer information, products, or services for new parents, don't forget that "pregnant" and "pregnancy" are both relevant keyword terms.

Search Engine Descriptor Tips

Although they're optional, entering search engine descriptors will significantly increase the likelihood that your Web site will be "noticed" by Web search services.

Search services maintain catalogs of Web pages, often compiled through the use of **crawlers** (also known as **spiders**) or other programs that prowl the Web collecting data on sites and their content. By including descriptive information and keywords, you'll assist these engines in properly categorizing your site.

The following tips will help you maximize your site's potential to attract visitors.

- **Keywords:** Jot down your choice of keywords. Perhaps use a **thesaurus** to identify similar words, also considering abbreviations or longer versions of words as well as different word forms and plurals. Note down common **misspellings** of your chosen words. Consider some **online research**: as a starting point, perform an Internet search for the phrase "good keywords." You can consider using free or paid-for services and software to extend your ability to choose the best keywords for your site. Additional research will give you the benefit of seeing which keywords are most commonly used in search terms; this will help you reach either a wider market with popular terms or a niche market with less-competitive terms.

Having carefully chosen a set of keywords, you need to know some important tips about how else they can be used—this is the important "meat"for search engine optimisation formed on the "bones" of having some keywords and a target audience in mind. Meta keywords (as discussed above) are stored hidden away from view in your HTML source code once the site is published. But the **visible text** carries more weight when a search engine decides how to rank your site. Many search engines, notably including Google, do not use meta tag keywords in their search engine technology, so you'll need to go beyond the **Site** and **Page Properties** dialogs.

The coloured HTML snippet shows a **meta tag** with the HTML name keywords. The site description would also have been stored in a different meta tag (called **description**) if we had entered one before previewing the page.

```
<title>Stainless Steel Sculpture and Design</title>
<meta name="keywords" content="sculpture,
stainless steel sculpture, dragon sculpture,
stainless steel, bespoke sculpture, custom
sculpture, bespoke design, custom design, hand-
crafted metal, metalwork, installation">
```

Thanks to WebPlus you don't really need to worry about the site's HTML code or how these meta tags are generated; it's all taken care of for you!

If you wish, however, you can open any HTML page in a simple text editor like Notepad and type in additional keywords specific to that page.

- **Body text (copywriting):** The main **body text** or **copy** of each page is crucial. Make sure your chosen keywords are well represented in the body text. If your site's keywords cover stainless steel sculpture, for instance, it would be wise for those exact words to appear in your body text.

  Don't get caught out just writing finer detail in the copy, also include those broader descriptions and terms frequently in your writing. Writing engaging content is the first stop for improving search results. You may also like to include keywords in your copy text with **bold** or *italicised* formatting and give them prominence in your first body text paragraph. These attributes may in turn lead to those words being given more prominence in search rankings. It's not difficult to write copy with the keywords in mind, and it's far more attractive and effective to include those words in your main copy rather than cheekily adding them as a list somewhere on the page. Using your keywords in your main copy can also make up for any key terms used on buttons or menus that are published as graphics—search engine crawlers can't read text that has been converted to a picture.

  Giving careful consideration to keywords in copy text is always recommended but may only impact search engine rankings for less competitive search terms. There are ranges of books dedicated to copywriting—even copywriting specifically for Internet search engine optimisation—so we're obviously simplifying the issue here. Again, perform an Internet search for references on "SEO Copywriting."

- **Page title:** Each page's name appears throughout WebPlus to help you manage and identify your pages. This page name normally becomes the **title** stored both in the hidden published HTML code and in the visible title bar of viewers' Web browsers. If you want the public to see a page title other than the WebPlus page name, you can enter one on the **Page** tab of the **Site Properties** dialog. Your choice of page title will be a factor in search engine optimisation and it sits between the copy text and filename in importance.

- **File name**: Each page you create in your WebPlus site has a title and a file name. For instance, the file name for the first page is usually always **index.html**—by default, that's what Web browsers look for if directed to a folder rather than to a specific page. For your other pages you have total freedom in choosing what the published HTML filename will be. Again, you can set the file's name on the **Page** tab of the **Site Properties** dialog.

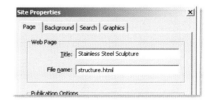

- **Hyperlinks and anchor names**: You can design navigation bars to help your site's visitors find their way from page to page, but you should also consider some text-based hyperlinks to other pages on your site and to important sections of long pages. The hyperlink names, as well as words either side of them in the copy, are analysed by search engine technologies and will add weight to your content's credibility.

Search Engine Optimisation

- **Image ALT and TITLE tags**: You can add descriptors to individual images using the **Web Export Options** dialog, available via **Tools/Web Picture Manager...**

ALT text is displayed before the image downloads and **TITLE text** is displayed when the mouse is hovered over a picture. Using pertinent keywords for these text strings adds further weight to your site's content.

Advanced Tips

Let's now consider what happens once your site is finished and published—how will search engines find it?

Some search engine companies accept submissions of sites for inclusion in their search results. Others use automated systems, such as spiders, to find and help rank sites. These electronic programs follow links to your site from known resources (or find your site in the search engine's own directory) and analyse your site's keywords as well as other content.

You can rely on spiders to find your site if you wish, or you can submit your site for inclusion in a search engine's listings, sometimes at a cost.

- **Search engine submissions:** You should try to get your site listed in the free **Open Directory Project** (http://www.dmoz.org). DMOZ is a totally free online directory used heavily by other search engine companies, so getting listed there will help make your site appear in a greater number of search results.

  Submitting your site to the Open Directory Project and having it approved by one of the volunteer staff may take some time, perhaps months, but is worth the effort. Be aware that your site may be rejected if there is no unique content; if the content is illegal; if your site is under construction; if you have suggested an inappropriate category for your submission; if you have used an automated submission program or service; if your description is not accurate, concise, or is too "promotional" in nature; or of course if your site is already listed.

  Choosing the right keywords before publishing and applying for inclusion on www.dmoz.org is likely to prove more effective than submitting your site to multiple search engines at length— although you do need to be listed somewhere to get the ball rolling! Take care to try and get your site's description right first time—DMOZ volunteer staff are so busy that an edit to your entry may be unachievable.

- **Keyword analysis**: Some Keyword Density Analysis may shed further light on the success of your site in search engine results. Search for this phrase on the Internet for further information and helpful software. You can use such software or online services to compare the frequency with which a chosen keyword occurs on your site in comparison with one of your competitors—choose a competitor with high-ranking search results for a worthwhile comparison.

Search Engine Optimisation

The analysis often differentiates between words in titles, image tags, copy text, hyperlinks, the domain name and, of course, official meta tag keywords. This will help determine if you can improve on the current frequency and usage of keywords. Search engines may favour a site against its competitors because of a higher density of keywords in the copy text and other areas.

- **Spider simulators**: There are some applications and Web sites that offer a view of your own Web site comparable to that of a search engine spider. A spider's-eye-view of your site might help you determine if you have made good use of keywords.

  Consider Google's approach by viewing your site through a text-only Web browser such as the Lynx Browser (perform an Internet Search to obtain this browser). A range of spider simulators can be found with a search for the phrase **spider simulator**.

  While these tips will make your site search-engine-friendly, you may find that full optimisation is required if your desired search terms are already very popular on the Web. If you have thought about keywords, their use in different ways and have checked your site's suitability for search engines by using a spider simulator, what else can you do? There are lots of doors open to you, including the following:

- **Fees and payment:** As mentioned previously, you can submit your site to search engines and directories (sometimes at a cost). You can also pay a service fee to have guaranteed frequent "spidering" so your entry with a search engine is updated regularly. Alternatively, consider pay-per-click advertising such as **Google's Adwords**.

- **Link building:** You should make efforts to build links, to get other sites to link to yours—preferably reputable sites with content relevant to your own. Look at some niche directories, and avoid signing up to "link farms"—sites that focus purely on offering links to other sites that are irrelevant to their own content, as these may be ignored by search engine companies (your site ranking may even be harmed by association).

  Some links to your site will carry more weight or relevance when a search engine ranks your site. A site's **Google Page Rank**™, for instance, can be ascertained by installing the Google Toolbar (found via Google's home page); you should aim to have links to your site on other relevant sites that already have a respectable Google Page Rank (five or higher). Sites with a high Page Rank are "spidered" more often so your site in turn will be found and spidered more often if you have links from such respectable sites.

  These link-building methods will increase the chances of your site being included in more search engine results, while the relevance of links and the content (use of keywords) will contribute to your ranking.

- **Link analysis:** You can also consider **Link Analysis** services or software—tools which will analyse successful sites and report on their optimisation methods. As you move forward with the evolution of your online presence, you may want to know detailed information about your visitors' habits—if and when they leave your site, how they found your site and much more.

  Web trackers and analysis software and services abound; your Internet Service Provider or Web host may be able to offer basic information as part of your hosting package, or you could consider external services.

External services are often able to offer a far greater level of accuracy and detail (for instance, at a basic level just differentiating between unique and repeat visitors is a great distinction).

Last but by no means least, you can learn from professionals with an expertise in search engine optimisation (**SEO**) and search engine marketing (**SEM**).

- **Consultancy:** Although the Internet is new to many people, some are already seasoned experts and have grown up with finding ways to improve their (and others') use of the Internet.

  Whether you wish to use paid services or not, you should examine some consultancy services and resources for advice, further learning, and often guaranteed better results.

We hope you've found these tips and links useful and here's hoping we see your site at the top of our next Google search!

Beyond the Basics: Special Effects

Expanding on the ideas discussed in the "Adding Graphic Flair" tutorial, these steps offer a range of fun graphical effects for text and objects in your publications and culminate with storing some of the effects as a reusable **object style**. So hop on board as we explore the editing capabilities of several key tools.

1 From PagePlus's Startup Wizard, select **start from scratch,** select an A4 or Letter size publication from the **Regular/Normal>Portrait** category, and then click **Finish.**

2 Select the **A Artistic Text tool** and drag out the initial text size to approximately 1 cm or half an inch high and type a sentence such as "**Artistic Text on a Path Looks Fantastic!**"

3 With the object selected, click the **Path** flyout on the Context bar and select the Wave preset. Using the Pointer tool, hover over the small red square at the start of the sentence. Click and drag to move it; it sprouts a control handle. Yes, the path you've applied to the text is a basic curve with two end nodes and can be manipulated like any other curved line. Move it downwards a little and move the right-hand node up a little, so the text is running 'uphill.'

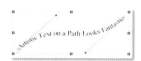

4 Still working with the path text object, notice the small handle at the left of the sentence. It has a dot which serves as a slider.

Drag the slider to adjust the **baseline shift**: the elevation of the characters in relation to the curved line. If your text were on a tight circle, this adjustment could make the words easier to read.

> You can also adjust the start and end points using the small grey arrows at each side of the sentence. The effect is reversible, by the way, using **Tools/Remove Path from Text.**

5 On the ⊠▾ **Mesh Warp** flyout on the toolbar, select the ▽ **Cone Down** preset. Double-click a couple of points inside the warped object, then click the ☐ **Hide/Show Grid** button on the Context bar to display the dot grid for the current warp.

 Using this tool you can deform any of your objects in PagePlus and using the ▨ **Warp Fills** button you can warp and unwarp the object's fill, too.

Special Effects

The points you double-clicked are now movable nodes. Experiment by moving your nodes and adjusting the control handles flying out from them. You can also grab and move the splines—the segments between your nodes. The Grid will help you see how your object is being warped.

6　Move the text up towards the top of the page. We'll come back to it in a moment.

7　On a clear area of your page, draw a **Quick Rectangle** approximately 7 x 4 cm in size. Move the slider to the left of the shape down to round the corners. On the **Styles** tab, in the **Materials** section, open the **Wood** category and apply the **Basswood** preset.

If you want to take a side trip to explore the mathematics behind the computer-generated wood effect shown here, right-click the object and choose **Filter Effects**. Browse the **3D Bump Map**, the **3D Pattern Map**, and the **3D Lighting** categories and subcategories. The settings for each category are shown in the right pane. Go ahead and adjust some settings to see how it affects your object.

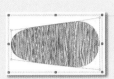

8　Apply the ◁ **Cone Left** warp preset to the lozenge. Then modify the position of the left-hand warp nodes and adjust all the node handles so that what started out as a Quick Rectangle looks like our illustration above. Using a warp envelope, we've quickly introduced a bit of fake perspective.

9　Increase the size of your warped wooden shape so that it is larger than the path text object we created earlier.

Click the ▣ **Send to Back** button on the toolbar, then position the shape behind your text.

10　Deselect the shape by clicking on a blank area of your page, then click on the path text object to select it. Click the _fx_ **Filter Effects** button on the **Attributes** toolbar.

In the dialog, check **Bevel and Emboss**, and then set the various parameters for the Bevel and Emboss filter to match those illustrated.

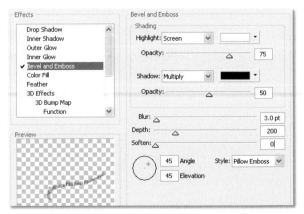

To finish, we'll define an object style based on the way this text object now appears.

11 Right-click your warped text object and choose **Format/Object Style/Create**.

An **object style** is a cluster of many attributes (the ones you see listed in the **Style Attributes Editor** dialog) saved under a particular name. Besides the predefined styles —which you can easily modify—you can create and customise your own object styles, which will also display on the **Styles** tab. If you update a style definition the change is propagated (as with schemes or text styles) to all the objects sharing that style.

To modify an attribute setting, you simply double-click the attribute.

12 Try it: double-click the black swatch next to the **Fill** entry. Click **Cancel** to return to the dialog without changing anything (in order to leave our text object unaltered).

Let's create an object style that includes the **Fill** and **Filter Effect** only.

13 Clear all the boxes except for **Fill** and **Filter Effect**. Name your setting something like "Custom Pillow Emboss."

14 Click the **Browse** button at the bottom right of the dialog to choose a category where you want to store the style preset. Expand the **Text Styles** category, click on **Abstract**, then click **OK**. Finally, click **OK** again to save your custom object style.

Your design should now resemble our illustration and you can use this predefined object style for any of your future designs!

Create a Sales Flyer

Work with text and graphics objects to create a single-sided "Car for Sale" flyer from scratch.

Create a Sales Flyer

Whether you're selling your car, organizing an event, or opening a new business, a flyer is an easy to produce, inexpensive, yet highly effective marketing tool.

The PagePlus Page design templates include a selection of ready-made flyer publications, which you can customize to suit your needs (click **File/New... /New from Startup Wizard**, then click **use a design template**).

In this tutorial, however, you'll create a "Car for Sale" flyer from scratch using sample images. The sample images are located in your PagePlus installation directory (usually **C:\Program Files\Serif\PagePlus\11.0\Tutorials**), in the **Workspace\Sales Flyer** directory. Of course, you can use your own images if you prefer.

In this exercise, you'll learn how to:

- Create and position text frames.

- Type text directly into a publication.

- Apply text formatting and adjust text leading.

- Apply a shadow filter effect to heading text.

- Import, position, resize, and crop images.

- Adjust image brightness and contrast.

- Create and position QuickShapes.

- Adjust line and border settings.

- Apply a transparency effect to a shape.

Create a Sales Flyer

In this tutorial, we'll assume that you're selling your car from home, and that you'll be printing your flyer on A4 paper, on a home printer. If you want to use your own images, they should be clear and should show the car from different angles.

We'll start by creating and saving a blank A4 document. We'll insert a standard text frame, type a headline, apply some basic text formatting, and create a drop shadow filter effect.

To create and save a new publication

1 In PagePlus, click **File**, point to **New**, click **New from Startup Wizard**, and then click **start from scratch**.

2 In the dialog, click **Regular/Normal**, and then click **Portrait**. Click the A4 or Letter template, and then click **Open**.

3 To save your new document, click **File/Save**. Save the file as **CarForSale.ppp**.

We want our heading to grab the reader's attention, so we need to make it large and bold. We've used **160 point Basic Sans Heavy SF**. You can use anything you like, but it's generally best to use a sans serif font for headings.

To create a heading

1 On the Tools toolbar, click the **Standard Frame** tool, then click and drag to insert a frame in the top left corner.

2 In the text frame, type "FOR SALE," and then click and drag to select the text (or press **Ctrl+A**).

3 On the Context bar, choose the font size and style for your heading.

4 With the text frame still selected, resize the text frame to fit the text— click one of the frame handles, hold down the left mouse button, and then drag to the new position.

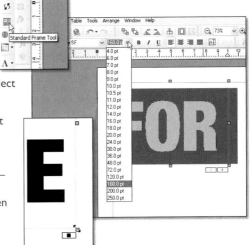

Next, we'll adjust the **leading**—the distance from one line of text to the next.

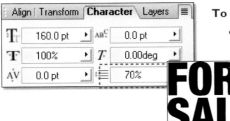

To adjust text leading

- Select the text, then on the **Character** tab, change the leading value to '70%.'

  Our headline words now sit snugly one on top of the other.

Create a Sales Flyer

PagePlus provides a variety of filter effects, which you can use to transform any object. We can make our headline text 'stand out' even more by applying a diffused shadow.

To apply a drop shadow

1 With the text frame selected, on the Attributes toolbar, click *fx* **Filter Effects**.

2 In the **Filter Effects** dialog, click **Drop Shadow**, enter the values as illustrated right, and then click **OK**.

The headline now appears to be shadowed, giving it more impact.

The **Styles** tab provides predefined styles that you can apply to objects, or customize to suit your own taste. Each object style can include settings for multiple attributes such as line colour, line style, fill, transparency, filter effects, font, and border. For an overview, see the "Using object styles" topic in online Help. **Note:** You can apply styles to **artistic text**, but not to **standard text**.

Now for the photographs of the car. We'll use four different images for this flyer. They'll need some adjustment though. In these next steps, we'll be resizing, cropping, and adjusting brightness and contrast levels.

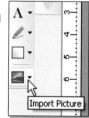

To import and resize an image

1 Click outside the text frame to deselect it. On the Tools toolbar, click ▣ **Import Picture**.

2 In the **Import Picture** dialog, browse to the **Workspace\Sales Flyer** folder and open the **CFSfront.png** file.

3 When the cursor changes to a ⊹▥, click in your page and then drag to insert the image. (Note that the Picture tools are displayed in the Context bar.)

4 Resize and move the image until it fits into the space to the right of the headline.

Notice that this image is a little dark. We'll use the **Image Adjustments** dialog to adjust it.

Create a Sales Flyer

To adjust image brightness and contrast

1 Select the image, and then on the Context bar, click **Image Adjustments**.

2 In the **Image Adjustments** dialog:

- Click **Add Adjustment**, and then click **Brightness and Contrast**.

- Adjust the values by typing into the value boxes, or by clicking and dragging the sliders. Check the effects of your adjustments in the **Image Preview** pane. Click **OK**.

We'll now insert the main photo for our flyer. We could use the image just as it is. However, there's a lot of background and we're only interested in the car. Let's crop the image, and focus on the car.

The **Photo Optimizer** helps you improve the print quality of an image on a specific printer. You can print test samples and choose the best brightness and contrast settings. With the image selected, on the **Format** menu, click **Picture/Photo Optimizer**, and then follow the instructions in the Wizard.

To crop an image

1 Repeat steps 1 to 3 of the "To import an image" section to import the **CFSside2.png** file. Resize this image so that it sits beneath the headline and fills the width of the page.

2 With the image selected, on the Tools toolbar, click the ⊡ **Square Crop Tool**.

3 Click the handle in the upper centre of the image and drag down until you have cropped most of the background. Repeat the process to crop the background on either side of the car.

To fine-tune your cropped image: Click in the image (the cursor changes to ⌐), and then drag to reposition the image inside the crop boundary. To restore the cropped object to its original shape: Click ⊕ **Remove Crop** on the Tools toolbar's Crop flyout.

4 Repeat steps 1 to 3 of the "To import and resize an image" section to import the **CFSscenery.png** and **CFSside.png** files. Resize these images and position them in the lower right corner of the page, as illustrated.

Create a Sales Flyer

Great, our images are now in place. They show the car from different angles and give the reader a good idea of its appearance and condition. We'll now insert some text frames and add the car's details and key selling points.

☐ Click the **Standard Frame Tool** and insert some text frames in the space at the lower left of the page. Click inside the frames for an insertion point, and then type the car details into the boxes.

You could use just one text frame. We used three, however, to give us more flexibility with positioning—try dragging the frames around the page to experiment with different positions.

Now for the finishing touches. For a fun effect, we'll use a **QuickShape** and the **Transparency** effect to create four pieces of sticky tape to 'stick' our main photo to the page.

You should list the year, model and body style, and you might want to include the number of miles, engine size, or colour. Be honest. Avoid flowery phrases and stick to words that buyers will respond to—super clean, low mileage, one owner, etc. The clearer and more honest your ad, the easier it will be to sell your car.

To create and format a QuickShape

1 On the Tools toolbar, click the **QuickShape** button and select the **Quick Rectangle**.

2 Click and drag to create a rectangle about 2 x 0.75 cm.

3 Right-click the rectangle, click **Format**, and then click **Line and Border**.

4 In the **Line and Border** dialog, on the **Line** tab:

- in the **Weight** box, click '0.5 pt.'
- in the **Shade(-) Tint(+)** box, in the drop-down list, click '+50%.'
- Click **OK**.

We're halfway there—we've created our basic rectangle and lightened its border. To resemble tape, however, our shape has to be transparent.

Create a Sales Flyer

To add transparency to an object

1. Right-click the object (in this case, the rectangle), and then click **Format/Transparency**.

2. In the **Transparency** dialog, in the **Type:** drop-down list, click **Solid**.

3. In the % value box, type '40' (or drag the slider to adjust the value), and then click **OK**.

Now that we've created the template for our 'tape,' we can copy and paste it to quickly create another three identical shapes.

 Transparency effects are great for highlights, shading and shadows, and simulating "rendered" realism. They can make the critical difference between flat-looking illustrations and images with depth and snap.

To copy and paste an object

1. Select the object, right-click, and then click **Copy**.

2. Right-click again and click **Paste**.

3. Repeat steps 1 and 2 to create a total of four identical shapes. The copies will be pasted one on top of the other in the centre of the workspace.

You can also use the **Opacity** tab to add transparency to an object.

Now all we have to do is position our shapes—we want them to appear to be holding down the corners of our main image. To do this, we need to rotate them.

To rotate an object

1. On the Tools toolbar, click the ⟲ **Rotate** tool.

2. Click to select the object, then click one of its handles—the pointer changes to the Rotate cursor—and then drag to rotate the shape 90°.

3. Now click in the centre of the object—the pointer changes to the Move cursor—and drag the shape into the desired position.

4. Repeat steps 1 to 3 to rotate and position each of the shapes as illustrated.

 As a shortcut, you can position the cursor over an object handle, then press the **Alt** key. This temporarily switches to the **Rotate** tool.

Create a Sales Flyer

That's it! We've finished creating our flyer and are ready to view and print it First of all, let's change to Print Preview mode and look at our layout without frames, guides, rulers, and other screen items.

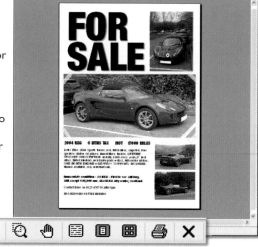

To preview the printed page

- Click the 📄 **Print Preview** button on the Standard toolbar (or on the **File** menu, click **Print Preview**.)

As you are designing your PagePlus publications, you might find it useful to occasionally switch to Print Preview mode to give you an idea of how your layout will look on the printed page.

To cancel Print Preview mode

- Click the ✕ **Close** button at the lower edge of the preview window.

Assuming you were happy with the way your flyer previewed, let's go ahead and print it out. For this exercise, you only require basic desktop printer output. However, PagePlus supports scaling, tiling, colour separations, and many other useful printing options. For more information, see "How to Print Your Publication" in online Help.

To print a publication

1 On the **File** menu, click **Print...**

2 In the **Print** dialog, on the **General** tab, do the following:

> In Print Preview mode, the lower toolbar provides a variety of options—for example, **Zoom**, **Pan**, and **Print**. The toolbar also includes a **Multipage View** button, which lets you preview multi-page publications using a page array.

- Select your desktop printer from the **Name:** drop-down list.

- Select the print range to be printed—in this case, we only have a single page, so click **Document**.

- Select the number of copies you want to print.

- Click the **Properties** button to set up the printer for the correct page orientation—**Portrait**.

Note: Depending on your printer driver, to print text with shading or custom settings, you may need to click the **Fonts** tab and select **Download TrueType Fonts as bitmap soft fonts**.

- When you are happy with your printer settings, click **Print**.

Your sales flyer will print in colour on a colour printer or in shades of grey on a black and white printer.

Congratulations, you have successfully created and printed a sales flyer from scratch!

We've covered a lot of ground in this tutorial, and you should now be feeling more familiar with some of PagePlus's powerful desktop publishing tools and features. We hope that you have enjoyed the exercise, and have learned a few things in the process.

What's next? Well, that depends on what you want to do. If you want more hands-on experience with graphic objects, try the "Create a Greeting Card" tutorial. If you're feeling adventurous and want to try your hand at creating a multi-page publication, see the "Create a Newsletter" and "Create a Photo Scrapbook" tutorials.

Create a Photo Scrapbook

Preserve your holiday memories by combining special photos with text
and graphics to create a holiday scrapbook.

Create a Photo Scrapbook

Every scrapbook is unique. Some are specifically for school events, others for vacations, while many simply record memories of children growing up and of family celebrations. Whatever memories they record, scrapbooks provide an ideal way for you to display and show your favourite photographs.

In this tutorial, you'll create a holiday scrapbook. We've provided sample photographs, but you can use your own snapshots if you prefer.

In this exercise, you'll learn how to:

- Create a multi-page document.
- Work with master pages to create backgrounds.
- Create QuickShapes.
- Work with colour, transparency, filter effects, and fills.
- Import, position, resize, and crop images.
- Create and apply object styles.
- Work with standard and artistic text.
- Wrap text to image borders.
- Adjust image colour, brightness, and contrast.

Create a Photo Scrapbook

In this exercise, you'll create a three-page holiday scrapbook, which you can print on a home printer. Our sample images were taken on a family holiday In Scotland, so you'll notice a Scottish theme to the layout. The images are located in your PagePlus installation directory—usually **C:\Program Files\Serif\PagePlus\11.0\Tutorials**, in the **Workspace\Scrapbook** folder.

You can use your own images and theme if you prefer. Your photographs don't have to be perfect—we'll show you how to crop them and make various adjustments later.

Let's begin by creating and saving a blank document. We'll then create a cover page and show you how to apply a background design using a master page.

> Try to avoid importing very large image files. Even if these are scaled down on the publication page, the original file size is preserved. As a rule, downscale your images first using photo-editing software (such as PhotoPlus), then import them into PagePlus.

To create and save a new publication

1   In PagePlus, click **File**, point to **New**, click **New from Startup Wizard**, and then click **start from scratch**.

2   In the dialog, click **Regular/Normal** and then click **Portrait**. Click the A4 or Letter template and click **Open**.

3   To save the new document, click **File/Save**. Save the file as **Scrapbook.ppp**.

First, we'll design an attractive cover for the scrapbook using a stylised version of the St. Andrew's Cross as a background. We'll create this part of the layout on a master page.

> Master pages are part of the structure of your publication, and provide a flexible way to store background elements that you'd like to appear on more than one page—for example a logo, background, header/footer, or border design.

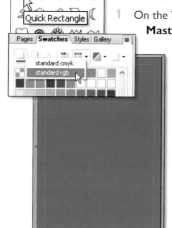

To create a master page

1   On the **View** menu, click **Master Page**. The master page view opens and 'Master A' is now displayed.

2   On the Tools toolbar, click the **QuickShape** button and select the **Quick Rectangle**.

3   Click and drag to create a rectangle to cover the entire page.

4   With the rectangle selected, on the right of the workspace, click the **Swatches** tab.

5   On the **Palette** drop-down list, select the **standard RGB** palette, and then click the blue swatch.

This solid blue rectangle will form the background of our St. Andrew's Cross, which will sit behind text and photos on our cover page. Rather than being solid, we want to give it a more transparent appearance.

Create a Photo Scrapbook

6 With the rectangle still selected, click the **Opacity** tab, click the **Gradient** button, and then click the **Linear Transparency 40** swatch. (Hover the cursor over the swatches to view their labels.)

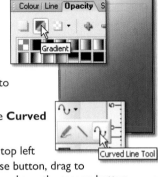

We've applied a blue to white transparency gradient. We'll now use the **Line** tool to create the white cross to complete our flag.

7 On the Tools toolbar, on the **Line** tools flyout, click the **Curved Line Tool**.

8 Draw a diagonal line across the page—click once at the top left corner of the page to start the line, hold down the mouse button, drag to the lower right corner, and then release the mouse button.

9 Click the **Pointer** tool, then click on the line and drag it to create a curve, as illustrated.

10 With the line selected, click the **Line** tab (or choose **Line and Border** from the **Format** menu), and increase the line weight to 64 pt.

11 Click the **Swatches** tab, click the **Line** button, and then click the white swatch. You should now have a heavy white line.

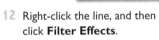

12 Right-click the line, and then click **Filter Effects**.

13 In the **Filter Effects** dialog, select the **Feather** checkbox, and increase the blur to 12 pt. Click **OK**.

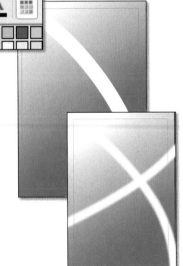

14 Repeat steps 6 to 13 to create and format a second line, as illustrated.

Create a Photo Scrapbook

Great, we've finished the flag design so let's now assign it to the cover page—page 1 of our publication. With our master page safely in place, we'll then be able to add and manipulate other PagePlus objects without disturbing our carefully created background elements.

To assign a master page

1 To the right of the Hintline toolbar, click the 📄 **Page Manager** button, and then click the **Set** tab. (You can also choose **Master Page** from the **View** menu.)

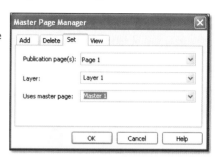

2 In the **Publication page(s):** drop-down list, select 'Page 1.'

3 In the **Uses master page:** list, select 'Master A.'

4 Click **OK**, and then switch back to Normal page view by selecting **Normal** from the **View** menu, or by clicking Master A at the lower left of the workspace.

In this next section, you'll import images, and add an interesting 'Polaroid' effect using the **Filter Effects** and **Lines and Borders** dialogs. You'll also use standard text frames to create a title.

To import and position an image

1 On the Tools toolbar, click 🖼 **Import Picture**.

2 In the **Import Picture** dialog, browse to the **Workspace\Scrapbook** folder and open **23_2338_small.jpg**.

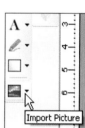

3 When the cursor changes to a ⊹🖼 click on the page to insert the image. Note that the Picture tools are displayed in the Context bar.

4 Resize the image—click one of its corner handles and drag it to a new position. You'll want this image to be about 6 cm by 4 cm.

5 On the Tools toolbar, click the ↻ **Rotate** tool.

6 Click to select the photograph, click one of its handles (the pointer changes to the Rotate cursor) and then drag to rotate the shape.

7 Now click in the centre of the object (the pointer changes to the Move cursor) and drag the image into the desired position.

8 Repeat steps 1 to 7 to import and position the **116_1664_small.jpg** and **119_1927_small.jpg** images.

Create a Photo Scrapbook

The images look okay, but we can create more impact and visual interest by adding some creative effects. In these next steps, you'll see how adding a line and a drop shadow can really make a difference by giving the impression of depth. Although we're applying this effect to a photograph, you can use the same procedure to apply lines, borders, and filter effects to many other PagePlus objects—shapes, artistic text, etc.

To add a line and drop shadow to an object

1 Right-click the image, click **Format**, and then click **Line and Border**.

2 In the **Line and Border** dialog:

- In the **Style** drop-down list, select the single solid line.
- In the **Weight** list, type 5.
- In the **Colour** drop-down list, select the white swatch.
- Click **OK**.

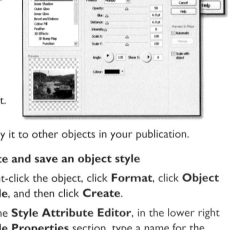

3 Right-click the image and then click **Filter Effects...**

4 In the **Filter Effects** dialog:

- In the **Effects** list, click the **Drop Shadow** check box.
- Set the **Opacity** to 50.
- Set the **Blur** and the **Distance** to 6 pt.
- Set the **Angle** to 135 and click **OK**.

You can save this new 'object style' and apply it to other objects in your publication.

To create and save an object style

1 Right-click the object, click **Format**, click **Object Style**, and then click **Create**.

2 In the **Style Attribute Editor**, in the lower right **Style Properties** section, type a name for the new style. For example, 'Polaroid.'

3 Click the **Browse** button and select a category in which to save the style. We've chosen 'Special Effects.' Click **OK**.

4 Now click the **Styles** tab, select **Special Effects** from the drop-down list, and then scroll down to find your new 'Polaroid' style. What could be simpler!

Let's apply our style to the other two photographs.

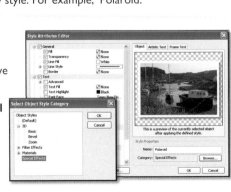

Create a Photo Scrapbook

To apply an object style to one or more objects

1 With the object(s) selected, click the **Styles** tab.

2 Select the style category from the drop-down list, and then click the style thumbnail to apply it to the object(s).

All we need now is a title and our cover page is complete.

It's often tempting to use large bold fonts for titles. When laying out a publication, however, try to keep the whole composition in mind. In this case, we don't want to detract from the background design and photos so we'll keep it simple.

Object styles benefit your design efforts in much the same way as text styles and colour schemes. Once you've created a set of attributes that you like— properties like line colour, fill, border, and so on—you can save this cluster of attributes as a named style. PagePlus remembers which objects are using that style, and the style appears on the **Styles** tab.

To create and format a title

1 On the Tools toolbar, click the **Standard Frame** tool, then click and drag to insert a frame to the right of the photos.

2 In the text frame, type "Scotland 2005" and then click and drag to select the text (or press **Ctrl+A**).

3 On the Context bar, choose the font size and style for your heading. We've used 36 pt Annie BTN.

4 With the text frame still selected, resize the text frame to fit the text—click one of the frame handles, hold down the left mouse button, and then drag to the new position.

5 In the text frame, double-click the word 'Scotland' to select it.

6 Click **Format**, and then click **Character**. In the **Character** dialog, in the **Text colour** drop-down list, select the white swatch. Click **OK**.

7 Repeat step 6 to change the colour of '2005' to blue.

8 Finally, repeat steps 1 to 6 to create a second text frame containing the words "holiday memories..." This time, use 20 pt Annie BTN and change the font colour to white.

Congratulations, you've completed the cover for your first scrapbook and can move on to the inside pages.

We'll use some of the features we've already worked with—master pages, text frames, object styles, etc. But we'll also introduce you to some others.

Create a Photo Scrapbook

We're now going to create a watermark effect, which we'll use as a background for our scrapbook. Our theme is Scotland, so we'll use an image of a thistle for the watermark. We'll show you how to import an image, apply a gradient fill, and change its colour.

To create a watermark design on a master page

1 Click the **Pages** tab, click the arrow to expand the **Master Pages** pane, and then click the ⊞ **Add** button. A blank page opens and 'Master B' is now displayed at the lower left of the HintLine toolbar.

2 On the Tools toolbar, click 🖾 **Import Picture**.

3 In the **Import Picture** dialog, browse to the **Workspace\Scrapbook** folder and open the **Thistle.jpg** file.

4 When the cursor changes to a ⌐🖾 click on the page to insert the image.

5 Resize the image so that the head of the thistle is approximately 6 cm high, and then move the whole image to the lower right of the page, as illustrated.

6 With the image selected, click the **Opacity** tab, click the **Gradient** button, and then click the **Ellipse Transparency 70** swatch.

7 Click the **Swatches** tab, click the **Fill** button, and then click the one of the light grey swatches at the top right of the swatches panel. We've used RGB (187, 187, 187).

8 Repeat steps 2 to 7 to import the same image (or use copy (**Ctrl+C**) and paste (**Ctrl+V**) to make a copy of the first image). Position the second image at the top left of the page.

Let's assign this master page (Master B) to the second page of our scrapbook.

To assign a master page

1 Click the 🗖 **Page Manager** button, then click the **Set** tab.

2 In the **Publication page(s):** drop-down list, select 'Page 2.'

3 In the **Uses master page:** list, select 'Master B.'

4 Click **OK**, and then switch back to Normal page view by clicking Master B at the lower left of the workspace, or by selecting **Normal** from the **View** menu.

💡 You can use this simple, but very effective, watermark technique in any type of PagePlus publication.

In this next section, you'll import some photographs and add titles and comments using standard and artistic text frames. We'll show you how to improve a photograph by adjusting brightness and contrast settings, and how to change a colour photograph into a dramatic black and white image.

You should now have 'page 2 of 2' open in the workspace. The page should be blank except for the watermark background. Let's begin by importing the four images we want to display on this page. As you've already imported and applied an object style to the images for the cover page, we'll summarise the following steps. However, go back to pages 87 and 89 if you feel you need to follow the more detailed step-by-step procedures.

To import and position images and apply an object style

1 On the Tools toolbar, click ▦ **Import Picture**.

2 In the **Import Picture** dialog, browse to the **Workspace\Scrapbook** folder and open **116_1621_small.jpg**.

3 Repeat steps 1 and 2 to import the **117_1781_small.jpg**, **119_1957_small.jpg**, and **120_2096._small.jpg** files.

4 Resize and position the photographs as illustrated.

5 Select all of the images (click on one, press and hold the **Shift** key, and then click each of the others in turn), click the **Styles** tab, and then apply the 'Polaroid' style.

We're now ready to add some text objects to the page. Let's first create a title using artistic text.

To create a title using artistic text

1 On the Tools toolbar, click the **Artistic Text Tool**, click in the top left corner, and then type "EASDALE ISLAND."

2 Click in the line of text and press **Ctrl+A** to select both words.

3 On the Context bar, choose the font style for your heading. We used 30 pt Humanst521 BT.

4 With the text frame still selected, click one of the frame handles and then drag the title until it overlaps the edge of the photograph at the top of the page. Click the upper centre frame handle to enlarge the height of the text.

5 Click the **Swatches** tab.

6 Click the **Gradient** button, and then select **Linear** from the drop-down list.

7 Select the **Linear Fill 186** swatch.

Create a Photo Scrapbook

Now let's add a comment for this first photo. We'll type text directly into a standard frame. We'll then change the font style and colour, and set text-wrapping options.

To create and format a photo comment

1 On the Tools toolbar, click the **Standard Frame Tool**, then click and drag to insert a frame under the title and to the left of the first photo.

2 In the text frame, type "View from Easdale Island to mainland on a misty morning" and then click and drag to select the text (or press **Ctrl+A**).

3 On the Context bar, choose the font size and style for your heading. We've used 14 pt Annie BTN. Resize the text frame to fit the text.

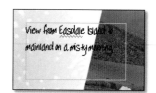

4 Click **Format**, and then click **Character**. In the **Character** dialog, in the **Text colour** drop-down list, select a dark grey colour swatch.

5 Click and drag the text frame to the right, so that it overlaps the edge of the photo.

We want our comment text to 'wrap' to the contours of the photograph. In PagePlus, you can easily do this by changing the wrap settings for the photograph.

To wrap text around an object

1 Select the photograph and click the **Wrap Settings** button on the toolbar (or right-click the photo and choose **Wrap Settings**).

You can wrap frame text around an artistic text object, a table or another frame, or even flow text inside a graphic (a circle, for example). For more information, see online Help.

2 In the ▣ **Wrap Settings** dialog, do the following:

- In the **Wrapping** section, click **Tight**.
- In the **Wrap To** section, click **Left**.
- In the **Distance from text** section, enter a value of **0.20 cm** in each of the four boxes.
  - Click **OK**.

❑ Repeat the previous steps to add comments for each of the other three photos, wrapping the text where necessary.

Create a Photo Scrapbook

Time to move on to the third and final page of this holiday scrapbook. Again, you'll be familiar with many of the following procedures, so we'll just summarise them here and let you go back to the previous sections if you need to. In this section, we'll show you how to get the best out of your photos using some new PagePlus features.

To lay out the final page

1 Click the 🗒 **Master Page Manager** button, click the **Set** tab, and assign Master B to Page 3 of your publication.

2 Click the 🖼 **Import Picture** button and import the following five images:

- 116_1657_small.jpg
- 116_1654_small.jpg
- 120_2097_small.jpg
- 118_1842_small.jpg
- 121_2132_small.jpg

3 Click the **Styles** tab and apply the 'Polaroid' object style to each photograph.

4 Add comments using 🖾 standard text frames and/or **A** artistic text. Add special effects if you wish.

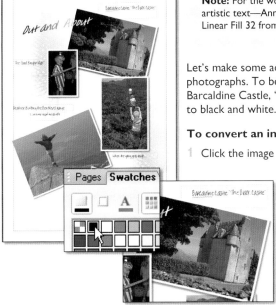

Note: For the words 'Out and About,' we used artistic text—Annie BTN italic font—and applied Linear Fill 32 from the **Swatches** tab.

Let's make some adjustments to two of the photographs. To begin, we'll take the image of Barcaldine Castle, "The Black Castle," and convert it to black and white.

To convert an image to black and white

1 Click the image to select it, and then click the **Swatches** tab.

2 On the **Swatches** tab, click the **Fill** button, and then click the black swatch in the upper left of the swatches panel.

Create a Photo Scrapbook

For our final task, we'll be working on the photo of 'Heather climbing the Ben Nevis range.' PagePlus now provides a host of features to allow you to perform common photo corrections such as adjusting contrast, modifying shadows and highlights, even fixing red eye. We'll use the PagePlus **Image Adjustments** dialog to adjust brightness and contrast.

To adjust image brightness and contrast

1 With the image selected, on the Context bar, click **Image Adjustments**.

2 In the **Image Adjustments** dialog, click **Add Adjustment**, and then click **Brightness and Contrast**.

3 Adjust the **Brightness** and **Contrast** values by dragging the sliders or typing directly into the boxes. Check the results of your adjustments in the **Image Preview** pane.

4 When you are happy with the image, click **OK**.

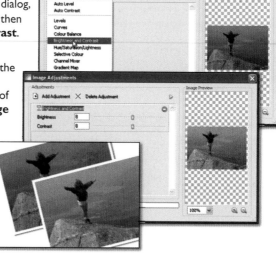

Let's crop some of the background so that Heather becomes the focal point.

To crop an image

1 With the image selected, on the Tools toolbar, click the ⊟ Square **Crop Tool**.

2 Click the handle at the centre left of the image (the cursor changes to ⊟) and drag towards the right until you have cropped most of the background.

> **Design Tip**
> To give your photos an 'aged' effect: On the Context bar, click **Recolour Picture**, and select a dark brown swatch, for example RGB (138, 90, 48). Instant sepia tone!

3 Repeat the process to crop the background to the right of Heather.

> 💡 To fine-tune your cropped image:
> Click in the image (the cursor changes to ✋), and then drag to reposition the image inside the crop boundary. To restore the cropped object to its original shape: Click ▣ **Remove Crop** on the Tools toolbar's Crop flyout.

Create a Photo Scrapbook

That's it—you've created the cover and the first two pages of your first holiday scrapbook. We hope you've enjoyed the process and have learned a few PagePlus tricks along the way.

When creating scrapbooks in the future, several different options are open to you:

Design Tip
Use QuickShapes and transparency to 'sticky tape' your photos to the page—For step-by-step instructions, see the "Create a Sales Flyer" tutorial.

- You can use this scrapbook layout as a template and import your own photos—simply right-click an existing photo, click **Replace Picture**, and then choose your new photo. Don't forget to change the photo captions too!

- You can use one of the pre-defined scrapbook layouts—click **File**, point to **New**, click **New from Startup Wizard**, and then click **use a design template**.

- If you're feeling adventurous, you can create a new scrapbook from scratch, designing your own cover and master pages.

Whichever option you choose, we're sure you'll enjoy creating beautiful scrapbooks to hold those special memories and share with friends and family.

Create a Greeting Card

Impress family and friends and make that special event even more memorable by making your own greeting card from scratch.

h a p p y   b i r t h d a y

Create a Greeting Card

Whether it's to celebrate a birthday, an anniversary, or a graduation, or simply to tell a friend you are thinking of them, we all enjoy sending and receiving greeting cards.

It may surprise you to know that UK consumers are the most avid card purchasers in the world—have you ever wondered just how much money you spend every year on greeting cards? With PagePlus, you'll spend time rather than money creating personalised greeting cards that your friends and family will want to keep.

You'll learn how to:

- Lay out a folded publication.

- Utilise minimal colour palettes to create clean, contemporary designs.

- Work with a variety of images to create very different effects.

- Format text to match an imported image.

- Adjust image colour and add transparency and reflection effects.

- Align objects on a page.

- Select the right paper for your greeting card.

- Print a greeting card.

Create a Greeting Card

In this tutorial, we'll create four different greeting card designs, which you can print on a home printer. We've supplied sample images for you to use; you'll find them in your PagePlus installation directory (usually **C:\Program Files\Serif\PagePlus\11\Tutorials**), in the **Workspace\Greeting Card** folder. Of course, you can use your own images or photographs if you prefer.

We'll start by creating and saving a blank document.

To create and save a greeting card document

1 In PagePlus, click **File**, point to **New**, click **New from Startup Wizard**, and then click **start from scratch**.

2 In the dialog, click **Folded Publications**, and then click **Greeting Cards**. Click the first template—Card—and then click **Open**.

3 To save the new document, click **File**, then click **Save**.

> PagePlus provides four different Greeting Card templates—Card; Side Fold, Quarter Size; Tent Card; and Top Fold, Quarter Size.

Now to import the image for our greeting card. We've supplied four different images; we'll use the flower for our first example.

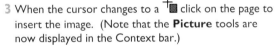

To import and position an image

1 On the Tools toolbar, click **Import Picture**.

2 In the **Import Picture** dialog, browse to the **Workspace\Greeting Card** folder and open the **Flower.jpg** file.

3 When the cursor changes to a ⊞ click on the page to insert the image. (Note that the **Picture** tools are now displayed in the Context bar.)

4 Resize the image by clicking one of its corner handles and dragging it to a new position. You'll want this image to be about 6 cm by 6 cm.

Design Tip
Before importing into PagePlus, an image of a detailed flower was opened in PhotoPlus. The background was then removed to produce a clean and contemporary design.

Let's add the title. We want it to match the look and feel of the image, so we'll use a modern font style.

To create a title using artistic text

1 On the Tools toolbar, click the **Artistic Text Tool**, click about 2 cm below the image and type "happy birthday."

2 Click in the text and press **Ctrl+A** to select both words.

3 On the Context bar, choose the font style for your heading. We used Arial 18 pt.

Create a Greeting Card

4 With the text frame still selected, click the **Character** tab at the lower right of the workspace.

5 Expand the character spacing to 10.0 pt.

You can do this by clicking the 'up' arrow, or by clicking the 'right' arrow and then dragging the slider.

h a p p y b i r t h d a y

Let's position our image and title so that they are centred horizontally on the page. PagePlus offers us a more precise method of aligning objects on a page using the **Align Objects** dialog.

To align objects on a page

1 Press and hold down the **Shift** key, then use the **Pointer** tool to click on the image and the text object. A blue bounding box appears around both objects.

2 Click the **Align Objects** button on the toolbar (or right-click and choose **Arrange/Align Objects...**).

3 In the **Align Objects** dialog, do the following:

- In the **Horizontally** section, click **H Centre**.

- Select the **Include margins** check box.

- Click **OK**.

h a p p y b i r t h d a y

For a quick and easy effect, we'll bold and change the colour of the first letters of the title words, we'll then add a subtle reflection.

You can also use the **Align** tab, located at the lower right of the workspace, to align objects.

h a p p y b i r t h d a y

To change font colour

1 In the text frame, click and drag to select the letter 'h.'

2 On the toolbar, click **Format**, and then click **Fill**.

3 In the **Fill** dialog, choose one of the pink swatches (we used RGB (255, 127, 255) on the **Standard RGB** palette), and then click **OK**.

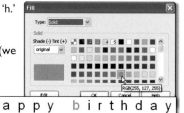

4 With the letter still selected, click the **B** **Bold** button on the Context bar.

h a p p y b i r t h d a y

Create a Greeting Card

Now to add a reflection. This effect looks impressive, but it's very simple to achieve. We're applying the reflection to an artistic text object, however, this effect works equally well on shapes, images, and other PagePlus objects.

To add a reflection effect to an object

1 Select the object, right-click, and then click **Copy**. Right-click again and click **Paste**.

2 Right-click the text object copy, click **Flip/Rotate**, and then click **Flip Vertical**.

3 Now click the new object and move it underneath the original.

4 Click in the text object and press **Ctrl+A** to select the whole line of text.

5 On the **Swatches** tab, click the **Fill** button, and select the pink colour swatch you used previously.

6 With both words still selected, click the **Opacity** tab, click the **Solid** button, and then click the **Solid Transparency 80%** swatch

You've just created the layout for your first greeting card! As you can see, it doesn't require complicated procedures, or professional graphic design skills. In fact, the simplest designs often work the best.

To further demonstrate this point, we'll show you a few more examples, all of which use simple techniques that you can adapt to suit your own needs. You'll find the sample images in your **Workspace\Greeting Card** folder.

For this party invitation, the main photo was taken at an interesting angle, giving the composition some depth.

Again, a minimal palette of colours was used, the colours of the image being reproduced in the title. We used the same technique described above to create the reflection effect.

💡 Try to avoid importing very large image files. Even if these are scaled down on the publication page, the original file size is preserved. As a rule, downscale your images first using photo-editing software (such as PhotoPlus), then import them into PagePlus.

Create a Greeting Card

For this textured abstract design, we started with an image of a vibrant textile. We cropped the photograph to show the detail of the fabric texture (you could do this with photo-editing software, or in PagePlus itself), and then placed it in the centre of the composition.

The colours of the text were then matched to the textile.

This example shows how you can turn an everyday photo of a pet or family member into a fun greeting card.

We imported our photo and then altered its colour properties by using the **Swatches** tab and the **Image Adjustments** dialog.

To recolour an image

1 With the image selected, on the Context bar, click the 🖼 **Recolour Picture** button, and then choose a colour from the palette—generally darker colours work best for this technique.

💡 You can quickly adjust brightness and contrast values of a selected image by clicking the appropriate button on the Context bar. Just hover the mouse cursor over each button to display the button name.

2 To adjust image brightness and contrast, on the Context bar, click **Image Adjustments**.

3 In the dialog, click **Add Adjustment** and then **Brightness and Contrast**.

4 Click and drag the sliders to achieve the desired effect.

To give the piece a more finished feel, we also added a thin border to the image.

To add a line to an image

1 Right-click the image, click **Format**, and then click **Line and Border...**

2 In the **Line and Border** dialog:

- In the **Weight** drop-down list, select 0.5 pt.
- In the **Style** drop-down list, select 'Solid.'
- In the **Colour** section, select a mid-grey swatch. Click **OK**.

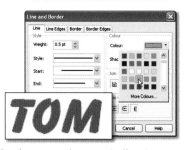

For the finishing touch we added a caption. A big bold fun font is used to good effect here.

Create a Greeting Card

When you are happy with your card layout, you can type a special greeting in the inside pages—even a verse if you're feeling really creative! When that's done, you're ready to print out your card.

You can buy packs of pre-folded greeting card paper and envelopes from most office suppliers. Usually, this paper is specifically intended to be used with ink jet home printers, and comes in 160 gsm weight.

When you select or define a **Folded Publication** (as we did at the beginning of this exercise), PagePlus automatically performs imposition of folded publications. The settings ensure that two or four pages of the publication are printed on each sheet of paper. This saves you from having to calculate how to position and collate pairs of pages on a single larger page.

It's obviously worth experimenting with printing your cards on normal A4 paper first, to get everything (margins, positioning etc.) set up correctly.

To produce double-sided sheets, use your printer's double-sided option or run sheets through twice, printing first the front and then the back of the sheet.

That's all there is to it! We've shown you four different examples of greeting cards to start you off, and hopefully inspire you to create your own unique designs. As you can see, all it takes is a little time and imagination.

Create a Business Card

Learn all about logos, branding, and identity as we show you the
secrets of effective logo and business card design.

Create a Business Card

You may have noticed that some business cards look better than others. Why is this? Is it the layout, the colours, the typeface, or a combination of all of these elements? Great designs are not a mystery and you don't need professional graphic design skills to produce a business card. By following some simple rules, however, you can ensure that your business cards look professional and convey the right image.

PagePlus tools give you the flexibility to lay out text and graphic objects, and design logos for your business cards—and it's easy to set up your printer to print multiple copies on one sheet. Creating your own design also allows you make modifications on the fly, and then preview and print out your results before choosing a final layout.

In this tutorial, you'll learn how to:

- Set up page and printer options.

- Use artistic text and graphics objects to design a logo.

- Use a variety of typefaces to create different effects.

- Use colour effectively in a layout.

- Position and align text and graphics objects.

- Group related objects together.

- Lay out a small publication.

Create a Business Card

In this exercise, we'll create a logo and design a business card for a fictitious recruitment company. We'll demonstrate five different logo designs and explain how the elements in each of them work together to convey a different image. To begin, let's create our publication and set up page and printer options.

To set up a business card publication

1 Open PagePlus, click **File**, point to **New**, click **New from Startup Wizard**, and then click **start from scratch**.

2 In the dialog, click **Small Publications**, and then click **Business Cards**. Click the **Wide Business Card** template, and then click **Open**.

3 On the **File** menu, click **Page Setup**, then click **Create Custom** to open the **Small Publication Setup** dialog.

• The left preview pane shows how the business cards will be laid out at print time.

• In the **Size** section, the default **Width** (8.50 cm) and **Height** (5.50 cm) of a 'wide business card' document are displayed.

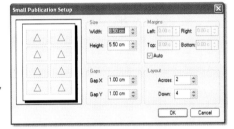

• The **GapX** and **GapY** values denote the size of the spaces that will be left between the business cards when they are laid out side-by-side on one sheet of paper.

• In the **Margins** section, clear the **Auto** box to set your own page margin size, or leave it checked to use the PagePlus default settings.

• The **Layout** section tells you how many business cards will fit across and down a single page, using the current margin and gap settings.

Let's remove the gap between the business cards so that we won't have to cut out each card individually after we have printed them.

4 Set both the **GapX** and **GapY** values to '0.' In the preview pane, you'll notice that the layout changes to reflect the new settings. Note also that we can now fit ten cards to a page, rather than eight.

5 Click **OK** to return to the **Page Setup** dialog. Click the **Print Setup** button.

When printing small publications such as business cards, try changing the orientation and then checking back in the **Page Setup** dialog to see which orientation will fit more copies on a single page.

6 In the **Print Setup** dialog, click the **Properties** button.

The dialog that opens is printer-specific—the settings depend on the printer you're using. The **Orientation** setting is generally available regardless of the printer and lets you choose to print your page in **Portrait** or **Landscape** style.

7 Click **OK** three times to close the printer, **Print Setup**, and **Page Setup** dialogs.

Create a Business Card

We've set up our business card publication. We're going to work on our logo design next, so we don't need the business card document at the moment. Let's save it and keep it open, but minimize it in the workspace so we can come back to it later.

- ❑ On the **File** menu, click **Save**. Save the document as **Business Card.ppp**.

- ❑ Click the document minimize button at the upper right corner of the publication.

- ❑ Follow the steps outlined previously to create a new blank document. This time select a **Regular/Normal** 'Portrait' size document.

You'll use this new document to experiment with your logo design. Once you've settled on a final layout, you can then copy it on to your business card.

In the following section, we'll show you the different techniques we used to create our five sample logos. We'll discuss the effectiveness of each, and give you some design tips to help you create your own.

A **logo** is a unique name, symbol, or trademark of a company or organization. Well-designed logos provide brand name recognition and promote a business presence. They achieve this because people process an image in their mind more easily than words. In addition, visual stimulation produces a more effective and long-lasting impact on the audience's memory than words alone.

Example 1

In this example, we used a modern font in two different sizes and colours. We expanded the text spacing and incorporated 'sunrise-coloured' graphic bars to give the impression of horizontal width—playing on the word 'horizon.' Let's break this down so you can see exactly how the effect was achieved.

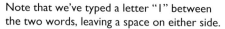

To create and format artistic text

1 On the Tools toolbar, click the **Artistic Text Tool**.

2 Click anywhere in the document and type "HORIZON I RECRUITMENT."

Note that we've typed a letter "I" between the two words, leaving a space on either side.

3 Click in the line of text and press **Ctrl+A** to select both words.

4 On the context bar, choose the font style for your text. We used Futura Lt BT.

5　In the text frame, click and drag to highlight the word 'HORIZON,' then on the **Format** menu, click **Character**.

6　In the **Character** dialog, click the **Font** tab, and then change the **Size** to 18 pt.

7　Repeat steps 5 to 7 to change the size of the letter 'I' to 24 pt, and the size of the word 'RECRUITMENT' to 12.5 pt.

8　Click in the line of text and press **Ctrl+A** to select both words.

9　Click the **Character Spacing** tab, in the **Spacing** drop-down list, select **Expanded** and enter a spacing value of 10 pt in the **By:** box. Click **OK**.

As you can see, by making these minor adjustments to font size and spacing, we have already created the impression of horizontal width and given a much more modern look and feel to the line of text.

Let's change the text colour of the word 'RECRUITMENT.' This is a quick and easy way to create visual interest and contrast in a layout.

Design Tip
Whether you're creating a business card, a newsletter, or even a greeting card, contrast is an important consideration when designing any publication layout. The simplest and most obvious contrast is black text on a white background, but you can be more adventurous and use opposite colours on the colour wheel—such colour pairs (e.g. red and green, blue and orange) are actually termed 'contrasting colours.'

To change font colour

1　In the text frame, click and drag to highlight the letter 'I' and word 'RECRUITMENT.'

2　On the **Format** menu, click **Character**. In the **Character** dialog, click the **Font** tab.

3　To the right of **Text** colour, click the arrow and then scroll to find a dark blue-grey colour swatch.

4　Click the swatch and then click **OK** to apply it to the text and close the **Character** dialog.

Create a Business Card

Now to introduce a graphic element to our design. In the following section, we'll show you how to create the coloured bars using a basic QuickShape. You'll be working at quite a detailed level, so it's a good idea to zoom in at this point.

To zoom into a publication

- On the toolbar, click the ⊕ **Zoom In** button.

  - or -

- Click the 🔍 **Zoom Tool**, and then drag out a rectangular bounding box on the page to define a region to zoom in to. The zoom percentage adjusts accordingly, fitting the designated region into the window. To zoom out, hold down the **Shift** key when dragging. Double-click the button to display the page at actual size (100%).

To create and format a QuickShape

1 Click the **QuickShape** button on the Tools toolbar and select the **Quick Rectangle** from the flyout.

2 Click and drag to create a rectangle under the first two letters of 'HORIZON.'

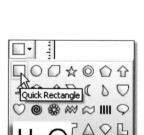

3 On the **Swatches** tab, click the **Palette** drop-down list and select the **standard RGB** palette.

4 Select the rectangle, then on the **Swatches** tab, click the **Fill** button and select the pink (RGB 255, 186, 255) swatch.

5 Right-click the rectangle again, click **Format**, and then click **Line and Border...**

6 In the **Line and Border** dialog, remove the border from the shape by choosing 'None' from the **Style** drop-down list.

7 Click **OK**.

Now that we've created the template for our shape, we can copy and paste it to quickly create another three identical shapes.

To copy and paste an object

1 Select the object, right-click , and then click **Copy**.

2 Right-click again and click **Paste**.

3 Repeat steps 1 and 2 to create four identical shapes. PagePlus pastes the copies one on top of the other.

4 Click on each of the copies in turn and position them so that they span the word 'HORIZON.' Don't worry about spacing them exactly—we can use PagePlus's alignment tools to do this for us.

To align objects on a page

1 Press and hold down the **Shift** key, then use the **Pointer** tool to click on each of the four bars. A blue bounding box appears around the group objects.

2 Click the  **Align Objects** button on the toolbar (or right-click and choose **Arrange/Align Objects**).

3 In the **Align Objects** dialog, do the following:

- In the **Vertically** section, click **Top**.

- In the **Distribute** section, click **Even Spacing**.

- If necessary, clear the **Include margins** check box.

- Click **OK**.

The bars are now perfectly spaced and aligned. Let's go ahead and change their colours.

To change the colour of an object

1 Click to select the object—in this case the second bar on the left.

2 Click the **Swatches** tab, click the **Fill** button, and then click one of the pale green colour swatches. We used RGB (188, 252, 184),

3 Repeat steps 1 and 2 to colour the other two bars. We used RGB (256, 136, 32)—orange, and RGB (0, 132, 132)—dark green.

Congratulations, you've just created a simple, but effective company logo. As you can see, it doesn't require complicated procedures, or professional design skills. In fact, the simplest designs often work the best.

To further demonstrate this point, we'll show you a few more examples, all of which use simple techniques that you can adapt to suit your own needs.

Create a Business Card

Example 2

In this example, we used a fluid modern font (Smudger LET) for the main company name 'Horizon,' contrasting it with a plainer font (Futura Lt BT) for the word 'Recruitment.' Playful loose fonts like this are often used for holiday agency companies.

As for Example 1, we expanded the text spacing slightly, We also created a colourful sun motif over the 'o.'

To do this, we used three capital 'I' letters, colouring, rotating, and resizing each of them individually.

Example 3

This example builds on the previous themes and ideas. Here, the focus is on the sunrise over the letter 'i.'

A clean and simple font was used (Prisoner SF), with the shade of each letter deepening towards the centre of the word. With this design, the letter 'i' and its sunrise motif could be used as a separate branding identity for the company.

This logo has a more 'technical' look and feel, more appropriate for an I.T. job agency for example.

Example 4

This example takes a very different direction. The heavy bold typeface (Arial Black) represents strength, while the colours were introduced to soften the company image. The letter spacing of the word 'RECRUITMENT' was expanded.

A simple, but effective technique—basic coloured QuickShapes were used to add colour behind the letters.

While this logo has quite a generic look and feel, it would be very recognisable.

Create a Business Card

Example 5

Here, we've created a **typographic letterform** logo formed by placing the letters 'h' and 'r' one on top of the other. Again, we've used QuickShapes for the coloured graphic bars.

Typographic letterform logos are preferred usually because of their effective means towards trademark development. This logo doesn't share the same themes as the previous examples (horizons, sunrises)—it's quite generic. It does, however, have strong distinctiveness, **retention**, **modularity**, and **equity**.

Equity: Refers to a logo's 'staying power' without the need to redesign. It is desirable to be modern and trendy—but not so much so that the logo may go out of fashion. It's generally better, therefore, to develop a more timeless identity.

Modularity: Describes how well a logo can be used across multiple applications (different printed media for example). In particular, how a typographic letterform logo can be used in conjunction with its more traditional full title logo (in our example, 'Horizon Recruitment').

Retention: Used to describe the process of a viewer's first interaction with the logo. If a symbol is too easy to read and figure out, the viewer feels no sense of discovery—no personal investment or connection with the logo. Having to digest the logo and work it out (in this case from the letters h + r within the letterform) ensures the logo stays with them in the subconscious.

Having covered how to design a company logo, we can now look at identity—how a company presents itself on printed media. Our focus will be the business card.

For this exercise we'll use the typographic letterform logo we created in Example 5.

Create a Business Card

A business card should be laid out in a way that is balanced. Different areas saying different things and presenting different information, all in order of appropriateness.

In our sample card for Horizon Recruitment, it's appropriate that the company logo is the focal point. The aim of this business card is to promote the company, whilst providing a means of direct contact with the person who gives away the card.

The person's name and job title is the secondary focus. This information is placed in the top left corner, using a 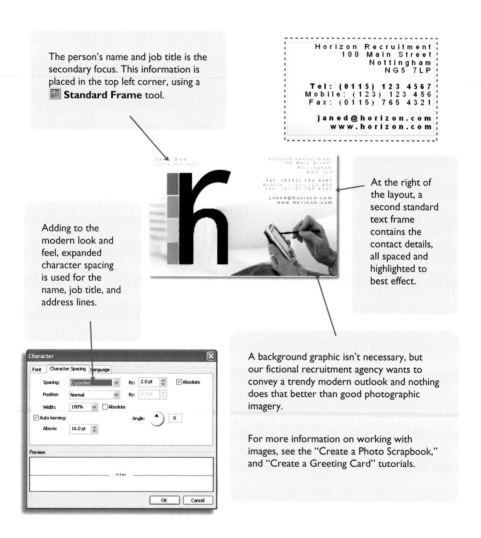 **Standard Frame** tool.

Horizon Recruitment
100 Main Street
Nottingham
NG5 7LP

Tel: (0115) 123 4567
Mobile: (123) 123 456
Fax: (0115) 765 4321

janed@horizon.com
www.horizon.com

At the right of the layout, a second standard text frame contains the contact details, all spaced and highlighted to best effect.

Adding to the modern look and feel, expanded character spacing is used for the name, job title, and address lines.

A background graphic isn't necessary, but our fictional recruitment agency wants to convey a trendy modern outlook and nothing does that better than good photographic imagery.

For more information on working with images, see the "Create a Photo Scrapbook," and "Create a Greeting Card" tutorials.

Create a Business Card

To lay out a business card

1 Return to your business card document by clicking the document maximize button.

2 On the Tools toolbar, click ▣ **Import Picture**.

3 In the **Import Picture** dialog, browse to the file containing the logo you want to use on your business card, highlight the file, and then click **Open**.

4 When the cursor changes to a ✛▣ click in the top left of your page and then drag to insert the image.

Note that the **Picture** tools are displayed in the Context bar.

5 With the logo selected, resize it by clicking one of the frame handles, holding down the left mouse button, and then dragging to the new position.

6 On the Tools toolbar, click the **Standard Frame** tool, then click and drag to insert a frame in the top left corner.

7 In the text frame, type your name, press **Enter**, and then type your job title.

8 In the text frame, click and drag to select the text (or press **Ctrl+A**).

9 On the Context bar, choose the font size and style for your heading, adjust the letter spacing if necessary.

10 Repeat steps 6 to 9 to add a second text frame to the right of the logo. Type in the company name and address, and your contact details.

Although a background graphic isn't necessary (and may sometimes be inappropriate), in our example, it certainly adds visual appeal and interest. It's easy to do this—simply click the **Import Picture** button and choose your image. Once you have the image in place, select it , and then on the toolbar, click the ▣ **Send to Back** button to place it behind all the other objects on the page.

💡 You can also add a background graphic to a master page. For more information on master pages, see the "Create a Photo Scrapbook" tutorial, or refer to the PagePlus online Help.

Create a Business Card

Well done! In these few pages, you've learned how to design an effective business logo and use it in a business card layout.

In this example we have clearly conveyed a fast-moving, modern, and powerful corporate image. But this is just the beginning. A well-designed logo can be used for many different purposes—business stationery, brochures, newsletters, and so on.

We hope we've given you an insight into logo and business card design and inspired you to create a logo that will work for your company to promote a distinct and recognisable identity.

Create a Newsletter

Learn about formats, using columns, font styles, and images in newsletter design. Whether producing simple one-page fliers or glossy multi-page publications, you'll find these design tips invaluable.

Create a Newsletter

The goal of good newsletter design is to entice the reader to read the information it contains. You can do this through your choice of layout style, nameplate, typefaces, and images—all of which should reflect the content.

In this tutorial, you'll create a four-page newsletter from scratch.

You'll learn how to:

- Create a multi-page document.

- Create master pages.

- Work with artistic text.

- Lay out standard and shaped text frames and flow text between frames.

- Import text from a word-publishing program.

- Work with grouped elements.

- Create and format a QuickShape.

- Import, position, resize, and crop images.

- Create and apply object styles.

- Wrap text around objects and fit text to a curve.

Create a Newsletter

In the following exercise, we'll create a newsletter for a kids' Karate Club. We'll explain how to lay out a newsletter publication, providing design tips along the way. We'll also show you some examples of good and bad newsletter design. Use your own images if you wish, or our sample images—located in your PagePlus installation directory (usually **C:\Program Files\Serif\PagePlus\11.0\Tutorials**), in the **Workspace\Newsletter** folder.

To begin, let's create our newsletter publication and set up the pages.

To create and set up a newsletter publication

1 In PagePlus, click **File**, point to **New**, click **New from Startup Wizard**, and then click **start from scratch**.

2 In the dialog, click **Regular/Normal**, and then click **Portrait**. Click the A4 or Letter template, and click **Open**.

3 At the lower left of the workspace, click the **Page Manager** button.

4 In the **Page Manager** dialog, click the **Insert** tab.

5 In the **Number of pages** box, type 3, and click **OK**. At the right of the workspace, the four pages display on the **Pages** tab.

6 On the **File** menu, click **Page Setup**.

7 The **Page Setup** dialog allows you to modify the publication dimensions and format. We're going to keep all the default settings except one.

8 At the lower left of the dialog, click to select the **Facing pages** check box. (Note that the **Dual master pages** box is automatically checked by default.) Click **OK**.

You'll notice now that pages 2 and 3 display together, as facing pages. This page setup is particularly useful when laying out multi-page publications because it allows you to see your pages exactly as they will be viewed in the document.

9 To save the document, click **File/Save**. Save the file as **Newsletter.ppp**.

Page size and **orientation** settings are fundamental to your layout, and are defined when a new publication is first created. You can adjust these aspects of a publication at any time—as a rule, however, make changes before you've gone too far with your layout. In practice, your working limit is likely to be set by the capabilities of your desktop printer.

Create a Newsletter

Our next job is to set up the master pages—pages that are shared by the entire publication. You can use master pages for objects such as background designs or watermarks that you want to appear on multiple pages of a publication (see the "Creating a Holiday Scrapbook" tutorial). We're going to use master pages to set up the page numbering of our newsletter.

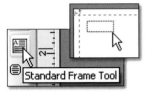

Standard Frame Tool

To insert page numbers on a master page

1 On the **View** menu, click **Master Page**. The master page view opens and 'Master A' is now displayed in the Hintline toolbar at the lower left of the workspace.

2 On the Tools toolbar, click the **Standard Frame** tool, and then click in the upper left corner of the page to insert a text frame.

3 Click in the text frame, on the **Insert** menu, click **Page Number**.

4 With the text frame still selected, on the toolbar, click the 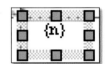 **Align Centre** button.

5 Repeat steps 2 to 4 to insert a page number in the upper right corner of the facing page.

6 On the **View** menu, click **Normal** to return to the main publication pages.

In the lower left corner of the workspace, click the **View previous page** and **View next page** arrows. You'll see that the page number now appears on all four pages of the document. As a general rule, the first page of a newsletter is not numbered. To remove the number from our front page, we'll simply assign the master pages to all pages *except* page 1.

To assign a master page

1 To the right of the Hintline toolbar, click the **Page Manager** button, and then click the **Set** tab. (You can also choose **Master Page** from the **View** menu.)

2 In the **Page Manager** dialog, in the **Publication page(s)** drop-down list, select 'Page 1.'

3 In the **Uses master page** list, select '(none).'

4 Click **OK**, and then switch back to Normal page view by selecting **Normal** from the **View** menu, or by clicking Master A at the lower left of the workspace.

5 Go the first page to confirm that the page number is no longer displayed.

Great, we've laid the groundwork for our newsletter publication and can now start to work on the layout.

Create a Newsletter

We'll begin on page 1, with the nameplate. We'll use artistic text for this.

The banner on the front of a newsletter that identifies the publication is its **nameplate**. The nameplate usually contains the name of the newsletter, possibly graphics or a logo, and perhaps a subtitle, motto, and publication information such as volume and issue number or date.

To create a nameplate using artistic text

1 On the Tools toolbar, click the **Artistic Text** tool.

2 Click in the document and type "karatecamp."

3 Click in the line of text and press **Ctrl+A** to select it, then on the **Format** menu, click **Character**.

4 In the **Character** dialog, in the **Font** drop-down list, choose 'Goudita Heavy SF.' In the **Size** box, type '90 pt.' Click **OK**.

5 In the text frame, click and drag to highlight just the word 'camp,' then on the Context bar at the top of the workspace, change the font to 'Goudita Light SF.'

6 Repeat steps 1 to 3 to insert a second artistic text frame containing the word 'Newsletter.'

7 This time, in the **Character** dialog:

- On the **Font** tab, choose 30 pt Goudita Heavy SF.

- On the **Character Spacing** tab, in the **Spacing** list, select 'Expanded' and then enter a value of 10 pt in the corresponding **By** box.

- Click **OK**.

8 Position this second text frame below the first one, as illustrated.

As you can see, by making these simple adjustments to font style, size, and spacing, we have created contrast—an important element in any type of publication layout.

We've created our newsletter nameplate out of two separate artistic text elements, which we've positioned carefully. We can now turn these two objects into a group object. We'll then be able to position, resize, or rotate them all at the same time—this is a useful feature to use when designing nameplates or logos that you might want to use repeatedly, across different types of printed media.

Create a Newsletter

To create a group from a multiple selection

1 Select the first object, press and hold the **Shift** key, and then select the next object.

   - or -

   Use the **Pointer** tool to draw a selection bounding box around both objects.

2 Click the ▣ **Group** button below the selection.

   - or -

   Choose **Group Objects** from the **Arrange** menu.

To turn a group back into a multiple selection

Click the ▣ **Ungroup** button below the selection.

- or -

Choose **Ungroup Objects** from the **Arrange** menu.

Let's add an image to the front page of our newsletter. When selecting an image or photograph for the first page of a newsletter, you should choose something that will grab the attention of your target audience. Make sure, however, that it is also representative of the content of your publication.

To import an image

1 Click outside the text frame group to deselect it. On the Tools toolbar, click the ▦ **Import Picture** button.

2 In the **Import Picture** dialog, browse to the **Workspace\Newsletter** folder and open the **15745851.png** file.

3 At the right of the dialog, click the **Embed picture** option, and then click **Open**.

4 When the cursor changes to a ⌖▦ click in your page and then drag to insert the image. Note that the Picture tools are displayed in the Context bar.

Embedded images become part of the publication file, while linking places a reference copy of the image on the page and preserves a connection to the original file. Each approach has its pros and cons (for more information, see online Help).

We're going to give this image more impact by adding a border effect. In PagePlus, a border is a repeating, decorative element that can be set to enclose an object. Borders work especially well with imported pictures.

To add a border to an image

1 Click the image to select it, then click the **Line** tab.

2 On the **Line** tab:

- In the line **weight** box, click the drop-down arrow and select a weight of 7.5 pt.

- In the line **style** box, click the drop-down arrow and select a dashed line.

- Adjust the **Dash Pattern** slider as illustrated.

You've no doubt noticed that we've left a space to the left of our image. We're going to fill this space with a **standard text frame** containing the address and contact details.

To create and format text

1 On the Tools toolbar, click the  **Standard Frame** tool, then click and drag to insert a frame to the left of the photograph.

2 In the text frame, type the address and contact details for the newsletter, pressing **Enter** between each line.

3 With the text frame selected, on the Context bar, click the **Align Right** button.

4 On the Context bar, choose the font size and style for your heading. We've used 10 pt Times New Roman.

5 Repeat the previous steps to add a caption for the photo.

2005 Annual Camp Review

💡 Keep it simple by using a single typeface or typeface family. Introduce contrast by adjusting size, style, letter spacing, colour, etc. Or use bold, italic, and light and condensed versions of the same family. Play with alignment and text leading. You can create very different effects simply by changing the amount of white space surrounding the text.

Create a Newsletter

In the next section, we'll create and format a QuickShape, which we'll then convert to a shaped text frame. We'll use this frame for our first piece of body text.

To create a QuickShape and convert it to a shaped frame

1 Click the QuickShape button on the Tools toolbar and select the **Quick Button**.

2 Keeping inside the blue page margins (if you can't see the margins, click **View/Guidelines**), click and drag to create a shape extending from the 17 cm mark on the vertical ruler, down to the bottom of the page.

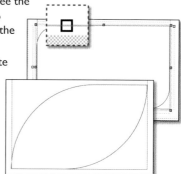

When the shape is selected you'll notice small white boxes—control handles—on each side. You can alter the shape by dragging these handles.

3 On the left side of the shape, click the handle and drag it down to the bottom of the shape. Then, drag the top handle across to the right. You're aiming to achieve the shape illustrated right.

4 With the shape selected, on the **Swatches** tab:

- Click the **Fill** button, and select a colour for your new shape (we used RGB(208,252,92) from the Standard RGB palette).

- In the lower right corner, adjust the **Tint** to 50%.

- Click the **Line** button, and select the same colour and tint you used for your fill.

5 Finally, right-click the shape, and click **Convert to Shaped Frame**.

6 To fill the frame with text, click inside and start typing! To fill with placeholder text, right-click and select **Fill with Placeholder Text** (you can also select the same command from the **Insert** menu).

We can create additional visual interest using filter effects to add a drop shadow to this text frame.

To apply a drop shadow

1 With the text frame selected, on the Attributes toolbar, click *fx* **Filter Effects**.

2 In the **Filter Effects** dialog, click **Drop Shadow**, and enter the values as illustrated right.

3 Click **OK**.

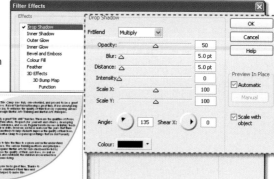

We now need to add a caption for this text box. For this, we'll make use of another PagePlus tool that allows us to fit a line of text to a shape or line. First, we need to create the caption and a shape to fit it to.

To fit artistic text to a shape

1 Create a new QuickShape, exactly the same as the first one but slightly bigger. This time, don't add colour or convert the shape to a shaped frame.

2 With this new shape selected, click the **Send to Back** button, and then position the shape behind the original shaped text frame.

3 Follow the steps outlined previously (p. 121) to create an artistic text object containing the words "A BIG thank you to all!" We used 34 pt Basic Sans Heavy SF. Position the text object as illustrated.

4 Select the text frame and the new shape (*do not* select the original shaped frame), then choose **Fit Text to Curve** from the **Tools** menu. The text now flows along the specified path and the original shape object disappears.

You'll notice that the text is not quite in the position we want. Fortunately, we can edit its path using the **Pointer** tool.

5 Select the text path object and zoom in. You'll notice that text paths have several unique "handles" not found on other objects. Hover over them and you'll see that the cursor changes for each.

- The **Baseline Shift** handle, indicated by a cursor, resembles a QuickShape handle with a tiny slider control. Drag the slider to raise and lower the text with respect to the path.

- The **Start** and **End** handles, indicated by and cursors, look like arrows. Drag them to adjust where the text begins and ends.

6 Click the **Start** handle and drag to the desired position.

7 **Optional:** You might also need to use the **Baseline Shift** slider to move the text closer to, or further from, the shape.

Our front page is starting to come together, but it still looks a little bare.

Let's liven it up by adding another photograph and a background graphic.

Create a Newsletter

☐ Repeat the steps outlined previously (p. 122) to import the **24275544.jpg** graphic file.

☐ Position the image in the lower right corner of the page.

☐ With the image selected, click the **Send to Back** button to place it behind the shaped text frame.

This image adds to the depth of the layout and sets the scene—even though it's not in full view.

Now for the final touch. We'll create a background image using another coloured QuickShape.

To create a background graphic

1   Click the **QuickShape** button on the Tools toolbar and select the **Quick Button** from the flyout.

2   Keeping inside the page margins, click and drag to create a shape to fill the entire page.

3   As you did previously, drag the handle on the left down to the bottom of the shape, and then drag the top handle across to the right.

4   With the shape selected, on the **Swatches** tab:

- Click the **Fill** button, and select a colour for your new shape. We used the same colour we used previously—RGB(208,252,92).

- In the lower right corner, change the **Tint** to 60%.

- Click the **Line** button, and select the same colour and tint you used for your fill.

- With the image selected, click the **Send to Back** button to place it behind the everything else on the page.

Congratulations! The first page of your newsletter is complete!

Let's now move on to the inside pages. Here, we're going to use a layout that is often used in newsletter publications—multiple columns. We'll set up our pages so that the body text flows through three columns.

To set up a multiple column frame layout

1 On the Tools toolbar, click the 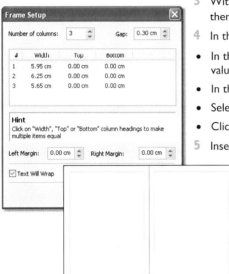 **Standard Frame** tool.

2 On page 2 of the publication, click the upper left corner of the page margin and drag to the lower right corner to create a text frame that completely fills the page.

3 With the frame selected, click **Format**, and then click **Frame Setup**.

4 In the **Frame Setup** dialog:

- In the **Number of columns:** box, enter a value of 3.

- In the **Gap:** box, enter a value of 0.30 cm.

- Select the **Text Will Wrap** check box.

- Click **OK**.

5 Insert an identical frame on page 3. Do this by copying and pasting the frame you just created (or repeat steps 1 to 4).

> You can drag the column guides or use the **Frame Setup** dialog to adjust the top and bottom column **blinds** and the left and right column **margins**.

At the moment, these two text frames are independent elements. However, we want to set them up so that text will flow between them.

When selected, a text frame includes a **Link** button at the lower right which allows you to import text files or control how the frame's story flows to following frames. The icon inside each frame's **Link** button denotes the state of the frame and its story text.

- **No Overflow**—The frame is not linked to a following frame (it's either a standalone frame or the last frame in a sequence). The end of the story text is visible.

- **Overflow**—The frame is not linked (either standalone or last frame). There is additional story text in the overflow area. An **AutoFlow** button displays to the left of the **Link** button.

- **Continued**—The frame is linked to a following frame. The end of the story text may be visible, or it may flow into the following frame.

  Note: The button icon will be red if the final frame of the sequence is overflowing, or green if there's no overflow.

Create a Newsletter

To flow text between text frames

1 Right-click the text frame on page 2 and select **Fill with Placeholder Text**.

 Notice the ▣ **Link** button indicating that there is no overflow.

2 Click anywhere in the text and press the **Enter** key a couple of times so that the last few lines of text no longer fit on the page.

 The **Link** button now indicates a text overflow.

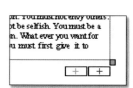

3 Click the right **Overflow** button, the cursor changes to a ⬚.

> The text in a frame is called a **story**:
> - When you move a text frame, its story text moves with it.
> - When you resize a text frame, its story text flows to the new dimensions.

4 Now move the cursor over to the frame on page 3, and then click in the text frame when the cursor changes to a ⬚.

 The missing lines of text now appear at the top of page 3's text frame. Notice too that the **Link** button on page 2's frame has changed to indicate that there is no overflow.

If you wish, you can add more placeholder text to the **story** in the frames. Or you can add your own text in any of the following ways:

- **WritePlus story editor**
  Right-click on a frame and choose **Edit Story** (or select the text and press **Ctrl+E**) to start WritePlus.

- **Importing text**
  Right-click on a frame and choose **Text File** to import a text file.

> 💡 Using **placeholder text** lets you concentrate on the visual arrangement of text frames without having to worry about their content.

- **Typing into the frame**
  Select the **Pointer** tool, then click for an insertion point to type text straight into a frame, or edit existing text.

- **Pasting via the Clipboard**
  Select the **Pointer** tool and click for an insertion point in the text, then press **Ctrl+V**, or click **Edit/Paste Special...** for a choice of formatting options.

- **Drag and drop**
  Select text (e.g. in a word processor file), then drag it onto the PagePlus page.

For more detailed information on these options, see online Help.

With our basic text column layout in place, we can now place our remaining images and create captions. In the following steps, we'll import four images and set their wrap settings so that the text story flows around them.

Create a Newsletter

To wrap text around an object

1 Click outside the text frames to make sure that nothing on the page is selected, then click the **Import Picture** button and open the **7690421.jpg** file.

2 Place this image in the upper right corner of page 2 so that it covers the right column and half of the centre column.

3 Right-click the image and choose **Wrap Settings** (you can also click the ⬚ **Wrap Settings** button on the **Arrange** toolbar, or click **Arrange/Wrap Settings**).

4 In the **Wrap Settings** dialog:

- In the **Wrapping** section, click 'Tight.'
- In the **Wrap to** section, click 'Left.'
- In the **Distance from text** section, enter '0.20 cm' in each of the four boxes.
- Click **OK**.

Back in the publication, your text now flows neatly around the image borders.

PagePlus lets you wrap frame text around the contours of a separate object. Usually, this means wrapping text to a picture that overlaps or sits above a text frame. But you can wrap frame text around an artistic text object, a table or another frame, or even flow text inside a graphic (a circle, for example). To wrap text, simply change the wrap setting for the object to which you want the text to wrap.

Now we'll add a caption to our image.

5 Click the **Standard Frame** tool and insert a text frame below the lower right corner of the image.

6 Type your caption—"Setting up the camp!"—and format it appropriately. We used 8 pt Times New Roman. Right-click the text frame and choose **Wrap Settings**.

7 In the **Wrap Settings** dialog:

- In the **Wrapping** section, click 'Square.'
- In the **Wrap to** section, click 'Left.'
- In the **Distance from text** section, enter '0.20 cm' in each of the four boxes.
- Click **OK**.

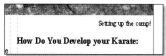

Create a Newsletter

☐ Repeat the previous steps to import the **7232572.jpg** file, this time applying a 'Tight, Right' wrap setting.

☐ Add an appropriate caption and apply a 'Square, All' wrap setting.

Now all we need is a title to finish this page. Again, we'll use a standard text frame for this.

To add a title

1 On the Tools toolbar, click the **Standard Frame** tool and insert a text frame in the upper left corner of the page.

2 Size the frame so that it is slightly smaller than the column.

3 Type the following: 'CAMPING TRAINING TOURNAMENTS ACTIVITIES TEAM BUILDING ADVENTURE,' pressing the **Enter** key after each entry so that each appears on a new line.

4 Select the text and on the Context bar:

- Apply a 24 pt Basic Sans Heavy SF typeface.
- Click the **Right Align** button.

5 If necessary, resize the frame to fit the text.

6 Right click the text frame and click **Wrap Settings**. Apply a 'Tight, Right' wrap setting, with '0.20 cm' distance from text on all sides.

7 Finally, select the main three-column text frame and drag the centre top handle down so that the text begins halfway down the photo.

Create a Newsletter

Well done, you've completed the second page of your newsletter—and you've now been introduced to all the PagePlus features you need to finish the publication.

We'll explain how we created the final pages, summarising the steps required. We'll let you go back to the previous sections if you need to.

To create page 3

1. On page 3, the second of our three-column pages, we imported two photographs—**7689511.jpg** and **15745776.jpg**.

2. We applied wrap settings to the images and added captions.

3. To the second image we applied the same border effect used for the cover photo.

4. The third column of this page contains a testimonial letter.

   We distinguished this from the rest of the text by applying an **italic** font style:

   - Select the text and on the Context bar, click *I*.

   - or -

   - Right-click the text, click **Text Format**, and then click **Character**. In the **Character** dialog, in the **Style** drop-down list, select 'Italic.'

5. Finally, we added the same background graphic used on page 1.

> You could also create a background graphic on a **master page** and then use the **Page Manager** dialog to apply it to multiple pages in your publication. For more information on working with master pages and background effects, see the "Create a Photo Scrapbook" tutorial and online Help.

Create a Newsletter

To create page 4

1 We copied the background graphic on to page 4, and then converted it to a shaped frame (click **Tools/Convert to Shaped Frame**).

2 We added a drop shadow effect to the shaped frame, applying the settings used on our cover page (see p. 124 for details).

3 We used two different font sizes for the text in this frame.

4 We added two images—**15745722.jpg** and **2425644.jpg**, applying wrap settings to both and our border effect to the first.

5 Finally, we created text frames for a large caption (52 pt Basic Sans Heavy SF), and contact details.

Before moving on to the next exercise, let's take a few moments to look at an example of a newsletter that doesn't work quite as well as ours. In doing so, you might be able to avoid some of the more common pitfalls that can occur when designing this type of publication.

In this example, while some advanced techniques have been used—such as the shaped text frame and text on a path, the overall composition misses the mark for the following reasons:

- The colours used are gaudy and not pleasing to the eye.

- The height spacing of the title needs adjusting, and the font used is not very imaginative.

- The white body text is hard to read against the bright green background.

- The image is not positioned well and would benefit from a border or frame.

- The overall look and feel of the layout does not convey the right image for the newsletter content, and would not appeal to the target audience.

You've reached the end of this tutorial. Well done! You've created an effective newsletter layout from scratch—we hope you've learned a few design tips too.

If you're interested in creating another type of multi-page publication, try the "Create a Photo Scrapbook" tutorial. If you enjoyed creating the masthead for this newsletter and want to try your hand at logo design, see "Create a Business Card."

Whatever you choose, you should now be more familiar with PagePlus's powerful desktop publishing features—features you'll put to good use in any type of PagePlus publication.

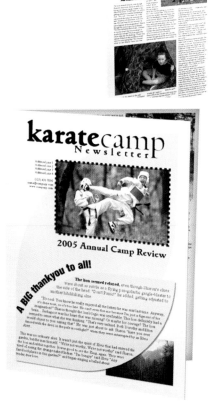

Create a PDF Form

Make use of powerful new PagePlus 11 functionality to create and publish an electronic-based Portable Document Format (PDF) business expense form.

Create a PDF Form

Portable Document Format (PDF) form creation is one of the exciting new features included in PagePlus 11.

You can use PDF forms for many purposes (order forms, subscription forms, billing forms, employee personal data forms, and so on) and to collect many different kinds of data from your audience. For example, on a product order form, you'd want to know the name, shipping address, and telephone number of your customer. You'd also need the details of the order—product type, quantity, price per unit, total price, and so on.

In this tutorial, you'll get the chance to work with a selection of the different form fields available in PagePlus. You'll create and publish a business expense claim form, which can then be accessed by your users, filled out online, and printed.

In this exercise, you'll learn how to:

- Design a layout for a functional form.

- Create and format text objects.

- Create, resize, and position form fields.

- Set form field properties.

- Work with grouped objects.

- Copy and paste form fields.

- Work with ruler guides and alignment to position objects.

- Create a calculated form field.

- Create a custom validation script.

- Specify tabbing order of form fields.

- Publish a PDF form.

Create a PDF Form

Let's assume that you want to create an employee expense claim form to be posted on company intranet. Employees will access the form from their own computers, fill in their expense details online, and then print out the form for processing.

Before you begin to lay out your form in PagePlus, there are couple of things you should do. Use a blank piece of paper to complete these initial steps.

First, you need to determine exactly what information you want to collect. Next, map out your design on paper. Decide on form size and structure (single or multi-page), and be sure to include graphics, text, and any other static objects.

Gathering the data

Let's think about the information we need to collect in order to process an expense claim. We'll need to know at least who is submitting the expense form, and what expenses they are claiming for. Let's assume then that we want to capture the following data:

Employee Information	Expense Information	Other Information
Employee name	Date	Reimbursement method — cheque or direct deposit
Employee number	Description—e.g. sales conference hotel bill	Whether or not receipt is attached
Employee department	Category—travel, meals, etc.	Total expenses amount
	Amount	Employee's signature date
		Manager's signature date

Mapping out the form design

The next step is to map out the form design with paper and pencil. It's tempting to skip this and just go ahead and start dropping form objects into PagePlus document. However, if you sketch your form layout on paper first, you'll end up with a better-designed form. You'll also save yourself the time and effort of having to recreate your form multiple times in PagePlus—it's very unlikely that you'll be happy with your first layout attempt!

When drafting out your form design, keep usability and visual appeal in mind. Use the following guidelines to help you:

- Keep your form simple and uncluttered.

- Group related form fields together.

- Give your form fields clear, meaningful labels and position them consistently relative to the object.

- Provide clear and simple instructions (use ToolTips too) to help users complete the form as easily as possible.

If users must complete certain information on the form, be sure to indicate that these fields are mandatory. For example, you could do this with an asterisk or with colour-coding.

Create a PDF Form

- If you will be collecting data via hardcopy printout, avoid unnecessary or complex graphics that will use up ink and take too long to print.

- Be careful when using colour on your forms. While useful for emphasizing and enhancing certain sections of your form, too much colour can be distracting. Again, if your form will be printed out, you should use colour sparingly.

Notice that we have placed the employee details together at the top of the form, while all of the expense information is grouped together in a table— we'll show you how to do this later. Grouping related items together will make your forms more legible and 'user-friendly.'

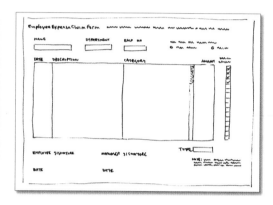

We drafted out the form design illustrated here, which we'll show you how to reproduce in PagePlus. You can use our design, or one of your own if you prefer. Let's get started.

To create and save new publication

1 In PagePlus, click **File**, point to **New**, click **New from Startup Wizard**, and then click **start from scratch**.

2 In the dialog, click **Regular/Normal**, and then click **Landscape**. Choose an A4 or Letter template, and then click **Open**.

3 Click **File/Save**, and save the file as **ExpenseForm.ppp**.

We'll now add the title of our form using a standard text frame.

To add and format title

1 On the Tools toolbar, click the **Standard Frame** tool, then click and drag to insert a frame in the top left corner.

2 In the text frame, type "Employee Expense Claim Form," and then click and drag to select the text (or press **Ctrl+A**).

3 On the Context bar, choose the font size and style for your title (we've used 14 pt Verdana), and click the **Bold** button.

4 Right-click in the text frame, click **Text Format**, and then click **Character**.

5 In the **Character** dialog, in the **Text colour** drop-down list, click the dark blue swatch and then click **OK**.

Create a PDF Form

6 If necessary, resize the text frame to fit the text—click one of the frame handles, hold down the left mouse button, and then drag to the new position.

The next step is to add the employee details: name, department, and employee number. It makes sense to include the reimbursement method in this group too. We want these four objects to sit beneath the form title, about 3 cm or so from the top of the page. We can use ruler guides to help us position the items initially. We'll also make use of PagePlus's alignment feature for fine-tuning.

PagePlus lets you set up horizontal and vertical ruler guides—non-printing red lines used to position layout elements.

To create and move ruler guide

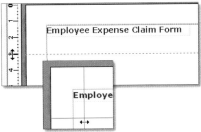

1 Click on the ruler running down the left side of the page. The dotted red ruler guide line appears.

2 Drag to position the ruler guide at the 3 cm horizontal mark. The dotted line changes to solid red.

3 Making sure you do not have any text frames selected, click on the ruler at the top of the page and insert a vertical guide 2 cm from the page edge.

- To move a guide, simply click and drag.
- To remove a guide, drag and drop it anywhere outside the page area.

If a text object is selected, clicking within the object's ruler region adds a tab stop. Clicking elsewhere on the ruler creates a guide.

Before continuing, let's check that **snapping** is turned on. This will ensure that any objects we create, move, or resize will jump to align with our ruler guides.

To turn Snapping on or off

- Click the ⊡ **Snapping** button on the HintLine toolbar. When the button is down (i.e. appears indented), snapping is on.

  When you are happy with the position of your ruler guides, move on to the next section and add the form field labels to the 'employee details' section of the form.

  Note: When choosing labels you should make them as clear and meaningful as possible.

💡 The snapping feature simplifies placement and alignment by 'magnetizing' grid dots and guide lines. When snapping is on, the edges and centres of objects you create, move, or resize will jump to align with the nearest visible grid dot or guide line. Objects normally snap to the page edge, too.

To set which visible elements are snapped to:

1 Choose **Options** from the **Tools** menu.

2 On the **Layout** tab, in the **Snap to** section, clear any elements you don't want to snap to.

Create a PDF Form

To add and format form field labels

1 On the Tools toolbar, click the **Standard Frame** tool, then click and drag to insert a text frame at the top left of the page, at the point where the ruler guides intersect.

2 In the text frame, type "Name," and then click and drag to select the text (or press **Ctrl+A**).

3 On the Context bar, choose the font size and style for your heading (we've used **10 pt Verdana**), and click the **Bold** button to bold the text.

4 Right-click in the text frame, click **Text Format**, and then click **Character**.

5 In the **Character** dialog, in the **Text colour:** drop-down list, click the dark blue colour swatch. Click **OK** to apply the colour.

Now that you have created the first form field label, you can use it as a template for the others. This will ensure that all labels are the same height, making it easier for you to align them. Let's use 'copy and paste' to make the other labels for our employee details section.

To copy and paste an object

1 Right-click the object and click **Copy**.

2 Right-click again and click **Paste**.

3 Repeat steps 1 and 2 to create the 'Department,' 'Employee No.' and 'Reimbursement requested by:' labels, adjusting the length of the text frames accordingly.

4 Position the labels by 'snapping' them to the ruler guide, as illustrated.

We've laid the groundwork for our first form fields, so now let's create them. We'll use the **Form** toolbar for this exercise (you can also click **Insert/Form Field)**. The **Form** toolbar is a floating toolbar, which you can drag to any position in the PagePlus workspace.

To view the Form toolbar

- On the **View** menu, click **Toolbars** and then click **Form**.

The buttons on the toolbar represent the form field types available. For our first field—Employee Name—we want users to type in their names, so it makes sense to use a **text field** here.

There are a variety of different types of form fields, some of which we will cover in this tutorial. For in-depth information and a list of all the form field types, see "Creating PDF Forms" in online Help.

To create a text field

1 On the **Form** toolbar, click the **Text Field** button.

2 Move the cursor just below the 'Name' label and click once to insert the field.

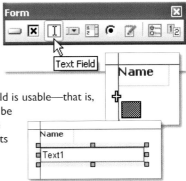

We now have a basic text field. As it stands, this field is usable—that is, if we were to publish the form as a PDF, we would be able to type into this box. However, we can change the way a form field looks and 'behaves' by editing its **properties**.

We'll use the **Form Field Properties** dialog to:

- Give a unique name to the field.

- Add a ToolTip.

- Format the line around the text box, and the text that the user types into the box.

- Limit the number of letters that can be typed into the box.

Text fields
Use a text field when you want the user to type their input—this can be textual or numerical. For example, names, addresses, phone numbers, e-mail addresses, or cash amounts.

Let's get started...

To set text field properties

1 Right-click the field, and then click **Form Field Properties**.

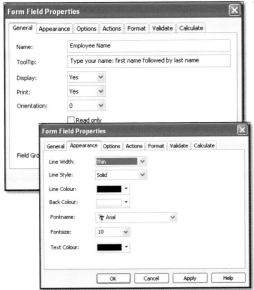

2 On the **General** tab:

- Overwrite the current **Name:** with your own name for this field. This name will serve as unique identifier for the field; so it should 'make sense.' We used 'Employee Name.'

- In the **ToolTip:** box, type a brief sentence telling the user what information they should type in this field.

3 On the **Appearance** tab:

- Change the **Line Style** to 'Solid.'

- Choose the format of the user-typed text by selecting values from the **Fontname** and **Fontsize** drop-down lists. (We used 10 pt Arial.)

Create a PDF Form

4 On the **Options** tab:

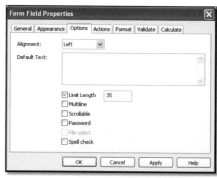

- The **Default Text:** box contains text that is displayed in the form field when the form user first opens the PDF form. We want our fields to be blank so leave this box empty.

- Select the **Limit Length** check box, and in the box to the right of this option, type '35.' This limits the number of characters allowed to be typed to 35, which should be sufficient for most names.

- Clear the **Scrollable** and **Spell check** boxes.

5 We don't need to change anything on the other tabs, so click **OK** to close the **Form Field Properties** dialog.

Our next form field, 'Department,' is slightly different. Rather than having users type their information into text box, we want them to be able to select a value from a list. This sounds complicated, but it isn't. We can easily do this with a **combo box**.

In this case, we want to present employees with list of departments. We'll create list items for Accounting, Sales, Human Resources, Shipping, and Customer Service.

Combo boxes
Use a combo box when you want to present the user with a drop-down list of items from which to choose.

To create a combo box

1 On the **Form** toolbar, click the **Combo Box** button.

2 Move the cursor just below the 'Department' label and click once to insert the field.

To set the properties of a combo box

1 Right-click the combo box, and click **Form Field Properties**.

2 On the **General** tab:

- Overwrite the **Name:** with your own identifier. We used 'Employee Department.'

- In the **ToolTip:** box, type a brief sentence telling the user what information they should enter in this field. For example, "Click the arrow and select your department."

3 On the **Appearance** tab:

- Change the **Line Style** to 'Solid.'

- In the **Fontname** and **Fontsize** drop-down lists, choose the format for the text that will be displayed in the combo box list.

You can choose any font, but your form will look better if you use a standard font style throughout. We suggest you select the same font you used for your text field.

4 Now click the **Options** tab. You'll notice that it looks different than the **Options** tab for our text field. This is where we add the list items for our combo box.

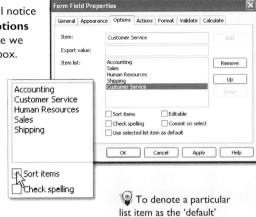

- In the **Item:** box, type 'Accounting,' and then click **Add**. 'Accounting' appears in the **Item list:** box.

- Repeat this process to add 'Sales,' 'Human Resources,' 'Shipping,' and 'Customer Service' to the list.

- Select the **Sort items** check box to sort the menu items alphabetically.

5 We don't need to change anything on the other tabs so click **OK** to close the dialog.

We'll look at the 'Employee No.' field next.

In our fictitious company, assume that employee numbers consist of two letters followed by three numbers—for example, JB007. We want to ensure that employees type this *exact* format, so we need to somehow validate the data entered. PagePlus PDF forms allow you to validate form data in two different ways, both by means of the **Validate** tab in the **Form Field Properties** dialog:

- **Simple validation**—Use this for numeric fields to restrict the number range that users can enter by setting minimum and maximum values. We'll demonstrate this later.

- **Custom validation**—This more advanced validation can be applied to text fields and editable combo boxes and requires use of JavaScript code. We'll use an example of JavaScript code to validate our 'Employee No.' field.

> To denote a particular list item as the 'default' value, select the item in the Item list: box, and then click **Use selected list item as default**.
>
> To allow users to enter their own items rather than selecting one from the predefined list, select the **Editable** check box.

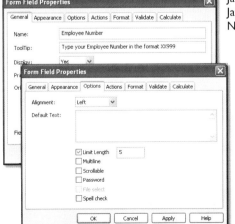

- ❑ Follow the steps outlined in "To create text field" (p. 141) to add a text field below the 'Employee No.' label.

- ❑ Follow the steps outlined in "To set the properties of text field" (p. 141) to set the properties on the **General** and **Appearance** tabs (your ToolTip should tell the user that they must enter the correct format).

- ❑ On the **Options** tab, set the **Limit Length** value to 5.

Create a PDF Form

We're now ready to add the validation.

To add a custom validation script

1 In the **Form Field Properties** dialog, on the **Validate** tab:

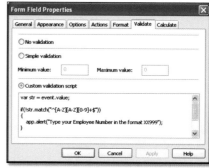

- Click **Custom validation script**.
- In the **Custom validation script** box, type the following JavaScript code *exactly*:

```
var str = event.value;
if(!str.match("^[A-Z][A-Z][0-9]+$"))
{
   app.alert("Type your Employee Number in the format XX999");
}
```

This code checks that users have typed the correct format, and presents them with an error message otherwise.

2 Click **OK** to close the **Form Field Properties** dialog.

For the 'Reimbursement Method' field, we could ask users to type their preferred method into text field, or select it from a list.

There is another type of form field, however, that is particularly suited to this type of data: the **radio button**.

The development of JavaScript code is beyond the scope of this tutorial. For more information, including the *Acrobat JavaScript Scripting Reference Guide*, go to http://partners.adobe.com/public/developer/pdf/topic_js.html

Some custom JavaScript may not be supported by certain versions of Acrobat Reader. You should test all forms in the Acrobat software used by your target audience.

We want employees to choose one of two methods of reimbursement—direct deposit or cheque. We'll create a radio button for each option.

To create a radio button

1 On the **Form** toolbar, click **Radio Button**.

2 Move the cursor below the 'Reimbursement requested by:' label, click once to add the field.

3 Repeat to insert a second button.

Radio buttons
Use radio buttons when you want the user to select a single mutually-exclusive option from a group of two or more options—Yes/No, Often/Sometimes/Never, etc.

Great, we've created our radio buttons. Now we need to set their properties.

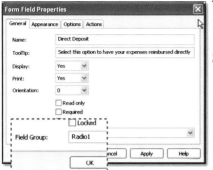

To set the properties of a radio button

1   Right-click the left radio button, and then click **Form Field Properties**.

2   On the **General** tab:

- In the **Name:** box, replace 'Radio1' with 'Direct Deposit.'

- In the **ToolTip:** box, type a brief sentence telling users how to use this field. For example, "Select this option to have your expenses reimbursed directly into your bank account."

- At the bottom of the **General** tab, In the **Field Group** box, delete 'Radio1,' and replace it with a new group name—'Reimbursement Method.'

Field Group: Reimbursement Method

The **Field Group** option is unique to radio buttons. To operate correctly, radio buttons that are intended to be grouped must belong to the same field group. We've just created a new 'Reimbursement Method' group, which will contain both of our radio buttons.

3   On the **Appearance** tab, change the **Fontsize** to 10 pt.

4   Click **OK** to close the **Form Field Properties** dialog.

5   Repeat the previous steps to set the properties for the second radio button:

- Name the button 'Cheque.'

- Add an appropriate ToolTip, e.g., "Select this option to have your expenses reimbursed by cheque."

- Add the button to the 'Reimbursement Method' field group by selecting it from the drop-down list.

- Change the font size to 10 pt.

On the **Options** tab, you can:

- Change the style of your radio button—choose from Circle, Check, Cross, Diamond, Star, or Square.

- Select **Checked by default** if you want the radio button to display as selected when the user opens the form.

Create a PDF Form

We've made and configured our radio buttons, now we need to label them appropriately.

❏ On the Tools toolbar, click the **Standard Frame** tool, then click and drag to insert a frame to the right of the first radio button.

❏ In the text frame, type "Direct deposit," and then click and drag to select the text (or press **Ctrl+A**).

❏ On the Context bar, choose the font size and style for your label (we've used **10 pt Verdana**), and click the **Bold** button to bold the text.

❏ Repeat these steps to create a second label for the 'Cheque' radio button.

Great, our employee details form fields and labels are in place, but the form would look better if the objects were aligned exactly. PagePlus provides precise method of aligning objects on a page using the **Align Objects** dialog.

Precise alignment is one key to professional layout. Use menu commands or the **Align** tab to align the edges of any two or more objects with one another; space them out at certain intervals; or align objects with a page margin.

To align objects using the Align Objects dialog

1 Press and hold down the **Shift** key, then use the **Pointer** tool to click on each of the four label text objects— 'Name,' 'Department,' 'Employee No.,' and 'Reimbursement requested by.'

2 Click the ⊞ **Align Objects** button on the toolbar (or right-click and choose **Arrange/Align Objects**).

3 In the **Align Objects** dialog, in the **Vertically**: section, click **Top**, and then click **OK**.

4 Repeat step 1 to select all the form fields, including the radio buttons and their labels.

5 Click **Align Objects**, but this time choose **Bottom** vertical alignment.

All of the text objects and form fields are now precisely aligned at the top of our page. Our employee details section is complete. Let's now move on to the expenses section.

We want to present this section of the form in tabular format. We'll begin by adding a ruler guide, then we'll add five text frames for our form field labels. These labels will act as the column headings for our expenses table.

To create and align column headings

1 Click the left ruler, and add a horizontal ruler guide at the 6 cm mark.

2 On the Tools toolbar, click the **Standard Frame** tool, then click and drag to insert a frame beneath the 'Name' form field, at the point where the ruler guides intersect.

3 In the text frame, type "Date," and then click and drag to select the text (or press **Ctrl+A**).

4 On the Context bar, choose the font size and style for your heading (we've used black **10 pt Verdana**), and click the **Bold** button to bold the text.

5 Using this text object as a template, copy and paste it to create text frames for the 'Description,' 'Category,' 'Amount,' and 'Receipt attached' labels.

6 Position the labels as illustrated.

7 Using the process you used in the previous section, align the column headings—**Shift**-click to select them all, and then click the **Align Objects** button. Select the vertical **Bottom** alignment option.

Our column headings are in place so we're ready to make our table. We'll use a few different types of form fields here—**text fields** for Date, Description, and Amount; a **combo box** for Category; and a **check box** for Receipt attached. We'll create the first row of our table and then copy and paste it to create the others.

> We'll summarise procedures that we've already explained, but go back and refresh your memory if you need to.

To create a text field and set its properties

1 On the **Form** toolbar, click the **Text Field** button and insert a text field under the 'Date' label.

2 Right-click the text field, and click **Form Field Properties**.

On the **General** tab:

- Overwrite the **Name:** with your own identifier.

- Add the following ToolTip: "Type the date of the expense in the format dd/mm/yyyy." (You'll understand why in minute.)

On the **Appearance** tab:

- Change the **Line Style** to 'Solid.'

- Choose the format of the user-typed text (we used 10 pt Arial).

Create a PDF Form

On the **Options** tab:

- Clear the **Default Text:** box.
- Select the **Limit Length** check box, and type '10' in the box.
- Clear all other options.

On the **Format** tab:

- In the **Format as:** drop-down list, select **Date**.
- In the **Date format:** list, select 'dd/mm/yyyy' (now our ToolTip makes sense!). Click **OK**.

3 Repeat these steps to create two more text fields for 'Description' and 'Amount,' and then position them under their respective labels.

4 Right-click the 'Description' text field, click **Form Field Properties** and make the following changes:

- On the **General** tab, type a name and an appropriate ToolTip for this field,
- On the **Appearance** tab, select a **Solid** line style; choose the font name and size you used for your 'Date' field.
- On the **Options** tab, delete the default text, set the **Limit Length** to 50, and clear all other options.

5 Right-click the 'Amount' text field, click **Form Field Properties** and make the following changes:

- On the **General** tab, type a name and an appropriate ToolTip.
- On the **Appearance** tab, select a solid line style; choose the font name and size you used for your 'Date' field.
- On the **Options** tab, in the **Alignment** list, select 'Right.' Clear all other options.
- On the **Format** tab:
  - **Format as:** Number
  - **Decimal places:** 2
  - **Separator style:** 9,999.99
  - **Currency symbol:** None
  - **Negative numbers:** Use red text

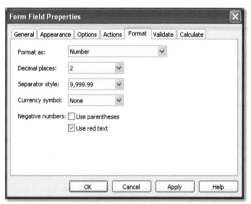

Our text fields are in place, but we still need to align them. Before we do this, let's create the form fields for 'Category' and 'Receipt attached.' We can then group all of these expense form fields and align them in one step. We'll use a combo box for the expense category because we want our users to select a category from a predefined list— Accommodation, Entertainment, Meals, Supplies, Telephone, Travel, and Other.

We've used a combo box for the 'Department' field so the process will be familiar to you.

To create a combo box and set its properties

1 On the **Form** toolbar, click the **Combo Box** button and add a combo box under the 'Category' label.

2 Right-click the combo box and click **Form Field Properties**.

On the **General** tab:

- Overwrite the current **Name:** with your own unique identifier. We used 'ExpenseCategory1.'

- Add the following ToolTip: "Click the arrow and select an expense category."

On the **Appearance** tab:

- Change the **Line Style** to 'Solid.'

- Choose the format of the list box text (we used 10 pt Arial).

On the **Options** tab:

- In the **Item:** box, type 'Accommodation,' and then click **Add**.

- Repeat this process to add 'Entertainment,' 'Meals,' 'Supplies,' 'Telephone,' 'Travel,' and 'Other' to the list.

- In this case, don't select the **Sort items** check box because we don't want the list items sorted alphabetically—we want 'Other' to appear at the bottom of our list.

- We don't need to change anything on the other tabs, so click **OK** to close the **Form Field Properties** dialog.

Our last item is 'Receipt attached.' We want to know if the user is attaching a receipt for a particular expense. We could use a text box, and ask users to type in 'Yes,' or 'No'; we could use a combo box and add No and Yes as list items; or we could use radio buttons, one for Yes and one for No. However, the best choice for this field is the check box.

Check boxes
Check boxes are boxes containing a simple check, cross, or other symbol. The form user clicks once to select or clear the box. Check boxes are great for simple Yes/No questions, such as "Do you want to be notified of any upcoming events in the future?" They are also ideal when you want your users to be able to multiple-select a series of options displayed side by side. For example, "Check all the events that are of interest to you."

Create a PDF Form

To create a check box

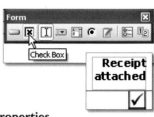

1 On the **Form** toolbar, click the **Check Box** button.

2 Move the cursor just below and to the right of the 'Receipt attached' label. Click once to insert the field.

To set the properties of a check box

1 Right-click the check box, and then click **Form Field Properties**.

2 On the **General** tab:

- Overwrite the current **Name:** with your own unique identifier. We used 'Receipt1.'

- In the **ToolTip:** box, type "Click this box if you are attaching receipt."

3 On the **Appearance** tab:

- Change the **Line Style** to 'Solid.'

- In the **Fontsize** drop-down list, choose the size you used for your other form fields.

4 On the **Options** tab:

- In the **Style:** drop-down list, select the style you want to use for your check box. We used 'Check.'

- Leave the **Checked by default** box cleared. (If you check this option, the check box will appear 'checked' when your users first open the form, i.e., they'll have to click to clear the box.)

- Click **OK** to close the **Form Field Properties** dialog.

You should now have all of your expense form fields in place. Earlier in this tutorial, we used the **Align Objects** dialog to align text objects and form fields. We'll now use the **Align** tab—a new PagePlus 11 feature—to align the top row of our expenses table.

To align objects using the Align tab

1 Press and hold down the **Shift** key, then use the **Pointer** tool to click on the 'Date' label and its corresponding text box.

2 At the lower right of the workspace, on the **Align** tab. Clear the **Include Margins** check box, and then click the **Left** button to left-align the objects.

The **Align** tab is one of series of tabs new to PagePlus 11. The tabs are accessible on the right of the workspace and are free-floating—just click and drag a tab to the most convenient position. To 'dock' a tab, click and drag it back to its original position. To hide or display a tab, on the **View** menu, click **Studio tabs**, and then select from the list. For more information, see online Help.

We can now use the 'Date' text object to align all the other form fields in the row.

3 Using the same process you used in step 1, **Shift**-click to select the 'Date' text field, the 'Description' text field, the 'Category' combo box, the 'Amount' text field, and the 'Receipt attached' check box. (You could also use the **Pointer** tool to click and drag a selection 'bounding box' around these objects.)

4 On the **Align** tab, clear the **Include Margins** check box, and then click the **Top** button.

5 Finally, **Shift**-click to select the 'Receipt attached' label and check box objects.

6 On the **Align** tab, clear the **Include Margins** box, and then click the **Right** button.

Great, all the hard work is done! All of the form fields are now neatly aligned under the red ruler guide. We can use this row of fields as a template for the rest of our table.

Some of the tools we'll be using in this section should be familiar to you—copy and paste, and alignment. However, before we continue, we'll show you another useful PagePlus feature—**grouping**.

Rather than copying and pasting each of the form fields individually, we can group them and then copy the group.

To create a group from a multiple selection

1 **Shift**-click to select all of the form fields in the row.

2 Click the ▣ **Group** button below the selection (or click **Arrange/ Group Objects**).

When objects are grouped, you can position, resize, or rotate the objects all at the same time.

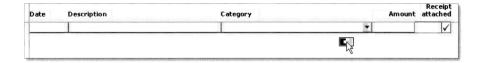

To ungroup (turn a group back into a multiple selection), click the ▣ **Ungroup** button below the selection (or click **Arrange/ Ungroup Objects**).

Create a PDF Form

We're now ready to copy and paste our group and create the rest of our expenses table.

To copy and paste a group of objects

1 Right-click the group of form fields, and then click **Copy**.

2 Right-click again and click **Paste**.

3 Click on this new group and drag it into position as the second row of the table. Use the **Zoom** tools on the toolbar to help you do this.

> 💡 Use the Zoom tools to help you fine-tune the positioning of objects on the page.
>
> 🔍 **Zoom Tool**—Click the button, then drag out a rectangular bounding box to define a region to zoom in to. The zoom percentage adjusts accordingly, fitting the designated region into the window. To zoom out, hold down the **Shift** key when dragging. Double-click the button to display the page at actual size (100%).
>
> 🔍 **Zoom Out**—Click to view more of the page in the window.
>
> 🔍 **Zoom In**—Click to view the page area more closely.

4 Click to select both groups of form fields, then on the **Align** tab, click the **Left** button.

This gives us two rows of form fields, aligned below their respective column headings.

We can continue to copy and paste the first row to build our table, or we can make the process even faster by grouping the two rows together, and then copying them. Let's do this.

5 With both groups selected, click the **Group** button. Right-click this new group, click **Copy**, and then click **Paste**.

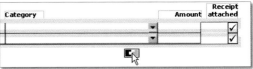

6 Repeat 3 steps and 4 to position and align this group of two new rows.

7 Now group all four rows together, and then copy, paste, and align them. This gives us eight rows.

8 Finally, group the eight rows and repeat the process to complete the 16-row table.

That's it, the table is finished! Now all we have to do is create the 'Total' field, and the signature and date text frames.

Let's get the tricky part over with first—creating the 'Total' field. We don't want the user to type into this field. Instead, we want the field to do all the work and automatically add up all the values that appear in the 'Amount' fields.

This may sound complicated, but it isn't. We'll use the **Calculate** tab in the **Form Field Properties** dialog to do this.

To create a calculated field

1 On the **Form** toolbar, click the **Text Field** button and insert a text field below the last 'Amount' field.

2 Resize the new field to match the column width—click one of its frame handles, hold down the left mouse button, and then drag to the new position.

3 Right-align the field with the 'Amount' column. (You'll need to 'ungroup' one of the table rows to do this.)

4 Right-click the field, click **Form Field Properties** and make the following changes:

- On the **General** tab, type a name for this field.; you don't need a ToolTip this time.

- On the **Appearance** tab, select a solid line style; choose the font name and size you want to use in this field.

- On the **Options** tab, in the **Alignment** list, select 'Right'; clear the default text and all other options.

- On the **Format** tab:
  + **Format as:** Number
  + **Decimal places:** 2
  + **Separator style:** 9,999.99
  + **Currency symbol:** Pound (£)
  + **Negative numbers:** Use red text

5 Now click the **Calculate** tab. The last time we used this tab, we created a custom calculation script to check user input. This time, we'll use **simple calculation** instead. Don't worry, no JavaScript required here! PagePlus will do all the hard work for us, all we need to do is tell it which fields to work with.

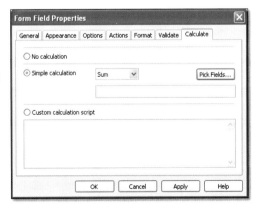

6 Click the **Simple calculation** radio button, select **Sum** from the drop-down list, and then click **Pick Fields**.

Create a PDF Form

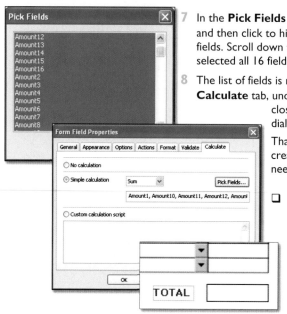

7   In the **Pick Fields** dialog, hold down the **Shift** key and then click to highlight all of the 'Amount' fields. Scroll down the list to make sure you have selected all 16 fields. Click **OK**.

8   The list of fields is now displayed on the **Calculate** tab, under the **Sum** box. Click **OK** to close the **Form Field Properties** dialog.

That's all there is to it. We've created our 'Total' field and just need to label it.

❑   Click the **Standard Frame** tool and add a text frame to the left of the 'Total' field. Type "TOTAL" in the frame and format the text appropriately (right-click, and then select **Text Format/Character**).

❑   Repeat the previous step to add text frames for the employee and manager signatures and dates. Position and align these objects at the bottom of the form, as illustrated.

Everything is in place, we've finished laying out our form.

Before we publish it as a PDF form, there are a couple of small but important tasks we should do—set the **tab order** of the form fields, and **lock** the form objects.

💡 You'll notice on our form that we have two 'notes'—one at the top of the form and another at the bottom (we just used standard text frames for these). Obviously these aren't mandatory. However, wherever possible, you should aim to provide any additional information that might help the user complete the form.

Our form users can navigate through the form fields in one of two ways—they can use the mouse and click each field in turn; or they can use the **Tab** key to jump from field to field. As forms are generally designed to be completed in sequential manner, 'tabbing' is considered the more efficient method. In addition, it's important to set a logical tab order so that users who are unable to use a mouse can complete the form easily.

The tab order is governed by the order in which the form designer adds the form fields to the page. As the form design may change during the design process, the tab order may be thrown out of sequence.

Fortunately, the **Tab Order** button on the **Form** toolbar can be used to reset the tab order at the end of the design process. In this tutorial, we added our form fields in the order in which we want our users to complete them. Because of this, you'll see that our tab order is already logically sequenced. For demonstration purposes, however, we'll show you how this feature works so you can make use of it in the future.

Note: Before you begin the following process, make sure that all of your form objects are *ungrouped*.

To change tab order

1 On the **Form** toolbar, click the **Tab Order** button. This reveals blue tab markers on all your form fields.

2 Click on the form fields in the order in which you want them to be assigned tab numbers. PagePlus automatically assigns a new tab number to the blue marker.

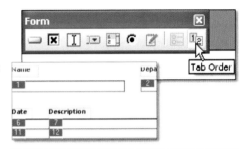

3 Click the **Tab Order** button again to switch off the blue tab markers.

> Go ahead and try it. To reset the tab order, click the **Tab Order** button and start again.

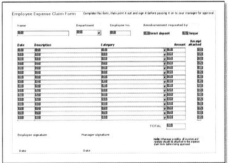

Happy with the form layout and tab order? Great. It's taken lot of time and effort to set up, so let's lock our form objects to prevent us from accidentally moving them.

We're going to lock all the objects on the form, but you can use the following procedure for single or multiple objects.

To lock objects

1 On the **Edit** menu, click **Select**, and then click **Select All** (or use the **Pointer** tool to draw a selection bounding box around all of the objects on the page.)

2 Right-click the selection, click **Arrange**, and then click **Lock Objects**.

3 Now click on one of your form fields and try to move it.

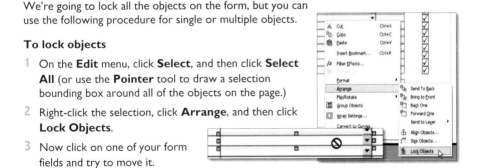

To unlock objects

• Right-click the object(s), then click **Arrange/Unlock Objects**.

Create a PDF Form

We're finally ready to save our form and publish it to PDF format.

You can export any PagePlus publication as a PDF file—not just forms. This tutorial covers the basic steps and options. For more information, see "Exporting PDF files" in online Help.

To publish a PDF form

1 On the **File** menu, click **Publish as PDF**.

2 On the **General** tab, in the **Compatibility** drop-down list, select the appropriate Acrobat version.

3 Select the **Preview PDF file in Acrobat** check box, and then click **OK**.

4 In the **Publish to PDF** dialog, type a file name for the PDF, and save it in a convenient location.

The **Publish to PDF** dialog closes and your form opens in Adobe Acrobat.

> PDF is a cross-platform file format, developed by Adobe, which has evolved into a worldwide standard for document distribution. PDF files work equally well for electronic or paper publishing—including professional printing. In recent years, print shops are moving away from PostScript and toward the newer, more reliable PDF/X formats expressly targeted for graphic arts and high quality reproduction. Several different "flavours" of PDF/X exist; PagePlus supports **PDF/X-1** and **PDF/X-1a**.

Your work is not quite finished yet—you still need to check your form to make sure that it works in the way you expect.

When checking your form, you should:

- Check the tab order.

- Hover over the form fields and make sure that ToolTips are spelled correctly.

- Make sure you can type into all text fields.

- Check that all fields are long enough to hold the typed text or predefined list item.

- Check the entries in the combo box drop-down lists—are the items spelled correctly, does all of the text display properly?

- Make sure that you can't select more than one radio button in a group.

- Verify that any calculated fields work correctly—if not, you've probably entered the wrong calculation type, or the wrong fields on the **Calculate** tab.

- Check any validation—e.g., make sure that incorrect data is not accepted and generates an error message.

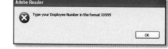

Well done! You've designed a business expense form from start to finish, and you've published it to PDF format. You can now post the PDF form on your company intranet and let your users take it for a test run! (Of course, you've already tested it thoroughly so there shouldn't be any surprises.)

Create Address Labels

Use PagePlus's Mail Merge features to import a simple address list and create mailing labels.

Create Address Labels

Use PagePlus's Mail Merge features to import a simple address list and create mailing labels.

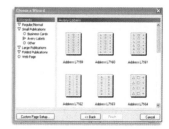

1 From the Startup Wizard, choose **start from scratch** and browse the **Small Publications/Avery Labels** category of blank documents.

   Depending on whether you chose a US or European setup at the time of installation, you'll encounter either US or European label definitions due to the differing paper size standards.

2 Choose either **Parcel L7165** (based on A4 paper) or **Namebadge 5095** (based on Letter paper) and click **Finish**. Your publication displays as a single label. Create a text frame to match the size of the page area within the blue margins—if you can't see the guidelines, click **View/Guidelines**.

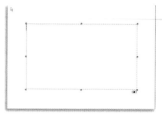

3 On the **Tools** menu, click **Mail and Photo Merge,** and then click **Open Data Source...**

4 In the **Open** dialog, in the **Files of Type** list (highlighted in blue in our illustration) and select **Text Files (*.txt, *.csv, *.tab, *.asc)**.

   Select the **Test.csv** file found in your Workspace folder (normally found at **C:\Program Files\Serif\PagePlus\11.0\ Tutorials\Workspace**) and click **Open**. The process of importing your data will begin.

5 In the **Data Format** dialog, click **Delimited**, select **First Line Contains Column Headers**, and then click **Next**. Select **Comma,** and then click **Finish**.

   The **Test.csv** file opens and is now your active **data source**. The **Merge List** dialog shows you the active data source and lets you further select, filter, or sort it for the impending merge operation.

Test.csv is a **comma-delimited file**—entries are separated by commas—and was created using an address book from an e-mail client program. Most address-management applications and database and spreadsheet programs can create such standard comma-delimited files, which you can import.

You can also take advantage of the **New Data Source...** command to create your own editable databases in PagePlus, or create data sources from a folder of images.

See the "Auction Catalog" tutorial for practice merging both text and photo data to a repeating page layout. Keep in mind that PagePlus can also open many data sources directly, saving you the trouble of exporting to an intermediate delimited or fixed-length format.

For example, you could prevent certain records from being merged, either by clearing the boxes one by one or by applying a filter (for instance, where City is Not equal to Nottingham).

6 For now, simply click **OK** to include all the data in your merge list. You should see the **Mail and Photo Merge** toolbar on your screen, indicating that there's an active data source.

7 Click the **Insert Text Field** button on the **Mail and Photo Merge** toolbar and the **Insert Mail Merge Text Field** dialog should be prominent in your display.

Highlight **First Name**, click **Insert**, press the spacebar. Highlight **Last Name** and click **Insert**. This inserts the First Name and Last Name data fields on the same line in your text frame with a space between them.

8 Now for the address: press **Enter**, select the **Address Line I** field, click **Insert**, then press **Enter**.

9 Repeat this process of selecting the field name, clicking **Insert** and pressing **Enter** until you have inserted each of the address fields on a line of its own in your text frame.

10 Click **Close** when you're done, then click the **AutoFit** button on the **Frame** toolbar (normally at the top of the PagePlus screen) to force the text to fill the available frame area. You can reformat these fields in your text frame as if they were normal text, except that each field will be treated as a single character.

This is all of the hard work done! With our help, PagePlus has created the database from an external file and has now also had a text frame set up to contain all of the mail merge data.

11 Click the **View Data** button on the **Mail and Photo Merge** toolbar. You can now use the arrow buttons on the toolbar (such as the ▶ **Next Record** button) to browse each of the database records in turn merged into your frame. When you're happy to proceed, you can click the **Print** button.

12 On the **Print** dialog's **Layout** tab, locate the **Multiple pages per sheet** section to the mid-left of the dialog.

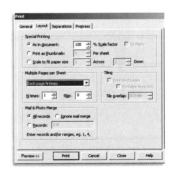

Pull down the menu and choose **Each page N times**, make sure that the **N times** box has a setting of 'I.'

Ensure that the **Mail Merge** settings are set to **All records**, then click **Print**.

You should find that you now have a printed page with addresses formatted as if they were on the label you chose at the beginning of this tutorial.

Create Address Labels

If your address database had consisted of more than eight records, the printed output would have continued on to subsequent pages. For instructions on how to print on partially-used label sheets, and how to select which addresses to print, see the "Mail Merge" and "Printing Special Formats" online Help topics.

Congratulations on successfully creating a mail-merged publication! The same principles can be used to create tailored newsletters, photo-based catalog layouts, and much more!

Create a Ticket Book

Combine page numbering using a master page, and powerful printing options to create pages for a ticket book.

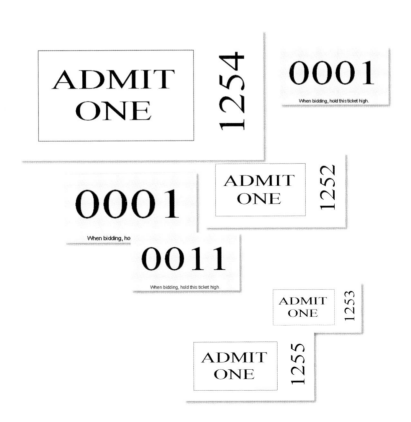

Create a Ticket Book

This exercise shows you a quick and easy way to create simple numbered tickets by using the PagePlus master pages and page numbering features.

1 For simplicity, before starting PagePlus you should begin by selecting a printer and page size. In Windows, **go to your Printers window** (this process differs slightly between versions of Windows), then right-click on your printer of choice and choose **Properties**.

In the dialog, select a suitable page size. You may regularly use **Letter** or **A4**, but this tutorial's example will be using an HP DeskJet 970Cxi desktop inkjet printer and **A5** paper (which is half the size of A4, roughly 6" x 8"). Make a comparable choice that's supported by your specific printer.

2 Open PagePlus and select **Cancel** from the Startup Wizard. This will open your default blank page. Choose **Page Setup** from the **File** menu. Set the page size to match your printer (A5 in this example). In the same **Page Setup** dialog, change the settings to **Small Publications** at the top left of the window. Click the **Create Custom** button near the bottom of the dialog.

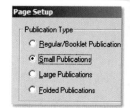

3 In the **Small Publication Setup** dialog, set the **Layout** values to **2 Across** and **5 Down**. In the **Margins** section, leave **Auto** selected.

PagePlus automatically calculates the small publication size required to fit this many "pages" on to the paper size you selected earlier. Selecting the **Auto** option ensures that PagePlus will not use the unprintable area of your paper in its calculations or printing. Click **OK** once to return to the **Page Setup** dialog and click **OK** again to return to the main PagePlus workspace.

Now your publication size will switch to the new settings. You can ignore the default blue margin indicated—or if you wish, right-click on your page, choose **Layout Guides**, then set your margins to zero.

4 Click the Current Page box at the lower left of the workspace to switch to the master page.

A brief aside about master pages and layers... As discussed in the Learning Lab's "Layout Tools" tutorial, **master pages** are background pages, like sheets of extra paper behind your main publication pages. Every page layer can have one master page assigned to it and a given master page can be shared by any number of main pages. The publication we're working with offers the simplest possible case: a single page with one layer. Objects on the master page show through to the main page—unless they're obscured or you've switched off **Master Page Objects** on the **View** menu.

Create a Ticket Book

Placing objects on a master page lets them appear on more than one page—useful for logos, headers, footers and auto-generated page numbers. For an overview of these important elements, see the online Help "Understanding master pages and layers" topic.

5   Using the A **Artistic Text** tool, click near the top left of the publication and drag out a fairly large square to set a large font size for a new text object. When you release the mouse button and can see a flashing text-insertion (I-beam) cursor, select **Page Number** from the **Insert** menu. You should see {n} or an actual page number appear on your page.

> **Optional extra step:** You can add an event name, logo, watermarked graphic or other object(s) to the master page if you would like them to appear on each "ticket." If you'd like to design a "stub" for the ticket, add a second Page Number object to the master page. You might also design an area for a name and address to be written on the stub and ticket.

6   Position the **{n}** in the centre of your publication and click the ☰ **Centred** button.

> 💡 Using **Centred** alignment with the text object in the centre of the page means that as your page number extends from 1 to 2 to 3 characters, the entire number will remain centred.

7   Add two short straight lines with a suggested weight of 2 pt to the bottom right corner of the page. These will help when it comes to scoring the tickets or trimming the pages ready to use as a ticket book.

Optional: If you designed a stub for the ticket, draw another line to score down after printing to make the stub and ticket easy to separate.

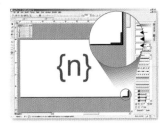

8   Click the Master Page indicator at the bottom left of the screen to switch back to your main publication page. On the **Pages** tab, click the **Page Manager** button, choose to insert 99 pages and click **OK**.

You now have a 100-page publication (printable on just 10 pieces of paper), with the publication automatically set at a size 1/10th that of your chosen printer page.

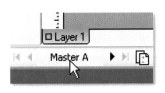

9   From the **File** menu, choose **Print Preview**.

Congratulations, you now have the beginnings of a sequentially-numbered "ticket book" with a paper size of your choice and automatically sized "tickets" based simply on the number of rows and columns specified! Now, where's that stapler?

Create an Auction Catalogue

Use PagePlus's Mail Merge features to import a simple address
list and create mailing labels.

Create an Auction Catalogue

In a "traditional" mail merge operation—for example, filling names and addresses into a batch of form letters—you start with a data source such as a contact list or address book. This tutorial demonstrates a mail merge operation, using a simple comma-delimited .CSV file as the data source.

You'll insert placeholder fields into your publication and specify which data field should map to each placeholder; then you'll print the publication a number of times. With each successive printout, data from the next record will be merged into the output.

PagePlus can perform this kind of merge operation pulling in not only text data but images (for example digital photos) whose path names are listed in the data source. That's why we call it **Mail and Photo Merge**!

You'll be merging both photos and text using a non-traditional merge operation where the result isn't a pile of printouts but a single new publication. Using this approach—ideal for a catalogue or photo album—you define a **repeating layout** with placeholder fields arranged in a grid. During the merge, PagePlus populates the grid fields with photo/text data, generating as many new pages as needed to accommodate the data set. As usual, we'll provide the sample data... so follow along as we produce a catalogue page for an auction house.

This will be a "learn-by-doing" example without a lot of additional comments—consult online Help later for the finer points.

The following steps will show you how to:

- Create a small database in PagePlus from a batch of photos.

- Annotate each photo with a caption.

- Design a repeating layout with a grid of "listings" where each listing includes a photo and its caption.

- Merge to a new publication that will display all the listings.

Creating the data source

1 Click **File/New/New Publication** to create a new, single-page publication using default settings.

2 On the **Tools** menu, click **Mail and Photo Merge, and** then select **Create Photo Data Source from Folder Contents...**

The **Photo Data Source Wizard** opens.

> **Photo Data Source Wizard**
>
> This wizard will help you create a Database containing a list of files within a folder. This Database can then be used as a Mail Merge Data Source.

Create an Auction Catalogue

3   Click the **Browse...** button and locate the **Pieces** subfolder of your **Workspace** folder (typically **C:\Program Files\ Serif\PagePlus\11.0\Tutorials\Workspace**). Click **Next**.

4   Provide a full path name for the database file to be created. We suggest you browse to your **Workspace** folder and use the default filename provided (**pieces.sdb**). Click **Save**, then **Next**.

5   The Wizard should list six image files located in the specified folder. Make sure they're all selected, then click **Next**.

6   On the following screen, click **Select None** to clear all the summary items—these refer to digital camera EXIF information, which you might want for original snapshots but not in this case. Now click **Finish**.

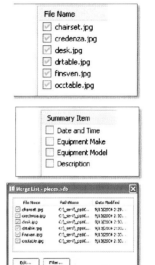

PagePlus creates a small Serif Database (.SDB) file and displays its records in the **Merge List dialog**.

The SDB format is the same used to store address list data for traditional mail merge, but in this case it consists of six records (one for each image), with three fields for each record: **File Name**, **Path Name** and **Date Modified**. The SDB file stores the full data and will be recorded as the active data source when you save this publication.

The **Merge List** dialog lets you filter, sort, or otherwise pare down the full SDB data set for the next merge operation. When you finally merge, only the items displayed and checked in your Merge List will actually be merged.

Adding caption data

An advantage of having the photos listed in an SDB database is that you can edit the accompanying data and PagePlus can save changes as part of the SDB file. Let's add some caption data to our mini image database.

1   Click the **Edit** button in the **Merge List** dialog.

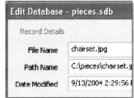

The **Edit Database** dialog opens, displaying data for the first record. From here, you can browse the records or use **Add** and **Delete** to expand or reduce the data set.

2   Click the **Customize** button. The **Customize Database** dialog displays the three fields. Click **Insert** and type "Description" as the new field name, then click **OK**.

Create an Auction Catalogue

3 Click the **Move Down** button if necessary to place the field at the bottom of the list. Now click **Insert** again, type "Appraisal," and then click **OK**. Again, move the field to the bottom. If your list looks like ours, right, click **OK**.

Now we've got two new fields available in the database and the next step is some basic data entry.

4 Open **AuctionData.rtf** in your **Workspace** folder. As an RTF (Rich Text Format) file, by default it should open in a word processor or text editing program.

Use copy and paste to transfer the information to your database. Click the buttons in the **View Records** section of the dialog to step through the numbered records.

5 When you're done, click **OK** to save changes to the data source. In the **Merge List** dialog, you'll see the data you entered displayed in two new columns.

6 Click **OK** to close the **Merge List** dialog (the current merge list data remains active for the next merge operation). You'll see that the **Mail and Photo Merge toolbar** has opened to assist you with your next steps.

| File Name |
| Path Name |
| Date Modified |
| Description |
| Appraisal |

#	Description	Appraisal
1	Jens Risom: Four early KNOLL blond-wood side chairs with spring seat support, re-upholstered in gray tweed fabric. Early Knoll Associates label.	$600-900
2	Florence Knoll: KNOLL maple credenza, 1949, with two sliding doors with leather tab pulls, enclosing four shelves and single fitted drawer, on tubular black metal legs. Refinished, veneer repair. Unmarked.	$1,500-2,000
3	Knoll: Desk, early design for Knoll Associates, ca 1940's. Birch construction throughout. Three drawers with tilt front styling. Early Knoll Associates label in top drawer.	$600-900
4	George Nakashima: KNOLL blond-wood extension dining table on flaring legs. Includes 2-9" leaves. Unmarked.	$1,500-2,000
5	Alvar Aalto: Rare and early FINSVEN lounge chair on laminated bentwood frame, with original orange tweed upholstery. (An example of one of Aalto's most iconic designs.) Unmarked.	$1,000-1,500
6	Knoll: Early blond-wood occasional table by an unknown designer, with bevel-edged rectangular top on four flaring legs. Early red/white Knoll Associates label.	$400-600

Description	Appraisal
Jens Risom: Fo...	$600-900
Florence Knoll: ...	$1,500-2,000
Birch constructi...	$600-900
George Nakashi...	$1,500-2,000
Alvar Aalto: Ra...	$1,000-1,500
Knoll: Early blon...	$400-600

Designing a repeating layout

To produce a repeating layout in a new publication, you need to specify a **repeating area** in the original document—basically a single cell whose unit size determines how many can be tiled across and down on a page. Within this repeating area, you can put placeholders—**picture fields** or **text fields** where you want merged data to appear—and other design elements such as artistic text or QuickShapes. At merge time, data from one record at a time will get merged into each cell of the resulting grid. You'll see how this works in a moment.

There are various ways to fine-tune the repeating area—you can read all about them in online Help.

1 On the **Mail/Photo Merge** toolbar, click the 🖹 **Create or Modify Repeating Area** button.

The **Tile Setup** dialog shows a page layout that consists of a 1 x 4 tiling grid: one repeating area across the page and four down. We have 6 images, so a 2 x 3 grid makes more sense.

2 In the **Tile Setup** dialog, in the **Layout** section, enter an **Across** value of 2 and a **Down** value of 3. In the **Size** section, use the spinwheel arrow buttons to increase the **Height** of the repeating area until the 2 x 3 grid occupies nearly all of the page area. When your preview region looks like our example (right), click **OK**.

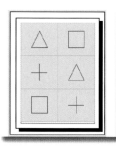

The repeating area appears as a single cell at the upper left of your blank page. Its inner text confirms that we can fit "2 across by 3 down" of these cells on the current page.

3 If you haven't saved your publication yet, do it now.

4 Click the 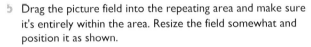 **Insert Picture Field** button on the **Mail/Photo Merge** toolbar. The dialog lists available picture fields in the current data source—in this case there's just one, "Path Name."

Click **Insert** once; the dialog stays open in case you want to insert more than one field. Click **Close**. A new picture field appears on the page (ensure you've added only one).

5 Drag the picture field into the repeating area and make sure it's entirely within the area. Resize the field somewhat and position it as shown.

If you select the repeating area at this point and move it slightly, you'll see that the picture field moves along with it. PagePlus treats any object fully inside a repeating area as part of the area. Be sure to undo the move operation.

6 Now click the 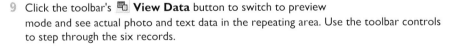 **Insert Text Field** button on the toolbar. This time, insert two fields—**Description** and **Appraisal**—in two successive clicks of the **Insert** button. Close the dialog and you'll see a new text frame on the page, with two text fields.

7 Drag the text field into position just as you did with the picture field, placing it as shown. Type a couple of returns to put the Appraisal field on a separate line.

8 Before proceeding, check the dimensions displayed in the upper left and lower right corners of the repeating area to check that your layout is still set up for a 2 x 3 grid. Confirm that your picture and text fields are within the repeat area. Save the publication again.

9 Click the toolbar's 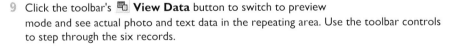 **View Data** button to switch to preview mode and see actual photo and text data in the repeating area. Use the toolbar controls to step through the six records.

Merging to a new publication

• Choose **Mail and Photo Merge** from the **Tools** menu and select **Merge Repeating Area to New Publication** from the submenu.

PagePlus generates a new publication in a separate window, replicating the repeating area as many times as there are records in the data (six in this case) and inserting new data into each region.

Create an Auction Catalogue

That's all there is to it! We'll leave you to experiment and consider the following additional pointers:

- The new publication is not yet saved, so if you think you can improve on the layout, simply close its window without saving, make changes in the original publication and merge again.

  Of course, there's nothing to prevent you merging and saving the results as many times as you like, using different file names. In fact one of the great advantages of repeating areas (as with form letters) is that you only need to design your "source" publication once—then you can reuse it with different data sources. This auction page will be just as useful when the next consignment of items makes its appearance.

> Had our data source included more than six records, additional pages would have been created after the first one.

- The new publication no longer contains any repeating areas, picture fields, or text fields. Everything on the page is a "regular" PagePlus object. Among other things, this is useful because each publication supports a *maximum of one repeating area*. In a situation where you need more than one, you could produce the publication in stages—merge from the first repeat area, then create the second one in the new publication, merge again, etc.

- The merged photos sit inside **picture frames**, which work much like text frames in that you can replace or edit their contents leaving the frame intact. To adjust display properties such as picture size and alignment for any individual picture frame, right-click it and choose **Frame Properties...**

We hope this exercise has cleared up any mysteries surrounding repeating areas and illustrated a novel use for traditional mail merge. For further information, see the relevant topics in online Help.

Design Templates

2

Introduction

This chapter provides you with useful previews of all of PagePlus 11's Design Templates. Design Templates are "instant publications"... creating a finished publication that you can be proud of is simple with PagePlus as most of the work is done by the automated Page Design Templates. There are two tutorials in the previous chapter—"Learning Lab 11: Web Publishing" and "Beyond the Basics: PDF Links"—that shows you how Design Templates work so that you can start publishing right now!

You'll need to install both the PagePlus 11 CD and the optional PagePlus 11 Resource CD to have access to the full set of Design Templates—when you see a design that you like, you can browse to and select your chosen Design Template publication using PagePlus's Startup Wizard. Click the Use A Design Template link to open the Choose a Design Template window. The category selector at the left of the Choose a Design Template window makes it easy to find the design you are looking for.

Double-click your selected design or select it then click Finish to close the window and open the design...

Landscape

Accounting & Finance

Antiques & Collectors

Beauty Bar

Builder

Business Vamp

Cellar Heat

Classy Expensive

Clean Squares

Cookies

Corporate Lime

Landscape

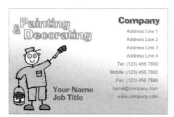

Decorating

Designer Minimal

Estate Agents

Fashion

Fitness

Floral Square

Florists

Freelance IT Support

Garden Centre

Go Karts

Landscape

Guitar School

Holiday Villas

Home & Furniture

Hotels

Life Assurance

Mirrorsaw

Mobile Phone

Music Technology

Network

Orange Optics

Landscape

Outside

Photographer

Pixelego

Platform

Portrait Photography

Pots

Ring

Solicitors

Tennis Club

Toy Shop

Landscape

Update

Venue

White Roses

Winebar

Portrait

Accounting & Finance

Antiques & Collector

Business Vamp

Cellar Heat

Corporate Lime

Designer Minimal

Fashion

Fitness

Floral Square

Portrait

Garden Centre

Holiday Villas

Home & Furniture

Hotels

Life Assurance

Mobile Phone

Orange Optics

Platform

Portrait Photography

Portrait

Pots

Property

Retro Electro

Ring

Robot

Toy Shop

Venue

White Roses

Winebar

Writer

Letterheads

Accounting & Finance

Antiques & Collectables

Artist

Beauty Bar

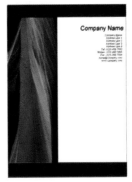

Business Vamp

Catalogue

Cellar Heat

Classy Expensive

Clean Squares

Letterheads

Corporate Lime

Designer Minimal

Fashion

Fitness

Flower

Garden Centre

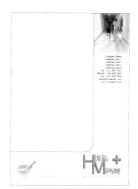

Health & Medicine

Holiday Villas

Home & Furniture

Letterheads

Hotels

Life Assurance

Mirrorsaw

Mobile Phone

Orange Optics

Outside

Pixelego

Platform

Pots

Letterheads

Property

Retro Electro

Solicitors

Sushi

The Gift Experience

Toy Shop

Update

Venue

Winebar

Blank Forms

Accounting & Finance

Beauty Bar

Classy Expensive

Clean Squares

Fashion

Fitness

Garden Centre

Health & Medicine

Holiday Villas

Blank Forms

Home & Furniture

Hotels

Mirrorsaw

Mobile Phone

Outside

Pixelego

Pots

Retro Electro

Solicitors

Blank Forms

The Gift Experience

Toy Shop

Update

Venue

Compliment Slips

Accounting & Finance

Antiques & Collectables

Artist

Beauty Bar

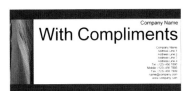

Business Vamp

Catalogue

Cellar Heat

Classy Expensive

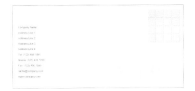

Clean Squares

Corporate Lime

Designer Minimal

Fashion

Compliment Slips

Fitness

Flower

Garden Centre

Health & Medicine

Holiday Villas

Home & Furniture

Hotels

Life Assurance

Mirrorsaw

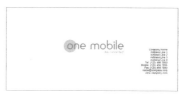

Mobile Phone

Orange Optics

Outside

Compliment Slips

Pixelego

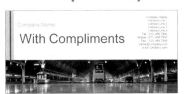

Platform

Pots

Property

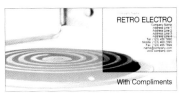

Retro Electro

Solicitors

Sushi

The Gift Experience

Toy Shop

Update

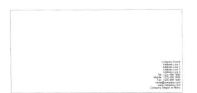

Venue

Winebar

C4/C5 Envelopes

Accounting & Finance

Antiques & Collectables

Artist

Beauty Bar

Business Vamp

Catalogue

Cellar Heat

Classy Expensive

Clean Squares

Corporate Lime

C4/C5 Envelopes

Designer Minimal

Fashion

Fitness

Flower

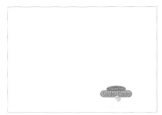

Garden Centre

Health & Medicine

Holiday Villas

Home & Furniture

Hotels

Life Assurance

C4/C5 Envelopes

Mirrorsaw

Mobile Phone

Orange Optics

Outside

Pixelego

Platform

Pots

Property

Retro Electro

Solicitors

C4/C5 Envelopes

Sushi

The Gift Experience

Toy Shop

Venue

Update

Winebar

DL Envelopes

Accounting & Finance

Antiques & Collectables

Artist

Beauty Bar

Business Vamp

Catalogue

Cellar Heat

Classy Expensive

Clean Squares

Corporate Lime

Designer Minimal

Fashion

DL Envelopes

Fitness

Flower

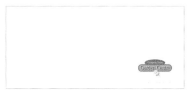

Garden Centre

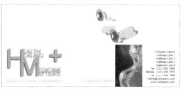

Health & Medicine

Holiday Villas

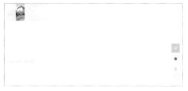

Home & Furniture

Hotels

Life Assurance

Mirrorsaw

Mobile Phone

Orange Optics

Outside

DL Envelopes

Pixelego

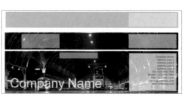

Platform

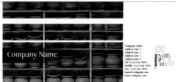

Pots

Property

Retro Electro

Solicitors

Sushi

The Gift Experience

Toy Shop

Update

Venue

Winebar

Artist

Fax Cover
Sheets

Gift
Voucher

Inventory
List

Invoice

Expense Report

Memos

Purchase
Order

Quotes

Time
Billing

Business Vamp

Fax Cover
Sheets

Gift
Voucher

Inventory
List

Invoice

Expense Report

Memos

Purchase
Order

Quotes

Time
Billing

Catalogue

Fax Cover
Sheets

Gift
Voucher

Inventory
List

Invoice

Expense Report

Memos

Purchase
Order

Quotes

Time
Billing

Cellar Heat

Expense Report

Fax Cover Sheets

Memos

Gift Voucher

Purchase Order

Inventory List

Quotes

Invoice

Time Billing

Corporate Lime

Expense Report

Fax Cover Sheets

Memos

Gift Voucher

Purchase Order

Inventory List

Invoice

Quotes

Time Billing

Designer Minimal

Expense Report

Fax Cover Sheets

Memos

Gift Voucher

Inventory List

Purchase Order

Invoice

Quotes

Time Billing

Flower

Expense Report

Fax Cover Sheets

Gift Voucher

Inventory List

Invoice

Memos

Purchase Order

Quotes

Time Billing

Life Assurance

Expense Report

Fax Cover Sheets

Gift Voucher

Inventory List

Invoice

Memos

Purchase Order

Quotes

Time Billing

Orange Optics

Expense Report

Fax Cover Sheets

Gift Voucher

Inventory List

Invoice

Memos

Purchase Order

Quotes

Time Billing

Platform

Company Name

Expense Report

Fax Cover
Sheets

Memos

Gift
Voucher

Purchase
Order

Inventory
List

Quotes

Invoice

Time
Billing

Property

Expense Report

Fax Cover
Sheets

Memos

Gift
Voucher

Purchase
Order

Inventory
List

Quotes

Invoice

Time
Billing

Sushi

Expense Report

Fax Cover
Sheets

Memos

Gift
Voucher

Purchase
Order

Inventory
List

Quotes

Invoice

Time
Billing

Winebar

Expense Report

Gift Voucher

Fax Cover Sheets

Inventory List

Invoice

Memos

Purchase Order

Quotes

Time Billing

A3/A4/Letter Side Half Fold

Front

Outside

Inside

Outside

Inside

Front

Front

Outside

Inside

Outside

Inside

Front

Front

Outside

Inside

Outside

Inside

Front

A3/A4/Letter Side Half Fold

Dental

Front

Outside

Inside

Outside

Inside

Designer Minimal

Front

Financial Consultant

Front

Outside

Inside

Outside

Inside

Fitness

Front

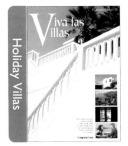

Holiday Villas

Front

Outside

Inside

Outside

Inside

Home & Furniture

Front

A3/A4/Letter Side Half Fold

Lite Assurance

Front

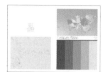

Outside

Inside

Outside

Inside

Music

Front

Orange Optics

Front

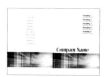

Outside

Inside

Outside

Inside

Outside

Front

Platform

Front

Outside

Inside

Outside

Inside

Retro Electro

Front

A3/A4/Letter Side Half Fold

Front

Outside

Inside

Outside

Inside

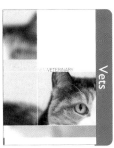

Front

Front

Outside

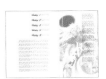

Inside

A4/Letter Side Tri Fold

Beauty Bar

Folded

Outside

Inside

Outside

Inside

Business Vamp

Folded

Cellar Heat

Folded

Outside

Inside

Outside

Inside

Classy Expensive

Folded

Cocktail Menu

Folded

Outside

Inside

Outside

Inside

Cookies

Folded

A4/Letter Side Tri Fold

Corporate Lime

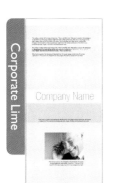

Folded

Outside

Inside

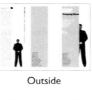

Outside

Inside

Folded

Designer Minimal

Fashion

Folded

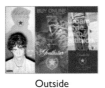

Outside

Inside

Outside

Inside

Folded

Florists

Garden Centre

Folded

Outside

Inside

Outside

Inside

Folded

Go Karts

A4/Letter Side Tri Fold

Hair Design

Folded

Outside

Inside

Health & Medicine

Outside

Inside

Folded

Honey Pot

Folded

Outside

Inside

Hotels

Outside

Inside

Folded

Juice

Folded

Outside

Inside

Life Assurance

Outside

Inside

Folded

A4/Letter Side Tri Fold

Medical

Folded

Outside

Inside

MEDICAL PUBLICATION

Outside

Inside

Mirrorsaw

Folded

Mobile Phone

Folded

Outside

Inside

Outside

Inside

Network

Folded

Orange Optics

Folded

Outside

Inside

Outside

Inside

Platform

Folded

A4/Letter Side Tri Fold

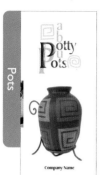

Pots

Outside

Inside

Outside

Inside

Tennis Club

Folded

Inside

Inside

Folded

Toy Shop

Outside

Inside

Outside

Inside

Update

Folded

Inside

Inside

Folded

Venue

Outside

Inside

Outside

Inside

Winebar

Folded

Inside

Inside

Folded

A4/Letter Side Z Fold

Outside

Outside

Business Vamp

Cafe

Inside

Inside

Folded

Folded

Outside

Outside

Cellar Heat

Corporate Lime

Inside

Inside

Folded

Folded

Outside

Outside

Cuisine 07

Designer Minimal

Inside

Inside

Folded

Folded

A4/Letter Side Z Fold

Farmers Market

Outside

Folded

Inside

Green English Cuisine

Outside

Inside

Folded

Indian

Outside

Folded

Inside

Outside

Inside

Life Assurance

Folded

Orange Optics

Outside

Folded

Inside

Outside

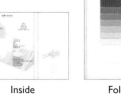

Inside

Oriental

Folded

A4/Letter Side Z Fold

Platform

Folded

Outside

Inside

Outside

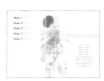

Inside

Winebar

Folded

World Cuisine

Folded

Outside

Inside

A4/Letter

Astronomy

Book Club

Business Newsletter

Church Newsletter

DIY

Green Fingers

Health Medicine

New Baby

School Newsletter

Science

Youth Club

A4/A5/A6/Letter Landscape

Business Vamp

Cellar Heat

Corporate Lime

Designer Minimal

Driving Instruction

Fashion

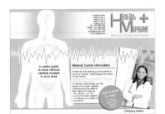

Health & Medicine

Holiday Villas

Life Assurance

Nursery

A4/A5/A6/Letter Landscape

Orange Optics

Platform

Portrait Photography

Pots

Sci_Fi

Venue

Winebar

Business Vamp

Cellar Heat

Corporate Lime

Designer Minimal

Farmers Market

Fashion

Health & Medicine

Holiday Villas

Language Tuition

A4/A5/A6/Letter Portrait

Life Assurance

Orange Optics

Perfume

Platform

Portrait Photography

Pots

Retro Electric

Snowblower Promo

Techtronic Clubnight

A4/A5/A6/Letter Portrait

Tennis Club

The Honey Pot

Venue

Winebar

Monthly (13 pages)

Families

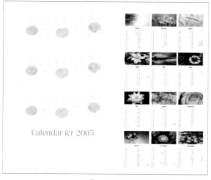

Flowers

Kids

Year On A Page

Business Gradient

Contemporary Abstract

Contemporary Cat

Contemporary Flower

Corporate

Clothing

Fluffy Bunny

Stag Night

Hen Night

Space Boy

Wind Me Up

Drink Thirst Quench

Yellow Flower

Coffee Mugs

2 Sugars

Best Mum

Daisy

Decorating

DJ Master

Halloween

Happy Easter

Lemon

My Dog

Screws

Mouse Mats

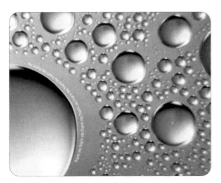

Bubbles

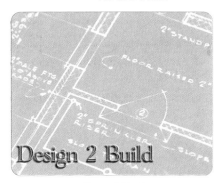

Design 2 Build

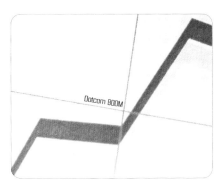

Dotcom BOOM

Mouse

Place Mats

Mountain Lake

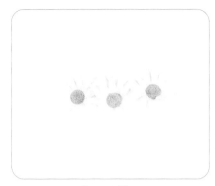

Summer Time

Growth Charts

Boy

Girl

Jungle

Little Angel

Outer Space

Scary

Space Boy

Sweets

Toys

Wildlife

Birthday

Birthday Greetings

Birthday Wishes

Daffodils

Spotlight

Have a Great Day

Spotlight

To Dad

Tulips

Youngster

Easter

Basket

Cross

Easter Frame 01

Easter Frame 02

Easter Greetings

Eggs

Happy Easter

Jesus

Father's Day

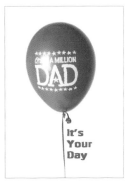

Balloon

Beer

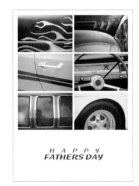

Custom Cars

Dad Tower

Drink Up

Fishing

Football

Happy Father's Day

To Dad

Mother's Day

Happy Mother's Day

Macro Flower

Mother's Day

Orchids

Piglets

Puppy

New Baby

Congratulations

New Baby

Nest

New Person

Small Hand

Valentines

Dark Mystique

Heart.

Lovebirds

Single Flower

Single Heart

Squares

Xmas

Christmas Greetings

Christmas tree

Holly Minimal

Merry Christmas

Seasons Greetings

Snow On Branches

Winter Reflection

Winter Scene

Zaney cherub

Zaney reindeer

CD

Eggs CD Label

Roses CD Cover

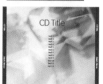

Star CD Cover

Swirl CD Label

Tomato CD Label

Tree CD Cover

Eggs DVD Label

Heart DVD Cover

Swirl DVD Label

Tomato DVD Label

Tree DVD Cover

Business

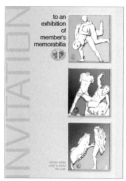

Antiques & Collectables

Art Exhibition

Photography

Team Building

The Gift Experience

Portrait Photography

Home

Afternoon Tea

Barbecue

Christening

Cool

Dinner Party

Floral Square

Garden Party

Hen Night

Open Gardens

Home

Open House

Parrots

Summer Fair

Wedding

White Roses

Home

Baby Boy Celebration

Baby Girl Celebration

Dinner Party

Halloween Party

Hen Night

Wedding

Wine Tasting

Home

Bear Tea Party

Boys Party

Bunny Party

Christmas Party

Christmas Tree

Dinner Party

Floral Square

Hen Night

House Party

Home

Little Devils

Masquerade Ball

My Birthday Party

New Years Eve

Princess Party

Santa Party Time

Skate Party

Wedding Day

Wedding

A3 Landscape

Antiques & Collectables

Fashion Specs

Fitness

Garden Centre

Halloween

Jane D Anderson

Joosh Juice

Masked Ball

Portrait Photography

Slouchie Retro Chairs

A3 Portrait

Antiques & Collectables

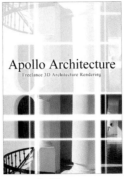

Architecture

Cafe

Dance School

Fitness

Garden Centre

Green English Cuisine

LePiano

Portrait Photography

A3 Portrait

World Cuisine

A5

Antiques and Collectables

Estate Agents

Garden Centre 1

Garden Centre 2

Garden Centre 3

Holiday Villas

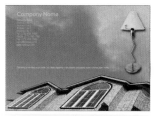

Home & Furniture 1

Home & Furniture 2

Sci-Fi

Note: US Content may vary

Balls

Business

Degree

Martial Arts

Medal

Medallion

Plasticine

Trohpy

Brass Monkeys

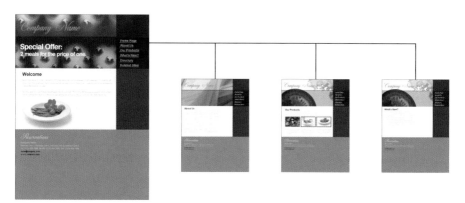

Business

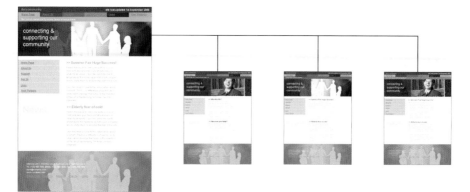

Community Spirit

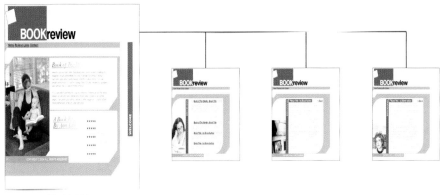

My Hobbies

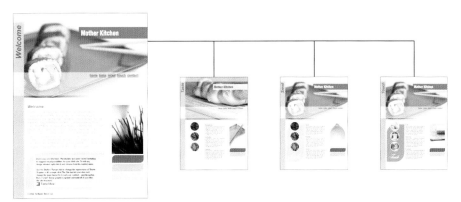

Natural Health

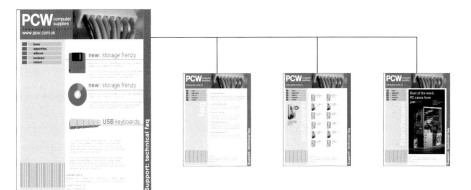

PC Whirl

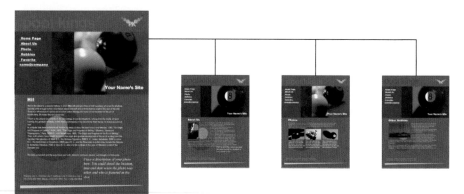

Pool Club

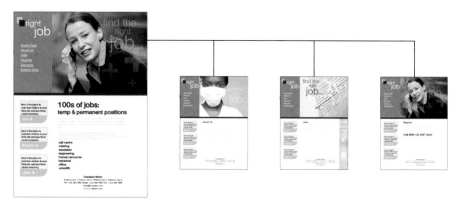

Recruitment

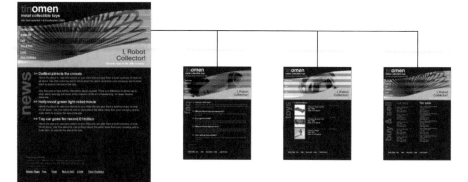

Tin Omen

The Honey Pot

World Cuisine

Sample Photo Gallery

Photo Gallery 1

Photo Gallery 2

Photo Gallery 3

Photo Gallery 4

Photo Gallery 5

Photo Gallery 6

Photo Gallery 7

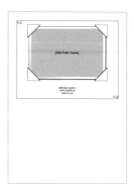

Photo Gallery 8

Photo Gallery 9

Sample Photo Gallery

Photo Gallery 10

Photo Gallery 11

Photo Gallery 12

Photo Gallery 13

Photo Gallery 14

Photo Gallery 15

Photo Gallery 16

Introduction

New to PagePlus 11 are the Photo Scrapbook Design Templates, which you can use to create your own scrapbook-style publications.

You can choose from a number of different scrapbook themes—for example 'Baby,' 'Wedding,' and 'Wildflower'—and 25 layout styles. As the themes are based on the PagePlus colour schemes, you can easily change the look of your page by simply clicking a different scheme on the **Schemes** tab.

Each layout includes *photo borders* and *text boxes*, which you can move, resize, and delete to suit your needs. These objects have predefined groups of attributes applied to them—drop shadow, inner shadow, font style and size, and so on. These attribute groups are stored as object styles on the **Object Styles** tab.

Each photo border has a *picture frame* associated with it, into which you import your pictures. The picture frames are square or rectangular (using a 4:3 ratio—a standard digital photograph format).

Note: If you're importing non-standard sized images, you can adjust the frame properties in the **Frame Properties** dialog (right-click the frame and choose **Frame Properties...**).

To import a photograph

- Double-click on a picture frame
- In the **Import Picture** dialog, locate and highlight the photo you want to use, and then click **Open**

Once you've laid out your first scrapbook page, you can add other pages to the publication.

To add a page to a photo scrapbook

- On the **Insert** menu, click **PagePlus** file
- In the **Choose a Template** dialog, select the page layout you want to use for your new page, and then click **Open**

The **Resources.ppp** file contains additional resources—colour schemes, photo borders, photo corners, etc, which you can use to customize any of your photo scrapbook publications.

Photograph Styles

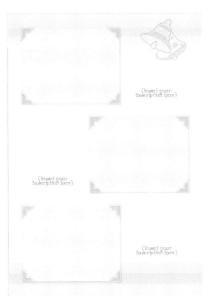

Standard Photograph

Photograph with border

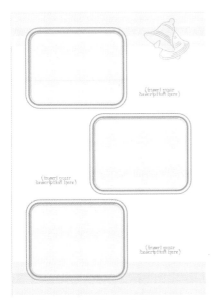

Photograph with rounded corners

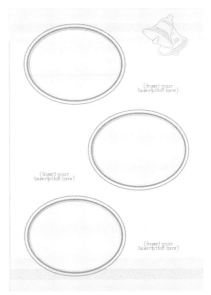

Vignette-style Photograph

Layouts

Wedding - Standard 1

Wedding - Standard 2

Wedding - Standard 3

Wedding - Standard 4

Wedding - Standard 5

Wedding - Standard 6

Wedding - Standard 7

Wedding - Standard 8

Wedding - Standard 9

Wedding - Standard 10

Wedding - Standard 11

Wedding - Standard 12

Layouts

Wedding - Standard 13

Wedding - Standard 14

Wedding - Standard 15

Wedding - Standard 16

Wedding - Standard 17

Wedding - Standard 18

Wedding - Standard 19

Wedding - Standard 20

Wedding - Standard 21

Wedding - Standard 22

Wedding - Standard 23

Wedding - Standard 24

Layouts

Wedding - Standard 25

Themes

Baby 1

Baby 2

Baby 3

Baby 4

Lawn

Notepad

Pinboard

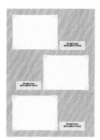

Sand 1

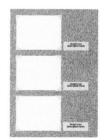

Sand 2

Stones

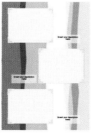

Striations

Stripes

Themes

Swirls

Wedding

Wildflower

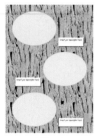

Wood

Colour Schemes
& Swatches

3

Introduction

This section provides previews of the PagePlus 11 colour schemes and swatches.

Colour Schemes

In PagePlus, a colour scheme is a group of five complementary colours that you can apply to elements in a publication. Colour schemes work like a paint-by-numbers system, where various regions of a layout are coded with numbers, and a specific colour is assigned to each region. The **Schemes** tab displays over 50 preset schemes, which you can select at any time during the design process.

The five complementary scheme colours—as shown in each preview here—are also available as numbered colours in the lower left corner of the **Swatches** tab. This means that you can design using schemes—simply select a numbered scheme colour for your object fills, rather than a fixed hue. Then, when you change your scheme your whole document will update automatically.

PagePlus design templates are excellent examples of publications designed to use colour schemes—open a design template, then on the **Schemes** tab, simply click to select a different colour scheme. Elements in the design will change colour to match the chosen scheme.

You can even edit the preset colour schemes and create new schemes of your own. For more information, see the "Using Colour Schemes" topic in online Help.

Swatches

On the **Swatches** tab, the **Palette** button provides preset gallery colours from a series of standard palettes, including RGB and CMYK.

The first swatch, 'None,' represents either no colour (a transparent fill for objects with line/fill properties) or 'Original' (for pictures only, to reset the object to its original colours).

Use the **Palette** button's drop-down menu to select the palette to use in a publication.

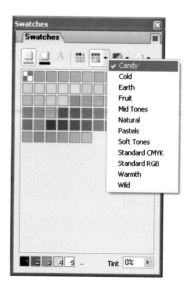

Colour Schemes

Abacus

Abstract

Apple

Aqua

Astro

Baby

Baby Colours

Bee

Colour Schemes

Blossom

Blue Berry

Carrot

Cavern

Chill

Citrus

Cocktail

Cuba

Colour Schemes

Cuddle

Danger

Dead Pool

Desert

dot.com

Fashion

Flesh

Floral

Colour Schemes

Fruit Cocktail

Fun Fair

Garden

Gardentime

Glacier

Gloom

Grays

Heather

Colour Schemes

Hessian

Honey

Hot

Ice

Island

Kitchen

Lab

Lagoon

Colour Schemes

Liquorice

Mahogany

Marine

Meadow

Mint

Mist

Moscow

Mountain

Colour Schemes

Olive

Orange

Parrot

PC Whirl

Pebbles

Primary

Punch

Purple

Colour Schemes

Raspberry

Recruitment

Reef

Sage

Science

Shamrock

Snowball

Sorbet

Colour Schemes

Spice

Stonehenge

Sunset

Superwave

Terracotta

Tin Omen

Tortilla

Tropical

Colour Schemes

Tropics

Turtle

Vineyard

Warp

Waterfall

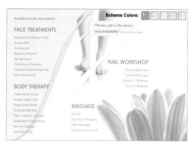

Wedding

Wheat

Wild

Colour Schemes

Wildflower

WWW1

WWW2

WWW3

WWW4

WWW5

WWW6

WWW7

Colour Schemes

WWW8

WWW9

Swatches

Candy

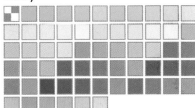

Cold

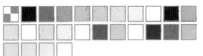

Earth

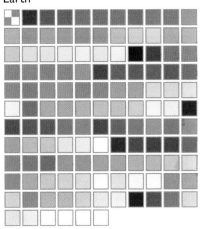

Fruit

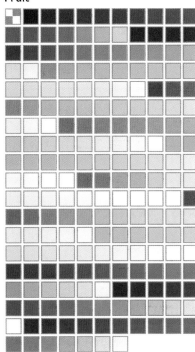

Mid Tones

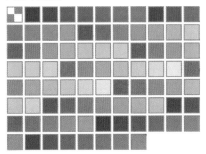

Natural

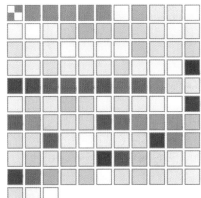

Swatches

Pastels

Standard CMYK

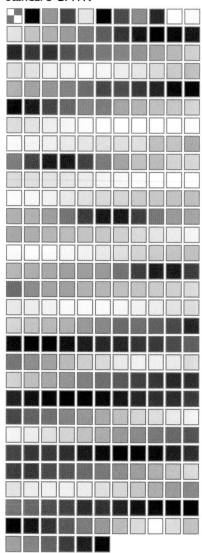

Soft Tones

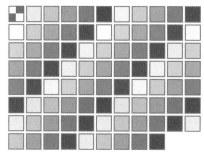

Swatches

Standard RGB

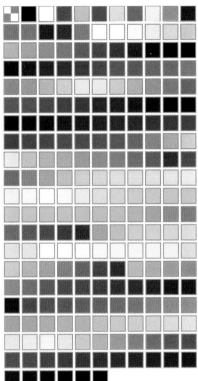

Warmth

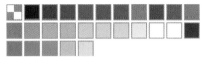

Wild

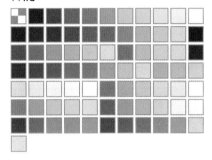

Object Styles

4

Introduction

The **Styles** tab includes galleries of predesigned graphical styles that you can apply to any object. Each object style can include settings for a multitude of object attributes, including line colour, line style, border, transparency, fill, filter effects (and individual filter effect settings), mesh warping effect, instant 3D effect, and font and other text attributes. The freedom to include or exclude certain attributes, and the nearly unlimited range of choices for each attribute, makes this a powerful tool in the designer's arsenal.

As with text styles and colour schemes, object styles help bring consistency to your design, and save both time and effort when you need to apply and change formatting. When you change an object style, you instantly update any element in the publication that uses it.

- To apply a style to one or more objects, simply select the object(s) and then click a style thumbnail.

- To modify an object style, hover the cursor over a style thumbnail, click the down arrow, and then click **Edit...**

- To create a new style based on a copy of an existing one, choose **Copy...** from the drop-down menu.

- To remove an object style from a gallery, choose **Delete** from the drop-down menu.

- To create a new style based on an existing object's attributes, right-click the object and choose **Format/Object Style/Create**.

Using object styles is a quick and easy way to save your favourite object attributes for future reuse.

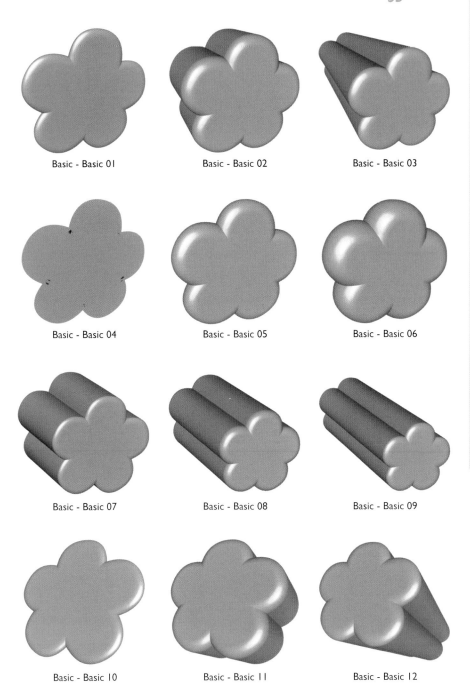

Basic - Basic 01

Basic - Basic 02

Basic - Basic 03

Basic - Basic 04

Basic - Basic 05

Basic - Basic 06

Basic - Basic 07

Basic - Basic 08

Basic - Basic 09

Basic - Basic 10

Basic - Basic 11

Basic - Basic 12

3D

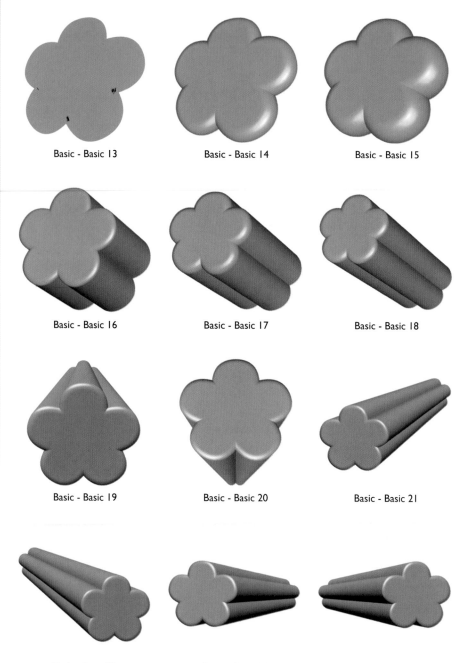

Basic - Basic 13

Basic - Basic 14

Basic - Basic 15

Basic - Basic 16

Basic - Basic 17

Basic - Basic 18

Basic - Basic 19

Basic - Basic 20

Basic - Basic 21

Basic - Basic 22

Basic - Basic 23

Basic - Basic 24

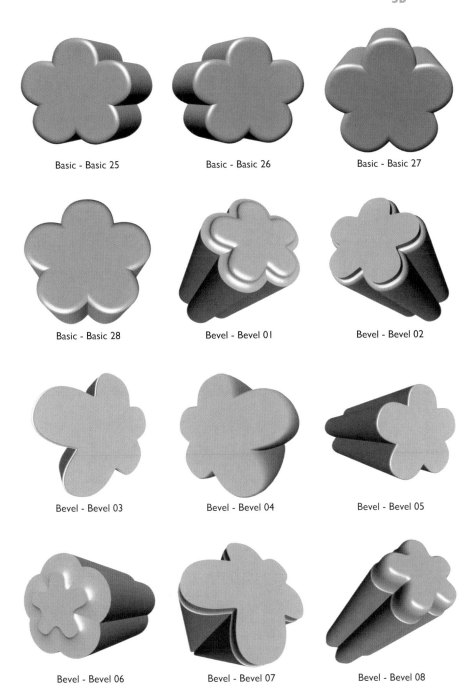

Basic - Basic 25

Basic - Basic 26

Basic - Basic 27

Basic - Basic 28

Bevel - Bevel 01

Bevel - Bevel 02

Bevel - Bevel 03

Bevel - Bevel 04

Bevel - Bevel 05

Bevel - Bevel 06

Bevel - Bevel 07

Bevel - Bevel 08

3D

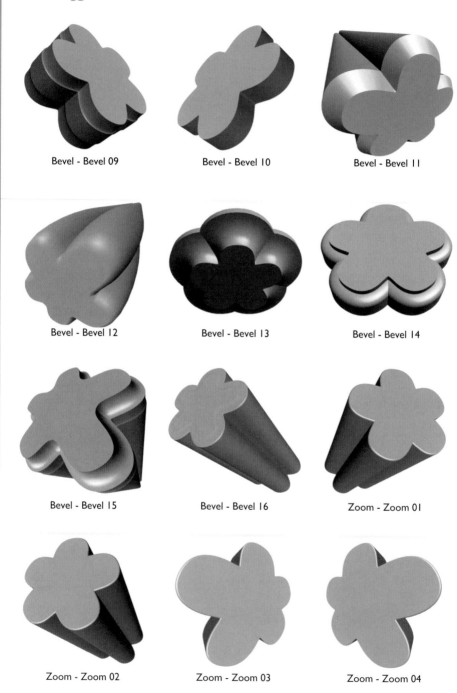

Bevel - Bevel 09

Bevel - Bevel 10

Bevel - Bevel 11

Bevel - Bevel 12

Bevel - Bevel 13

Bevel - Bevel 14

Bevel - Bevel 15

Bevel - Bevel 16

Zoom - Zoom 01

Zoom - Zoom 02

Zoom - Zoom 03

Zoom - Zoom 04

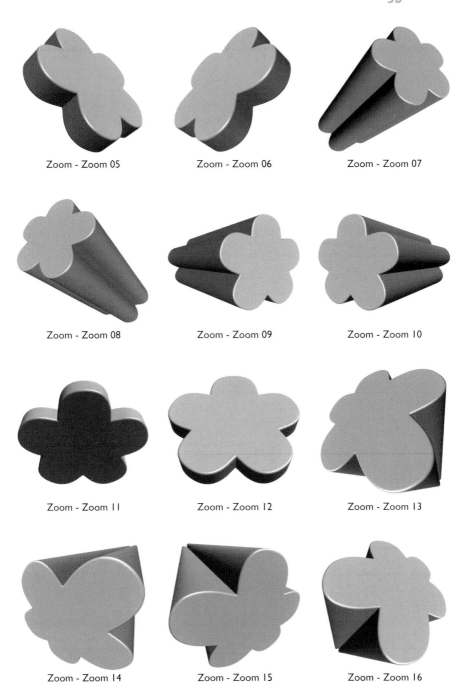

Zoom - Zoom 05

Zoom - Zoom 06

Zoom - Zoom 07

Zoom - Zoom 08

Zoom - Zoom 09

Zoom - Zoom 10

Zoom - Zoom 11

Zoom - Zoom 12

Zoom - Zoom 13

Zoom - Zoom 14

Zoom - Zoom 15

Zoom - Zoom 16

Filter Effects

Glow - Glow 01

Glow - Glow 02

Glow - Glow 03

Glow - Glow 04

Glow - Glow 05

Glow - Glow 06

Glow - Glow 07

Glow - Glow 08

Glow - Glow 09

Glow - Glow 10

Glow - Glow 11

Glow - Glow 12

Glow - Glow 13

Glow - Glow 14

Glow - Glow 15

Glow - Glow 15

Shadows - Shadows 01

Shadows - Shadows 02

Shadows - Shadows 03

Shadows - Shadows 04

Shadows - Shadows 05

Shadows - Shadows 06

Shadows - Shadows 07

Shadows - Shadows 08

Filter Effects

Shadows - Shadows 09

Shadows - Shadows 10

Shadows - Shadows 11

Shadows - Shadows 12

Shadows - Shadows 13

Shadows - Shadows 14

Shadows - Shadows 15

Shadows - Shadows 16

Shadows - Shadows 17

Shadows - Shadows 18

Shadows - Shadows 19

Shadows - Shadows 20

Shadows - Shadows 21 Shadows - Shadows 22 Shadows - Shadows 23

Shadows - Shadows 24 Shadows - Shadows 25 Shadows - Shadows 26

Shadows - Shadows 27 Shadows - Shadows 28 Shadows - Shadows 29

Shadows - Shadows 30 Shadows - Shadows 31 Shadows - Shadows 32

Filter Effects

Shadows - Shadows 33

Shadows - Shadows 34

Shadows - Shadows 35

Shadows - Shadows 36

Shadows - Shadows 37

Shadows - Shadows 38

Textures - Texture 01

Textures - Texture 02

Textures - Texture 03

Textures - Texture 04

Textures - Texture 05

Textures - Texture 06

Textures - Texture 07

Textures - Texture 08

Textures - Texture 09

Textures - Texture 10

Textures - Texture 11

Textures - Texture 12

Textures - Texture 13

Textures - Texture 14

Textures - Texture 15

Textures - Texture 16

Textures - Texture 17

Textures - Texture 18

Materials

Abstract - Amber

Abstract - Chocolate

Abstract - Chocolate Fancy

Abstract - Dots

Abstract - Marble Crumble

Abstract - Plasma

Abstract - Towers

Abstract - Wood

Active - Build

Active - Cultivate

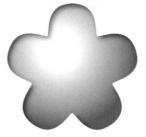

Active - Green Baize

Active - High Dive

Materials

Active - Non-slip

Active - Sky Dive

Active - Sporting Blue

Active - Sporting Red

Active - Sports Emblem

Active - Sportstripe

Active - Swim

Active - Swirl

Cloth & Paper - Blobs

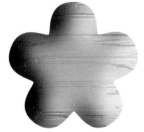

Cloth & Paper - Board

Cloth & Paper - Card

Cloth & Paper - Pulp

Materials

Cloth & Paper - Quilt

Cloth & Paper - Recycled

Cloth & Paper - Retro

Cloth & Paper - Silk

Cloth & Paper - Tea Towel

Cloth & Paper - Weave Board

Designer - ArtDek

Designer - Class

Designer - Decor

Designer - Fashion

Designer - Honey

Designer - Marine

Designer - Pine

Designer - Plastic

Designer - Pop

Designer - Punch

Designer - Spa

Designer - Trench

Elements - Altocumulus clouds

Elements - Cirrostratus clouds

Elements - Cirrus clouds

Elements - Fire

Elements - Fire storm

Elements - Nimbostratus clouds

Materials

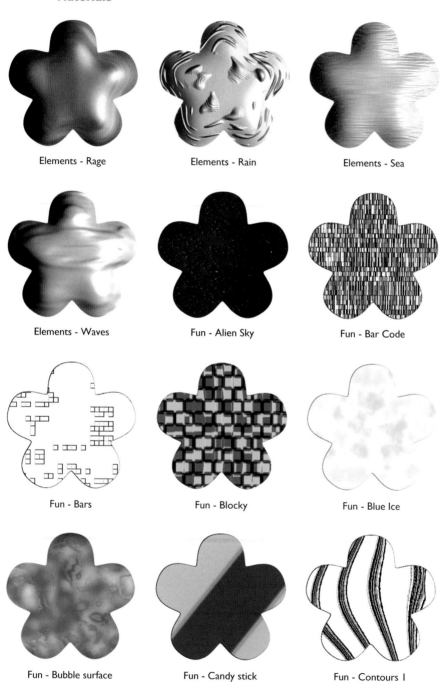

Elements - Rage

Elements - Rain

Elements - Sea

Elements - Waves

Fun - Alien Sky

Fun - Bar Code

Fun - Bars

Fun - Blocky

Fun - Blue Ice

Fun - Bubble surface

Fun - Candy stick

Fun - Contours 1

Fun - Contours 2

Fun - Contours and colours

Fun - Crazy

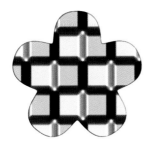

Fun - Cube

Fun - Dirty surface

Fun - Fine contours

Fun - Light speckled

Fun - Marble

Fun - Maze

Fun - Mellow yellow

Fun - Paper bag

Fun - Party

Materials

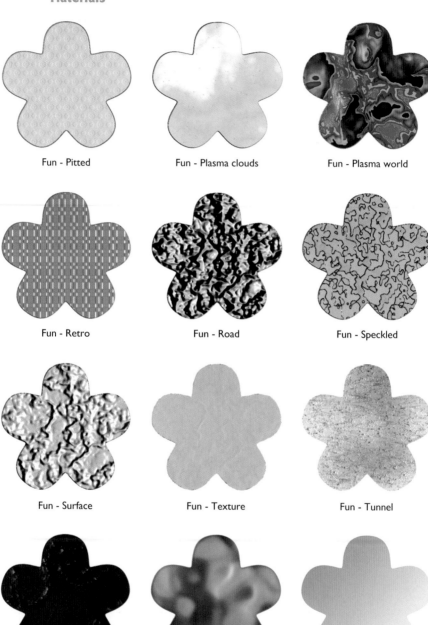

Fun - Pitted

Fun - Plasma clouds

Fun - Plasma world

Fun - Retro

Fun - Road

Fun - Speckled

Fun - Surface

Fun - Texture

Fun - Tunnel

Fun - Virus

Fun - Wiggle

Funky - Blimey

Funky - Blow-up

Funky - Bump

Funky - Candy Basket

Funky - Cool

Funky - Horizon

Funky - Mr. Soft

Funky - Pastel

Funky - Purple Passion

Funky - Red Shift

Funky - Streak

Funky - Tangy

Glass - Amber rain

Materials

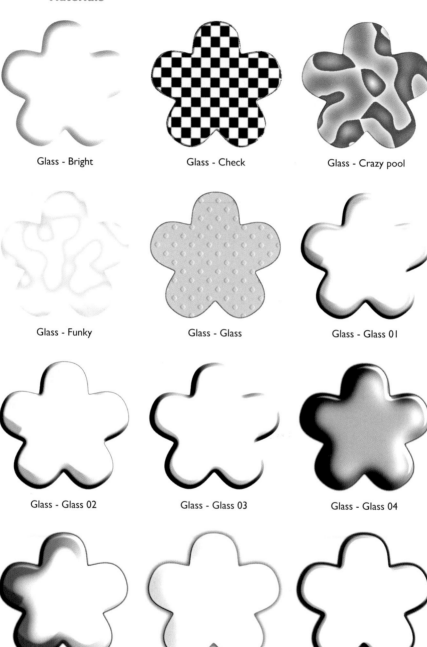

Glass - Bright

Glass - Check

Glass - Crazy pool

Glass - Funky

Glass - Glass

Glass - Glass 01

Glass - Glass 02

Glass - Glass 03

Glass - Glass 04

Glass - Glass 05

Glass - Glass 06

Glass - Glass 07

Materials

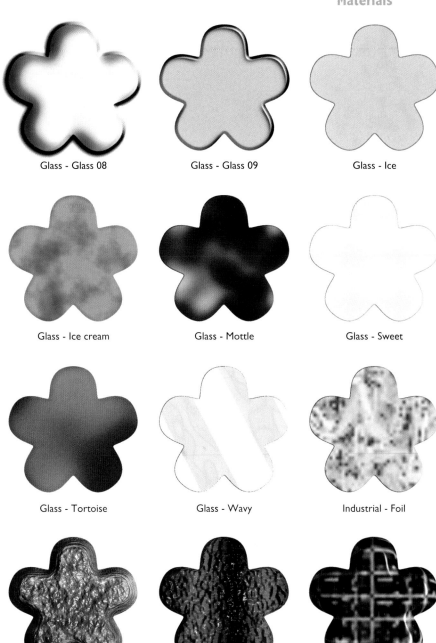

Glass - Glass 08	Glass - Glass 09	Glass - Ice
Glass - Ice cream	Glass - Mottle	Glass - Sweet
Glass - Tortoise	Glass - Wavy	Industrial - Foil
Industrial - Furnace	Industrial - Fusion	Industrial - Grid

Materials

Industrial - Liquify

Industrial - Mesh

Industrial - Nails

Industrial - Rivet

Industrial - Rust

Industrial - Steel

Industrial - Tin

Industrial - Wire

Lifestyle - Beach

Lifestyle - Bliss

Lifestyle - Chocolate

Lifestyle - Classical

Lifestyle - Cool Blue

Lifestyle - Cupid

Lifestyle - Embers

Lifestyle - Garden

Lifestyle - Lavender

Lifestyle - Raffia

Lifestyle - Spring

Lifestyle - Stainless

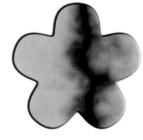

Marble - Blue marble

Marble - Deep marble

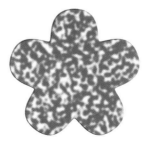

Marble - Fine marble

Marble - Lightning marble

Materials

Marble - Marble

Marble - Red marble

Marble - Royal marble

Marble - Thin marble

Marble - Vein marble

Media - Advert

Media - Commerce

Media - First Place

Media - Headline

Media - Ink

Media - Monitor

Media - Novel

Media - Radio

Media - Regal

Media - Seal

Media - Spectrum

Media - Static

Metal - Bars

Metal - Beaten Copper

Metal - Blocks

Metal - Corrugated

Metal - Drain

Metal - Grill

Metal - Iron Filings

Materials

Metal - Metal 01

Metal - Metal 02

Metal - Metal 03

Metal - Metal 04

Metal - Metal 05

Metal - Metal 06

Metal - Metal 07

Metal - Metal 08

Metal - Metal 09

Metal - Metal 10

Metal - Metal 11

Metal - Metal 12

Metal - Metal 13

Metal - Metal 14

Metal - Non-slip

Metal - Oxidized copper

Metal - Ribbed

Metal - Ridged

Metal - Rust

Metal - Rusty

Metal - Rusty holes

Metal - Sheet

Metal - Speaker

Metal - Steps

Materials

Mood - Blue

Mood - Demonic

Mood - Envy

Mood - Fruity

Mood - Gentle

Mood - Happy

Mood - Mellow

Mood - Muddled

Mood - Passion

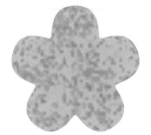

Mood - Serene

Mood - Tough

Mood - Tranquil

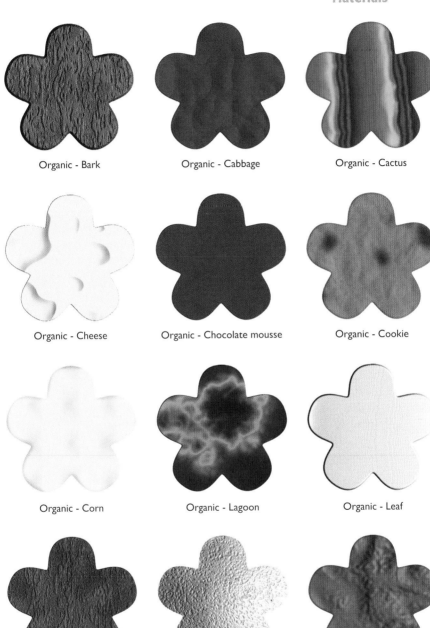

Organic - Bark

Organic - Cabbage

Organic - Cactus

Organic - Cheese

Organic - Chocolate mousse

Organic - Cookie

Organic - Corn

Organic - Lagoon

Organic - Leaf

Organic - Moss

Organic - Orange

Organic - Plant

Materials

Organic - Pond

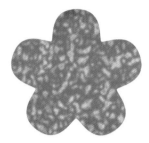

Organic - Salami

Organic - Strawberry ice

Organic - Tree tops

Plastic - Plastic 1

Plastic - Plastic 2

Plastic - Plastic 3

Plastic - Plastic 4

Plastic - Plastic 5

Plastic - Plastic 6

Plastic - Plastic 7

Plastic - Plastic 8

Plastic - Plastic 9   Sci-fi - Alien   Sci-fi - Cluster

Sci-fi - Cosmic   Sci-fi - Cyber   Sci-fi - Droid

Sci-fi - Eclipse   Sci-fi - Martian   Sci-fi - Moon

Sci-fi - Nebula   Sci-fi - Neon   Sci-fi - Slime

Materials

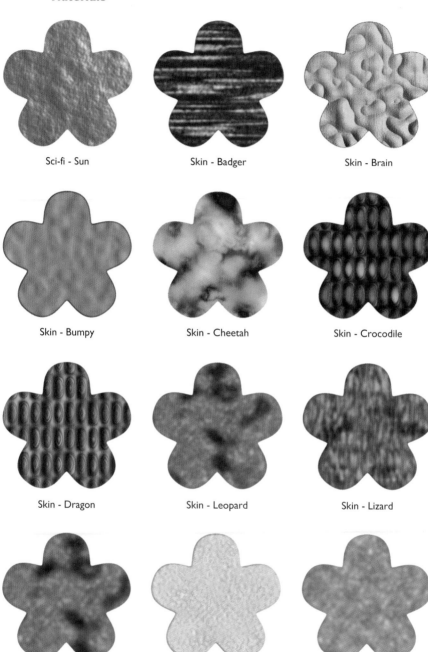

Sci-fi - Sun

Skin - Badger

Skin - Brain

Skin - Bumpy

Skin - Cheetah

Skin - Crocodile

Skin - Dragon

Skin - Leopard

Skin - Lizard

Skin - Leopard

Skin - Makeup

Skin - Mink

Skin - Mottle

Skin - Panther

Skin - Purple haze

Skin - Reptile

Skin - Ripple

Skin - Smooth

Skin - Snake skin

Skin - Tiger

Skin - Veins

Skin - Zebra

Stone - Basalt

Stone - Clay

Materials

Stone - Concrete

Stone - Crumble

Stone - Diabas

Stone - Dolomite

Stone - Gneiss

Stone - Gravel

Stone - Jasper

Stone - Mudstone

Stone - Polished stone

Stone - Sandstone

Stone - Slate

Wood - Basswood

Wood - Boxwood

Wood - Cocobolo

Wood - Dark wood

Wood - Distressed wood

Wood - Good wood

Wood - Lime

Wood - Mahogany

Wood - Oak

Wood - Rosewood

Wood - Teak

Wood - Walnut

Wood - Woodworm

Special Effects

Effect 01

Effect 02

Effect 03

Effect 04

Effect 05

Effect 06

Effect 07

Effect 08

Effect 09

Effect 10

Effect 11

Effect 12

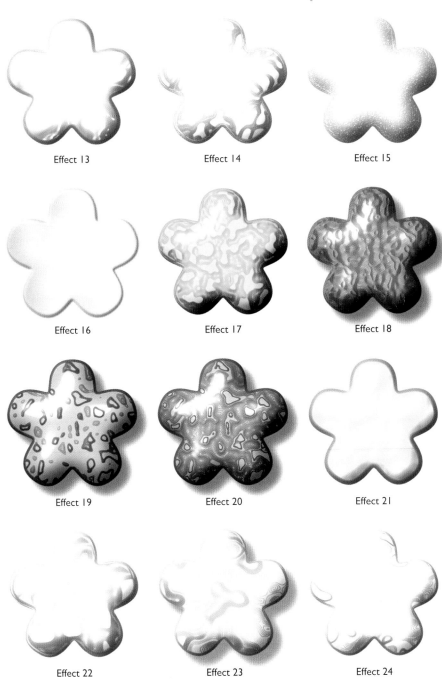

Effect 13

Effect 14

Effect 15

Effect 16

Effect 17

Effect 18

Effect 19

Effect 20

Effect 21

Effect 22

Effect 23

Effect 24

Special Effects

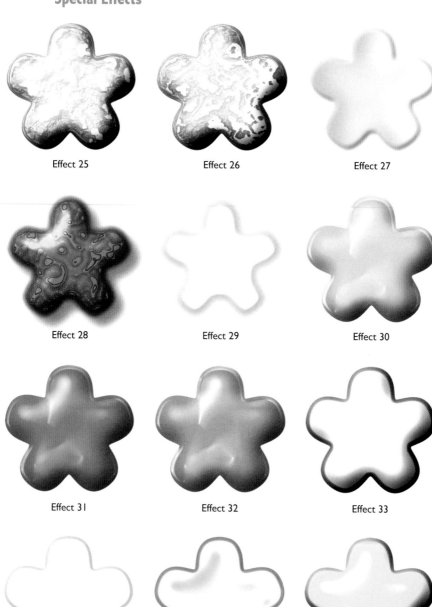

Effect 25

Effect 26

Effect 27

Effect 28

Effect 29

Effect 30

Effect 31

Effect 32

Effect 33

Effect 34

Effect 35

Effect 36

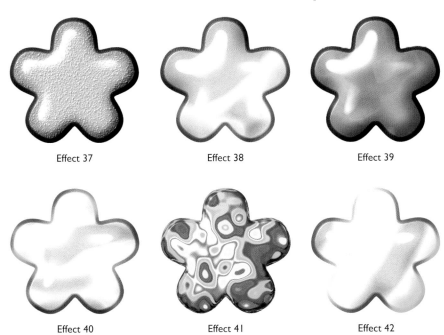

Effect 37 Effect 38 Effect 39

Effect 40 Effect 41 Effect 42

Image Gallery

5

Introduction

PagePlus 11 is supplied with a range of interesting photo-style clipart images (also used by the Design Template publications). You can use these images in your own designs.

To import an image from this collection into a PagePlus publication, click the Import Picture button and browse the hard drive that has PagePlus installed on it to locate the Design Template Images folder. This is typically found at C:\Program Files\Serif\PagePlus\11.0\Wizard\Images. Select an image and click Open. Click and drag your mouse on your page to import the image at the desired size.

These images are of a screen resolution and are suitable for home printing and Web sites.

0001h1006.png

0001h1016.png

0002h1036.jpg

0003h1004.png

0006h1070.jpg

0006h1079.png

0037h0043.png

0037h0044.jpg

0037h0044.png

0039h0001.png

0050h1028.jpg

0051h1043.jpg

0087h0115.jpg

0087h0126.png

0110h1031.png

0129h0007.png

0140h0001.jpg

0156h0002.png

0167h0002.jpg

0170h1006.png

Images

0181h0008.jpg

0182h1006.jpg

0184h0004.png

0188h1006.png

0189h0001.png

0189h0001_b.png

0189h0002.jpg

0202h0005.jpg

0202h0011.jpg

0206h1062.png

0206h1068.png

0244h0001.jpg

0287h0027.png

0289h1081.png

0289h1091.png

0307h1062.png

0311h0024.jpg

0321h1045.png

0333h1014.png

0347h1080.jpg

Images

0357h0101.jpg

0357h0224.jpg

0357h0233.jpg

0357h0250.jpg

0387h1051.png

0387h1054.jpg

0387h3051.png

0401h1030.png

0414h0253.png

0428h0242.png

0430h0059.jpg

0435h1037.png

0458h1013.png

0467h1021.jpg

0471h1013.jpg

0481h0044.jpg

0481h1025.jpg

0482h1059.jpg

0489h0025.jpg

0489h0032.png

Images

0490h0052.png

0490h0061.png

0490h0075.png

0490h0077.png

0493h1095.jpg

0490h0091.png

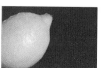
0496h0020.png

0500h0005.jpg

0500h0015.jpg

0500h0021.jpg

0500h0027.jpg

0500h0046.jpg

0500h0054.jpg

0500h0056.jpg

0500h0101.jpg

0500h0107.jpg

0501h0001.jpg

0510h0016.jpg

0524h0019.jpg

0530h0006.png

Images

0530h0047.jpg

0537h0119.png

0545h0100.jpg

0548h0102.jpg

0548h0130.png

0548h0136.png

0549h0043.png

0552h0062.jpg

0552h0197.png

0552h0285.jpg

0552h0286.jpg

0578h0004.jpg

0578h0019.jpg

0580h0055.jpg

0596h0493.png

0596h0534.jpg

0615h0007.jpg

0617h0001.jpg

0617h0052.jpg

0623h0046.jpg

Images

0644h0090.png

0655h0133.png

0657h0220.jpg

0670h0304.jpg

0676h0202.jpg

0677h0007.jpg

0688h0235.jpg

0688h0567.jpg

0705h0022.png

0718h0003.jpg

0718h0014.jpg

0727h0027.jpg

0732h0005.jpg

0739h0006.png

0740h0003.png

0743h0009.jpg

0743h0016.jpg

0743h0041.jpg

0746h0030.jpg

0746h0040.png

Images

0750h0003.jpg

0753h0023.png

0767h0013.jpg

0768h0028.png

0768h0031.jpg

0768h0059.jpg

0769h0016.jpg

0770h0004.jpg

0770h0017.jpg

0771h0182.jpg

0771h0278.jpg

0775h0876.jpg

0775h2525.jpg

0775h3088.jpg

0781h0037.jpg

0781h1004.jpg

0783h0001.jpg

0783h0002.jpg

0783h0003.jpg

0793h0004.jpg

Images

0793h0010.png

0793h0010_b.png

0793h0030.png

0796h0001.jpg

0797h0005.jpg

0797h1191.png

0797h1245.png

0797h1288.png

0800h0042.jpg

0800h0644.png

0800h1323.jpg

0800h1652.png

0800h1924.jpg

0800h2449.jpg

0800h2942.png

0800h2952.png

0800h3057.png

0800h3067.png

0800h3600.jpg

0800h3760.png

0800h3885.png

0800h4430.jpg

0800h4459.jpg

0800h6100.jpg

0801h0202.jpg

0801h1350.jpg

0803h0013.jpg

0804h0004.jpg

0804h0015.png

0804h0020.jpg

0808h0711.png

0808h1073.jpg

0808h1097.jpg

0808h1110.jpg

0808h1256.jpg

0809h0015.jpg

0819h0157.jpg

0832h0119.png

0832h0170.jpg

0852h0013.jpg

Images

0897h3956.jpg

0898h8769.png

0900h1011.jpg

0915h1019.jpg

0939h0002.png

0954h0010.jpg

0956h1014.png

0970h0012.jpg

0986h1026.jpg

0992h0024.jpg

0997h0095.jpg

0998h0348.jpg

1000h0274.jpg

1000h1002.jpg

1007h0078.jpg

1007h0515.jpg

1014h0004.jpg

1015h0186.jpg

1015h0344.jpg

1015h0448.jpg

Images

1023h0006.jpg

1036h0067.png

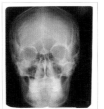
1049h0050.jpg

1081h2061.jpg

1081h3158.jpg

1081h3171.jpg

1081h4920.jpg

1081h4935.jpg

1081h4936.jpg

1105h0001.jpg

1105h0006.jpg

1111h0006.jpg

1111h0008.jpg

1118h0006.jpg

1121h0016.jpg

1125h0005.jpg

1128h0206.jpg

1140h0008.jpg

1158h0032.jpg

1158h0036.jpg

Images

1159h0007.jpg

1159h0014.jpg

1159h0015.png

1160h0009.jpg

1161h0006.jpg

1162h0009.jpg

1164h0014.jpg

1168h0027.jpg

1172h0002.jpg

1178h0001.jpg

1180h0005.jpg

1182h0022.jpg

1182h0023.jpg

1184h0009.png

1196h0002.png

1202h0022.jpg

1208h0022.png

1208h0027.png

1211h0010.jpg

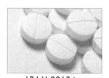
1211h0013.jpg

1221h0014.jpg

1232h0015.jpg

1234h0013.png

1238h0001.jpg

1245h0006.png

1266h0055.jpg

1266h0057.jpg

1270h0004.jpg

1276h0007.png

1276h0015.jpg

1276h0055.png

1278h0061.png

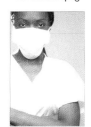

1279h0046.jpg

1279h0052.png

1279h0107.jpg

1279h0120.jpg

1279h0122.png

1279h0138.jpg

1286h0015.jpg

1292h0162.jpg

Images

1292h0163.jpg

1292h0186.jpg

1293h0002.png

1294h0002.png

1294h0004.png

1306h0006.png

1311h0018.png

1311h0023.png

1311h0036.png

1326h0018.jpg

1328h0003.png

1333h0013.jpg

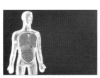

1334h0011.jpg

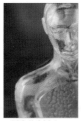

1334h0024.jpg

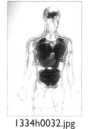

1334h0032.jpg

1339h0064.jpg

1357h0036.jpg

1357h0037.jpg

1367h0732.jpg

1369h0012.jpg

Images

1369h0062.jpg

1373h0008.jpg

1375h0016.jpg

1375h0051.jpg

1376h1088.png

1377h0010.jpg

1382h0013.png

1382h0048.png

1382h0072.jpg

1386h0004.jpg

1386h0008.jpg

1394h0029.jpg

1397h0001.jpg

1397h0002.jpg

1397h0005.png

1399h0005.png

1401h0014.jpg

1409h0017.jpg

1410h0040.png

1410h0043.png

Images

1410h0043_b.png

1410h0045.jpg

1411h0275.jpg

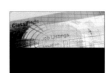
1416h0032.jpg

1429h0281.jpg

1431h0060.png

1434h0007.jpg

1437h0029.png

1453h0017.jpg

1453h0025.png

1455h0007.jpg

1455h0027.jpg

1467l0093.png

1477h0004.png

1477h0004_b.png

1477h0142.jpg

1477h1007.jpg

1480h0022.jpg

1480h0024.jpg

1481h0003.jpg

1482h0024.png

1483h0012.png

1484h0008.png

1485h0024.jpg

1495h0046.png

1499h0062.png

1505h0025.png

1510h0044.png

1513h0004.jpg

1514h0030.png

1514h0045.png

1519h0046.png

1524h0020.jpg

1525h0013.jpg

1528h0032.jpg

1529h0044.png

1533h0002.jpg

1536h0051.jpg

1537h0008.jpg

1537h0012.png

Images

1537h0040.jpg

1537h0058.jpg

1542h0008.png

1542h0022.jpg

1542h0030.jpg

1550h0036.jpg

1552h0014.jpg

1554h0037.jpg

1554h0057.jpg

1560h0011.jpg

1565h0029.jpg

1565h0040.jpg

1573h0014.jpg

1575h0009.jpg

1592h0029.jpg

1592h0084.jpg

1593h0001.png

1596h0029.jpg

1596h0073.jpg

1600h1008.jpg

Images

1600h2082.jpg

1600h2336.jpg

1604h0109.png

1607h0036.jpg

1607h0037.jpg

1608h0026.jpg

1608h0051.jpg

1618h0219.jpg

1620h0032.jpg

1620h0039.jpg

1620h0056.jpg

1620h0063.jpg

16252224.jpg

1628h1035.jpg

1647h0023.jpg

1647h0079.png

1655h0081.png

1655h0085.png

1660h0019.jpg

1660h0094.png

Images

1671h0041.png

1671h0044.png

1672h0170.png

1676h0014.png

1678h0008.png

1681h0066.jpg

1684h0017.png

1684h0058.png

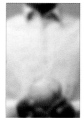
1684h0058_b.png

16891259.jpg

1692h0047.jpg

1694h0027.png

1696h0062.jpg

1701h0036.jpg

1701h0042.jpg

1702h0037.jpg

1704h0003.jpg

1704h0004.jpg

1706h0006.png

1707h0003.jpg

Images

1708h0028.png

1721h0001.jpg

1732h0023.jpg

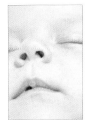
1736h0037.jpg

1740h0017.jpg

1751h0467.jpg

1755h0052.jpg

1756h0035.jpg

1757h0048.jpg

1757h0088.jpg

1758h0091.jpg

1774h0003.jpg

1786h0004.jpg

1796h0022.jpg

1809h0004.jpg

1834h0084.png

1835h0010.jpg

1835h0041.png

1835h0106.png

1841h0041.jpg

Images

1841h0045.jpg

1847h0008.jpg

1852h0006.jpg

1852h0011.jpg

1852h5019.jpg

1852h5031.jpg

1857h0004.jpg

1857h5152.jpg

1862h0003.jpg

1862h5034.jpg

1862h5038.jpg

1862h5051.jpg

1862h5071.jpg

1865h0003.jpg

1867h1003.png

1874h5123.jpg

1875h5036.jpg

1875h5043.jpg

1875h5059.jpg

1875h5070.jpg

Images

1875h5088.jpg

1875h5096.jpg

1877h0008.jpg

1877h0009.jpg

1881h0423.jpg

1881h0500.jpg

1881h0534.jpg

1882h0578.jpg

1882h0621.jpg

1883h0239.jpg

1883h5059.jpg

1891h0056.jpg

1897h0066.jpg

1899h5021.jpg

19067138.jpg

19098712.jpg

19213476.jpg

19256128.jpg

1940h1113.png

1941h0392.jpg

Images

1941h1902.jpg

1941h1967.jpg

1941h1979.jpg

1941h4036.jpg

1941h4628.jpg

1941h5202.jpg

1941h5287.jpg

1941h5414.jpg

1941h5458.jpg

1941h6379.jpg

1941h6518.jpg

1942h0621.jpg

1942h1012.jpg

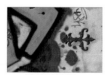
1942h2325.jpg

1942h2668.jpg

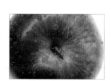
1942h3044.jpg

1942h3059.jpg

1942h3139.jpg

1942h3152.jpg

1942h3154.jpg

Images

1942h4170.jpg

1942h4392.jpg

1942h4697.jpg

1942h4953.jpg

1942h5800.jpg

1942h6105.jpg

1942h6394.jpg

1952h0480.jpg

1952h0524.jpg

1952h0729.jpg

1952h1036.jpg

1952h1739.jpg

1952h3064.jpg

1952h3164.jpg

1952h3190.jpg

1952h3243.jpg

1952h4081.jpg

1952h4352.jpg

1952h4419.jpg

1952h5184.jpg

Images

1952h5535.jpg

1956h0202.jpg

1956h0268.jpg

1956h0301.jpg

1956h0384.jpg

1956h0416.jpg

1956h0693.jpg

1956h0722.jpg

1956h0723.jpg

1956h0724.jpg

1956h0855.jpg

1956h0890.jpg

1956h0943.jpg

1956h0970.jpg

1956h0981.jpg

1956h1048.jpg

1956h1083.jpg

1956h1305.jpg

1956h1330.jpg

1956h1546.jpg

Images

1956h1549.jpg

1956h1640.jpg

1956h1669.jpg

1956h2043.jpg

1956h2298.jpg

1956h2333.jpg

1956h2552.jpg

1956h2553.jpg

1956h2569.jpg

1956h2608.jpg

1956h2609.jpg

1956h2687.jpg

1956h2764.jpg

1956h2942.jpg

1956h3120.jpg

1956h3185.jpg

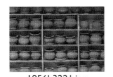
1956h3221.jpg

1956h3223.jpg

1956h3232.jpg

1956h3236.jpg

Images

1956h3459.jpg

1956h3484.jpg

1956h3485.jpg

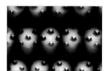
1956h3582.jpg

1956h3598.jpg

1956h3681.jpg

1956h3683.jpg

1956h3686.jpg

1956h3687.jpg

1956h3688.jpg

1956h3789.jpg

1962h0004.jpg

1962h0178.jpg

1962h0416.jpg

1962h0561.jpg

1962h0843.jpg

2039h1007.png

2040h1026.jpg

2040h1127.png

24231676.jpg

Images

24271375.jpg

2489h1001.jpg

2498h1009.png

2502h1032.png

2669h1002.jpg

2672h1031.png

2672h1035.png

2672h1037.png

2672h1046.png

2797h1016.png

2797h1047.png

2799h1023.png

3055h1036.png

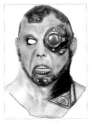
3758h1088.png

3760h1011.jpg

3764h1002.png

3828h1073.png

3834h1078.png

4030h1005.png

4085h1018.jpg

Images

4253h1089.png

4258h1057.png

4274h1010.png

4276h1011.png

4276h1058.jpg

4750h1009.jpg

9580h1024.jpg

9929234.jpg

c067h0048.png

c140h0025.jpg

c141h0038.jpg

c157h0062.jpg

c169h0074.jpg

c214h0033.jpg

c247h0023.png

c275h0001.png

c291h0060.jpg

c294h0076.png

c295h0068.jpg

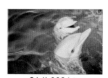

c314h0096.jpg

c364h0054.png

c510h0091.jpg

c541h0070.png

c574h0011.jpg

c574h0018.jpg

c574h0096.jpg

c591h0031.jpg

c658h0009.png

c664h0001.png

c664h0072.png

c703h0092.jpg

c706h0011.jpg

c706h0045.jpg

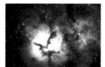

c706h0050.jpg

c758h0038.jpg

c759h0082.png

c771h0080.png

c802h0009.png

c832h0068.jpg

c845h0038.jpg

Images

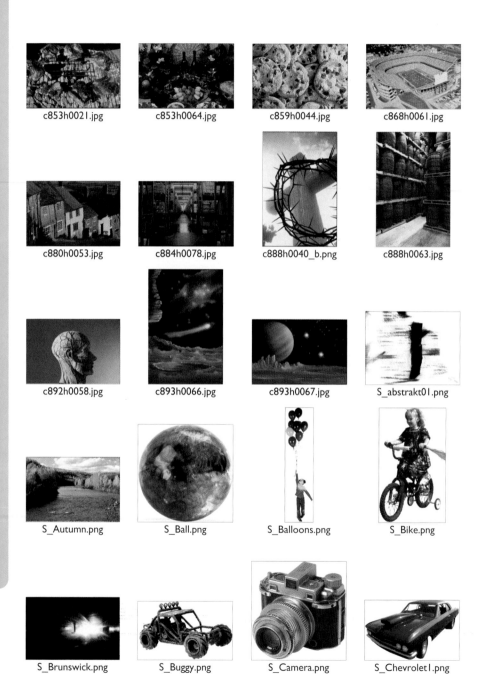

c853h0021.jpg

c853h0064.jpg

c859h0044.jpg

c868h0061.jpg

c880h0053.jpg

c884h0078.jpg

c888h0040_b.png

c888h0063.jpg

c892h0058.jpg

c893h0066.jpg

c893h0067.jpg

S_abstrakt01.png

S_Autumn.png

S_Ball.png

S_Balloons.png

S_Bike.png

S_Brunswick.png

S_Buggy.png

S_Camera.png

S_Chevrolet1.png

Images

S_Chevrolet2.png

S_Cocktail1.png

S_Cocktail2.png

S_Dancer.png

S_Drinks.png

S_Drop.png

S_Family1.png

S_Family2.png

S_Ferrari.png

S_Fist.png

S_Flowers.png

S_Food1.JPG

S_Food2.JPG

S_Hug.png

S_Jack.png

S_Keys.png

S_Lake.png

S_Man.png

S_Martini.png

S_Mobile.png

Images

S_Motocross.png

S_Motorcycle1.png

S_Motorcycle2.png

S_optic.png

S_Paintbrushes.png

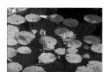
S_Plants.png

S_Present.png

S_Quad.png

S_Quebec.png

S_Rabbit.png

S_Ring.png

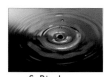
S_Ripple.png

S_Scooter.png

S_Sisters.png

S_Stuff.JPG

S_Sydney.png

S_Typewriter.png

S_Tyre.png

0678h1411.wmf

0678h1421.wmf

0713h0486.wmf

0713h0492.wmf

0713h1047.wmf

0834h0012.jpg

0866h4523.jpg

0867h2592.jpg

0867h2633.jpg

0876h4720.png

0878h6553.jpg

0879h4879.jpg

0881h1659.png

0881h5983.jpg

0881h6198.jpg

0883h1539.jpg

0883h2842.jpg

0890h5973.png

0892h2001.jpg

0894h0019.jpg

Illustrations

0973h0162.wmf

1056h0997.wmf

1063h0063.wmf

1063h0086.wmf

1067h3337.wmf

1068h2777.wmf

1072h6507.wmf

1075h2581.wmf

1075h7181.wmf

1075h7189.wmf

1075h7235.wmf

1075h8089.wmf

1078h2394.wmf

1078h2412.wmf

1078h2440.wmf

1078h2602.wmf

1102h1895.png

1229h0369.wmf

logos_08.png

S_baby1.png

S_baby2.png

S_baby3.png

S_Bottle.png

Fonts 6

Introduction

PagePlus 11 is supplied with a set of typefaces or fonts that can add variety to your design or a little flair to your headlines and flashes. The fonts you have installed on your PC will be previewed and are available to apply to your text objects via the Context Bar when text is selected.

When you install PagePlus 11, a basic set of over 200 fonts is normally included for use with the PagePlus 11 Page Wizards—fonts that Serif's designers have used in the creation of the Design Template documents.

In addition to the basic set of Design Template fonts, PagePlus also offers an optional set of approximately 200 font files on the Resource CD. Browse this chapter of the Resource Guide to preview and choose fonts that you wish to use, and then follow the steps below to install the fonts onto your PC:

1.   Insert your PagePlus 11 Resource CD.
2.   Choose **Start/Settings/...** and double-click the **Fonts** control panel.
3.   Choose **File/Install New Font**.
4.   In the **Drives** list, select the CD drive containing the PagePlus Resource CD and browse to the Program Files\Serif\Fonts\Optional folder in the Folders view.
5.   Select the fonts to install. To select more than one font, hold down the Control key on your keyboard and click each font with your mouse.
6.   Make sure the **Copy fonts to the Fonts folder** check box is selected then click **OK** to install the fonts.

This chapter is separated into two sections—the first previews the basic set of fonts installed with PagePlus and the second previews the optional fonts, which can be installed as outlined above.

Basic Fonts

Basic Fonts

Accent SF — Acce.ttf

The quick brown fox jumps over the lazy dog

Accord Heavy SF Bold — Accoh.ttf

The quick brown fox jumps over the lazy dog

Accord Light SF — Accol.ttf

The quick brown fox jumps over the lazy dog

Accord SF — Acco.ttf

The quick brown fox jumps over the lazy dog

Adamsky Outline SF — Admo.ttf

The quick brown fox jumps over the lazy dog

Adamsky SF — Adma.ttf

The quick brown fox jumps over the lazy dog

Adventurer Black SF — Adve.ttf

The quick brown fox jumps over the lazy dog

Adventurer Light SF — advlit.ttf

The quick brown fox jumps over the lazy dog

Ancestory SF — yosh.ttf

The quick brown fox jumps over the lazy dog

Annie BTN — Anniebtn.ttf

The quick brown fox jumps over the lazy dog

Arch Normal — arch___r.ttf

The quick brown fox jumps over the lazy dog

BacktalkSerif BTN — Backse__.ttf

The quick brown fox jumps over the lazy dog

Basic Sans Heavy SF Bold — saclb.ttf

The quick brown fox jumps over the lazy dog

Basic Fonts

Basic Sans Light SF — sacl.ttf
The quick brown fox jumps over the lazy dog

Basic Sans SF — sang.ttf
The quick brown fox jumps over the lazy dog

Bernstein SF — Bern.ttf
The quick brown fox jumps over the lazy dog

Blippo Light SF — roun.ttf
The quick brown fox jumps over the lazy dog

Blue Ridge Heavy SF Bold — denvh.ttf
The quick brown fox jumps over the lazy dog

Blue Ridge Light SF — denvl.ttf
The quick brown fox jumps over the lazy dog

Blue Ridge SF — denv.ttf
The quick brown fox jumps over the lazy dog

Blur Normal — blur___r.ttf
The quick brown fox jumps over the lazy dog

Bolts SF — Bolt.ttf
The quick brown fox jumps over the lazy dog

BruceOldStyle BT Roman — TT0965M_.TTF
The quick brown fox jumps over the lazy dog

Cairo SF — egyp.ttf
The quick brown fox jumps over the lazy dog

Candy Buzz BTN — Candbb__.ttf
The quick brown fox jumps over the lazy dog

Candy Square BTN Striped — Candsbst.ttf
The quick brown fox jumps over the lazy dog

Casablanca Heavy SF Bold — csabh.ttf
The quick brown fox jumps over the lazy dog

Basic Fonts

Casablanca Light SF — Csabl.ttf

The quick brown fox jumps over the lazy dog

Casablanca SF — csab.ttf

The quick brown fox jumps over the lazy dog

Caslon Bd BT — tt0443m_.ttf

The quick brown fox jumps over the lazy dog

Casper Light SF — caadl.ttf

The quick brown fox jumps over the lazy dog

Casper Open SF — cato.ttf

The quick brown fox jumps over the lazy dog

Casper SF — caad.ttf

The quick brown fox jumps over the lazy dog

CentSchbook BT Roman — tt0083m_.ttf

The quick brown fox jumps over the lazy dog

Chanson Heavy SF Bold — chalb.ttf

The quick brown fox jumps over the lazy dog

Cinema Gothic BTN Inline — Cinegbin.ttf

THE QUICK BROWN FOX JUMPS OVER THE LAZY DOG

Cinema Gothic BTN Shadow — Cinegbsh.ttf

THE QUICK BROWN FOX JUMPS OVER THE LAZY DOG

Clarity Gothic SF — cleg.ttf

The quick brown fox jumps over the lazy dog

Combat Ready BTN — Combrb__.ttf

The quick brown fox jumps over the lazy dog

Commerce SF Bold — city.ttf

The quick brown fox jumps over the lazy dog

Basic Fonts

ConcursoItalian BTN Bold — Concibb_.ttf
THE QUICK BROWN FOX JUMPS OVER THE LAZY DOG

ConcursoModerne BTN Lt — Concmbl_.ttf
THE QUICK BROWN FOX JUMPS OVER THE LAZY DOG

Copa Sharp BTN Bold — Copasbb_.ttf
The quick brown fox jumps over the lazy dog

CopprplGoth BT Roman — tt0420m_.ttf
THE QUICK BROWN FOX JUMPS OVER THE LAZY DOG

Crazy Girlz Blond BTN — Crazgbl_.ttf
The quick brown fox jumps over the lazy Dog

Crazy Loot BTN Inline — Crazlbin.ttf
THE QUICK BROWN FOX JUMPS OVER THE LAZY DOG

Dark Half BTN — Darkb____.ttf
The quick brown fox jumps over the lazy dog

Delta Italic — delta__i.ttf
THE QUICK BROWN FOX JUMPS OVER THE LAZY DOG

Diamond SF — diam.ttf
The quick brown fox jumps over the lazy dog

DomCasual BT — tt0604m_.ttf
The quick brown fox jumps over the lazy dog

Dragline BTN Dm — Dragbd__.ttf
The quick brown fox jumps over the lazy dog

Egyptian710 BT — TT0883M_.TTF
The quick brown fox jumps over the lazy dog

Elementary Heavy SF Bold — vwagh.ttf
The quick brown fox jumps over the lazy dog

Basic Fonts

Elementary SF — vwag.ttf
The quick brown fox jumps over the lazy dog

Elementary SF Black — elmhv.ttf
❄ ≋ ♏ ☐◆✣♏& ♌☐☐◻◆▪ ⚡☐☒ &⛢◆○☐◆
☐❖♏☐ ◆≋♏ ●☊⌘☐⌂ ♎☐♑

Embassy BT — TT0588M_.TTF
The quick brown fox jumps over the lazy dog

English157 BT — TT0840M_.TTF
The quick brown fox jumps over the lazy dog

Estelle Black SF — este.ttf
The quick brown fox jumps over the lazy dog

Excalibur SF — pald.ttf
The quick brown fox jumps over the lazy dog

Firenze SF — flot.ttf
The quick brown fox jumps over the lazy dog

Folio XBd BT Extra Bold — tt0853m_.ttf
The quick brown fox jumps over the lazy dog

Formal436 BT — TT1141M_.TTF
The quick brown fox jumps over the lazy dog

Freehand575 BT — TT1046M_.TTF
The quick brown fox jumps over the lazy dog

Freehand591 BT — TT1043M_.TTF
The quick brown fox jumps over the lazy dog

Gothic720 BT Roman — TT0993M_.TTF
The quick brown fox jumps over the lazy dog

Gothic720 Lt BT Light — TT0991M_.TTF
The quick brown fox jumps over the lazy dog

GothicNo13 BT — TT0120M_.TTF
The quick brown fox jumps over the lazy dog

Basic Fonts

Goudita Heavy SF — Bold goith.ttf

The quick brown fox jumps over the lazy dog

Goudita Light SF — goitl.ttf

The quick brown fox jumps over the lazy dog

Goudita Sans Heavy SF — Bold glawh.ttf

The quick brown fox jumps over the lazy dog

Goudita Sans Light SF — glawl.ttf

The quick brown fox jumps over the lazy dog

Goudita SF — goit.ttf

The quick brown fox jumps over the lazy dog

GoudyHandtooled BT — tt1053m_.ttf

The quick brown fox jumps over the lazy dog

Grenoble Heavy SF — Bold Grenh.ttf

The quick brown fox jumps over the lazy dog

Grenoble Light SF — Grenl.ttf

The quick brown fox jumps over the lazy dog

Grenoble SF — Gren.ttf

The quick brown fox jumps over the lazy dog

Handscript SF — cosc.ttf

The quick brown fox jumps over the lazy dog

Holiday Springs BTN Quill — Holisbq_.ttf

The quick brown fox jumps over the lazy dog

Humanst521 BT Roman — TT0290M_.TTF

The quick brown fox jumps over the lazy dog

Imperial BT Roman — TT0352M_.TTF

The quick brown fox jumps over the lazy dog

Impress BT — TT0209M_.TTF

The quick brown fox jumps over the lazy dog

Industrial736 BT Roman — TT1047M_.TTF

The quick brown fox jumps over the lazy dog

Invers SF — inve.ttf
The quick brown fox jumps over the lazy dog

Invite Engraved SF — hansb.ttf
THE QUICK BROWN FOX JUMPS OVER THE
LAZY DOG

Invite SF — hans.ttf
The quick brown fox jumps over the lazy
dog

Jagger SF — rols.ttf
The quick brown fox jumps over the lazy
dog

Jersey Normal — jerse__r.ttf
THE QUICK BROWN FOX JUMPS OVER THE LAZY DOG

Lapidary333 Blk BT Black — TT1052M_.TTF
The quick brown fox jumps over the lazy dog

Life BT Roman — TT0954M_.TTF
The quick brown fox jumps over the lazy dog

Liffey Script SF — baln.ttf
The quick brown fox jumps over the lazy dog

Lydian BT Roman — TT0841M_.TTF
The quick brown fox jumps over the lazy dog

Mackintosh SF — orga.ttf
THE QUICK BROWN FOX JUMPS OVER THE LAZY DOG

MattAntique BT Italic — TT1015M_.TTF
The quick brown fox jumps over the lazy dog

Minimal SF — orni.ttf
The quick brown fox jumps over the lazy dog

Mister Sirloin BTN Rare — Mistsbr_.ttf
THE QUICK BROWN FOX JUMPS OVER THE LAZY DOG

Basic Fonts

Monterey BT — TT0982M_.TTF
The quick brown fox jumps over the lazy dog

Mr Big SF — Mrbg.ttf
The quick brown fox jumps over the lazy dog

Napa Heavy SF Bold — napoh.ttf
The quick brown fox jumps over the lazy dog

Napa SF — napo.ttf
The quick brown fox jumps over the lazy dog

Native Normal — nativ__r.ttf
THE QUICK BROWN FOX JUMPS OVER THE LAZY DOG

Opera SF — sydn.ttf
The quick brown fox jumps over the lazy dog

Pagoda SF — nipd.ttf
The quick brown fox jumps over the lazy dog

Parisian BT — TT1064M_.TTF
The quick brown fox jumps over the lazy dog

ParkAvenue BT — TT0362M_.TTF
The quick brown fox jumps over the lazy dog

Piranesi It BT — TT0592M_.TTF
The quick brown fox jumps over the lazy dog

Plakette 4 SF — plk4.TTF
The quick brown fox jumps over the lazy dog

Plakette 5 SF — plk5.TTF
The quick brown fox jumps over the lazy dog

Prisoner SF — digi.ttf
The quick brown fox jumps over the lazy dog

PTBarnum BT — TT0720M_.TTF
The quick brown fox jumps over the lazy dog

Basic Fonts

Register Serif BTN SC Oblique — Regisbso.ttf
THE QUICK BROWN FOX JUMPS OVER THE LAZY DOG

Roller World BTN Bold Out — Rollwbo_.ttf
THE QUICK BROWN FOX JUMPS OVER THE LAZY DOG

Romana BT Roman — TT0896M_.TTF
The quick brown fox jumps over the lazy dog

Salsa Mangos BTN Lt — Salsmbl_.ttf
The quick brown fox jumps over the lazy dog

Seabird Heavy SF Bold — seagh.ttf
The quick brown fox jumps over the lazy dog

Seabird Light SF — seagl.ttf
The quick brown fox jumps over the lazy dog

Seabird SF — seag.ttf
The quick brown fox jumps over the lazy dog

Sliver Normal — slive__r.ttf
The quick brown fox jumps over the lazy dog

Smarty Pants BTN Bold — Smarpbb_.ttf
The quick brown fox jumps over the lazy dog

Smashed SF — smash.ttf
The quick brown fox jumps over the lazy dog

Sneakerhead BTN Shadow — Sneabs__.ttf
The quick brown fox jumps over the lazy dog

Sprint SF — sprn.ttf
The quick brown fox jumps over the lazy dog

Sprocket BT — TT1244M_.TTF
The quick brown fox jumps over the lazy dog

Staccato555 BT — TT1153M_.TTF
The quick brown fox jumps over the lazy dog

Basic Fonts

Stylistic SF — ente.ttf

THE QUICK BROWN FOX JUMPS OVER THE LAZY DOG

Sugarskin BTN Bold — Sugabb___.ttf

The quick brown fox jumps over the lazy dog

Super Black SF — Superb.ttf

The quick brown fox jumps over the lazy dog

Swis721 BT Roman — TT0003M_.TTF

The quick brown fox jumps over the lazy dog

Tennessee Heavy SF Bold — nashh.ttf

The quick brown fox jumps over the lazy dog

Tennessee Light SF — nashl.ttf

The quick brown fox jumps over the lazy dog

Tennessee SF — nash.ttf

The quick brown fox jumps over the lazy dog

Toledo SF — tole.ttf

The quick brown fox jumps over the lazy dog

Tropicali Script BTN Bamboo — Tropsb___.ttf

The quick brown fox jumps over the lazy dog

Troutkings BTN — Troub____.ttf

The quick brown fox jumps over the lazy dog

Unknown Caller BTN SC Bold — Unkcscb_.ttf

THE QUICK BROWN FOX JUMPS OVER THE LAZY DOG

VAGRounded BT — TT0756M_.TTF

The quick brown fox jumps over the lazy dog

Ultra Serif SF — corn.ttf

The quick brown fox jumps over the lazy dog

Verdict SF — veri.ttf

The quick brown fox jumps over the lazy dog

Basic Fonts

WeddingText BT — TT0985M_.TTF
The quick brown fox jumps over the lazy dog

Wicker SF — wici.ttf
The quick brown fox jumps over the lazy dog

Xpress Heavy SF Bold — exprh.ttf
The quick brown fox jumps over the lazy dog

Xpress SF — expr.ttf
The quick brown fox jumps over the lazy dog

Zanzibar SF — sigv.ttf
The quick brown fox jumps over the lazy dog

Zap Normal — zap_____r.ttf
THE QUICK BROWN FOX JUMPS OVER THE LAZY
DOG

ZapfHumnst Ult BT Ultra — TT0136M_.TTF
The quick brown fox jumps over the lazy dog

Zolano Sans BTN — Zolsab__.ttf
The quick brown fox jumps over the lazy dog

Zolano Serif BTN Bold — Zolasbb_.ttf
The quick brown fox jumps over the lazy dog

Optional Fonts

Arch-Condensed Normal — arch__cr.ttf

The quick brown fox jumps over the lazy dog

Archer Normal — arche__r.ttf

THE QUICK BROWN FOX JUMPS OVER THE LAZY DOG

Arch-Extended Normal — arch__er.ttf

The quick brown fox jumps over the lazy dog

Beeswax Normal — beesw__r.ttf

THE QUICK BROWN FOX JUMPS OVER THE LAZY DOG

Blur-Condensed Normal — blur__cr.ttf

The quick brown fox jumps over the lazy dog

Blur-Extended Normal — blur__er.ttf

The quick brown fox jumps over the lazy dog

Bunting 1 Normal — bunt1__r.ttf

THE QUICK BROWN FOX JUMPS OVER THE LAZY DOG

Bunting 1-Condensed Normal — bunt1_cr.ttf

THE QUICK BROWN FOX JUMPS OVER THE LAZY DOG

Bunting 1-Extended Normal — bunt1_er.ttf

THE QUICK BROWN FOX JUMPS OVER THE LAZY DOG

Bunting 2-Condensed Normal — bunt2_cr.ttf

THE QUICK BROWN FOX JUMPS OVER THE LAZY DOG

Bunting 2-Extended Normal — bunt2_er.ttf

THE QUICK BROWN FOX JUMPS OVER THE LAZY DOG

Catchup Normal — catch__r.ttf

The quick brown fox jumps over the lazy dog

Celtic Bold — celti__b.ttf

the QUICK BROWN fox JUMPS oveR the LaZy OOg

Chisel-Hollow Normal — chi_h__r.ttf

The quick brown fox jumps over the lazy dog

Chisel-Spiked Normal — chi_s__r.ttf

The quick brown fox jumps over the lazy dog

Chisel-Spiked-Condensed Normal — chi_s_cr.ttf

The quick brown fox jumps over the lazy dog

Chisel-Spiked-Extended Normal — chi_s_er.ttf

The quick brown fox jumps over the lazy dog

Chisel-Striped Normal — chi_x__r.ttf

The quick brown fox jumps over the lazy dog

Chocolate Normal — choco__r.ttf

THE QUICK BROWN FOX JUMPS OVER THE LAZY DOG

Chocolate-Condensed Normal — choco_cr.ttf

THE QUICK BROWN FOX JUMPS OVER THE LAZY DOG

Creepy Normal — creep__r.ttf

THE QUICK BROWN FOX JUMPS OVER THE LAZY DOG

Creepy Hollow Normal — cre_h__r.ttf

THE QUICK BROWN FOX JUMPS OVER THE LAZY DOG

Creepy Hollow-Condensed Normal — cre_h_cr.ttf

THE QUICK BROWN FOX JUMPS OVER THE LAZY DOG

Creepy Hollow-Extended Normal — cre_h_er.ttf

THE QUICK BROWN FOX JUMPS OVER THE LAZY DOG

Optional Fonts

Creepy-Condensed Normal — creep_cr.ttf

THE QUICK BROWN FOX JUMPS OVER THE LAZY DOG

Creepy-Extended Normal — creep_er.ttf

THE QUICK BROWN FOX JUMPS OVER THE LAZY DOG

Crest Normal — crest__r.ttf

The quick brown fox jumps over the lazy dog

Dingbats1 — dingb1_r.ttf

[dingbat glyphs]

Dingbats2 — dingb2_r.ttf

[dingbat glyphs]

Dingbats3 — dingb3_r.ttf

[dingbat glyphs]

Dingbats4 — dingb4_r.ttf

[dingbat glyphs]

Dingbats5 — dingb5_r.ttf

[dingbat glyphs]

Drips Normal — drips__r.ttf

THE QUICK BROWN FOX JUMPS OVER THE LAZY DOG

Drips-Condensed Normal — drips_cr.ttf

THE QUICK BROWN FOX JUMPS OVER THE LAZY DOG

Drips-Extended Normal — drips_er.ttf

THE QUICK BROWN FOX JUMPS OVER THE LAZY DOG

Eddy's Bones Normal — edbon__r.ttf

THE QUICK BROWN FOX JUMPS OVER THE LAZY DOG

Fanzee Normal — fanze__r.ttf

THE QUICK BROWN FOX JUMPS OVER THE LAZY DOG

Fanzee-Condensed Normal — fanze_cr.ttf

THE QUICK BROWN FOX JUMPS OVER THE LAZY DOG

Fanzee-Extended Normal — fanze_er.ttf

THE QUICK BROWN FOX JUMPS OVER THE LAZY DOG

Fatso Normal — fatso__r.ttf

THE QUICK BROWN FOX JUMPS OVER THE LAZY DOG

Fatso-Condensed Normal — fatso_cr.ttf

THE QUICK BROWN FOX JUMPS OVER THE LAZY DOG

Fin Normal — fin____r.ttf

The quick brown fox jumps over the lazy dog

Fin-CondensedNormal — fin___cr.ttf

The quick brown fox jumps over the lazy dog

Fin-ExtendedNormal — fin___er.ttf

The quick brown fox jumps over the lazy dog

FlowerPower Normal — flpow__r.ttf

The QUICK BROWN FOX JUMPS OVER THE LAZY DOG

FlowerPowerCondensed Normal — flpow_cr.ttf

The QUICK BROWN FOX JUMPS OVER THE LAZY DOG

FlowerPowerExtended Normal — flpow_er.ttf

The QUICK BROWN FOX JUMPS OVER THE LAZY DOG

Frantic Normal — frant__r.ttf

The quick brown fox jumps over the lazy dog

Optional Fonts

Frantic-Condensed Normal — frant_cr.ttf

The quick brown fox jumps over the lazy dog

Frantic-Extended Normal — frant_er.ttf

The quick brown fox jumps over the lazy dog

Gothic Normal — gothi__r.ttf

The quick brown fox jumps over the lazy dog

Gothic 32 Normal — got32__r.ttf

The quick brown fox jumps over the lazy dog

Gothic 32-Condensed Normal — got32_cr.ttf

The quick brown fox jumps over the lazy dog

Gothic 57 Normal — got57__r.ttf

The quick brown fox jumps over the lazy dog

Gothic 57-Condensed Normal — got57_cr.ttf

The quick brown fox jumps over the lazy dog

Gothic-Condensed Normal — gothi_cr.ttf

The quick brown fox jumps over the lazy dog

Gothic-Extended Normal — gothi_er.ttf

The quick brown fox jumps over the lazy dog

Greek Normal — greek__r.ttf

Τηε θυιχκ βροων φοξ φυμπσ οϖερ τηε λαζψ δογ

Gregory Normal — grego__r.ttf

The quick brown fox jumps over the lazy dog

Gregory-Condensed Normal — grego_cr.ttf

The quick brown fox jumps over the lazy dog

Gremlin Solid — greml__s.ttf

THE QUICK BROWN FOX JUMPS OVER THE LAZY DOG

Groovey-Cracked Normal — gro_c__r.ttf

The quick brown fox jumps over the lazy dog

Groovy Normal — groov__r.ttf

The quick brown fox jumps over the lazy dog

Groovy-Condensed Normal — groov_cr.ttf
The quick brown fox jumps over the lazy dog

Groovy-Extended Normal — groov_er.ttf
The quick brown fox jumps over the lazy dog

HotStuff Normal — hotst__r.ttf
The quick brown fox jumps over the lazy dog

HotStuff-Condensed — hotst_cr.ttf
The quick brown fox jumps over the lazy dog

HotStuff-ExtendedNormal — hotst_er.ttf
The quick brown fox jumps over the lazy dog

Initial Caps 3 Normal — icap3__r.ttf
THE QUICK BROWN FOX JUMPS OVER THE LAZY DOG

Initial-Caps1 Normal — icap1__r.ttf
THE QUICK BROWN FOX JUMPS OVER THE LAZY DOG

InitialCaps4 Normal — icap4__r.ttf
THE QUICK BROWN FOX JUMPS OVER THE LAZY DOG

Ironwork Normal — ironw__r.ttf
THE QUICK BROWN FOX JUMPS OVER THE LAZY DOG

Jazz Normal — jazz____r.ttf
THE QUICK BROWN FOX JUMPS OVER THE LAZY DOG

Jersey-Condensed Normal — jerse_cr.ttf
THE QUICK BROWN FOX JUMPS OVER THE LAZY DOG

Jersey-Extended Normal — jerse_er.ttf
THE QUICK BROWN FOX JUMPS OVER THE LAZY DOG

Jitter Normal — jitte__r.ttf
THE QUICK BROWN FOX JUMPS OVER THE LAZY DOG

Jitter-Condensed Normal — jitte_cr.ttf
THE QUICK BROWN FOX JUMPS OVER THE LAZY DOG

Optional Fonts

Jitter-Expanded Normal — jitte_er.ttf

THE QUICK BROWN FOX JUMPS OVER THE LAZY DOG

Keycaps 1 Normal — keycaps1.ttf

Keycaps 2 Normal — keycaps2.ttf

Keystone Normal — keyst__r.ttf

Magoo Normal — magoo__r.ttf

The quick brown fox jumps over the lazy dog

Magoo-Condensed Normal — magoo_cr.ttf

The quick brown fox jumps over the lazy dog

Magoo-Extended Normal — magoo_er.ttf

The quick brown fox jumps over the lazy dog

Neonz Normal — neonz__r.ttf

THE QUICK BROWN FOX JUMPS OVER THE LAZY DOG

Neonz-Condensed Normal — neonz_cr.ttf

THE QUICK BROWN FOX JUMPS OVER THE LAZY DOG

Neonz-Extended Normal — neonz_er.ttf

THE QUICK BROWN FOX JUMPS OVER THE LAZY DOG

Norman Normal — norma__r.ttf

The quick brown fox jumps over the lazy dog

Norman-Condensed Normal — norma_cr.ttf

The quick brown fox jumps over the lazy dog

Norman-Extended Normal — norma_er.ttf

The quick BROWN FOX JUMPS OVER the LAZY DOG

Notes Normal — notes__r.ttf

∞♩♫ ♩♪♩ ♩♭♩ ♫ f ♪ ⌐ jumps ♪♪♫ ▦♫♪ ♩♫ D.S.

Optical A Normal — opta____r.ttf

The quick brown fox jumps over the lazy dog

Optical B Normal — optb____r.ttf

The quick brown fox jumps over the lazy dog

Optical C Normal — optc____r.ttf

The quick brown fox jumps over the lazy dog

Orient2 Normal — orie2__r.ttf

THE QUICK BROWN FOX JUMPS OVER THE LAZY DOG

Orient2-Condensed Normal — orie2_cr.ttf

THE QUICK BROWN FOX JUMPS OVER THE LAZY DOG

Orient2-Extended Normal — orie2_er.ttf

THE QUICK BROWN FOX JUMPS OVER THE LAZY DOG

Primer-Spiked Normal — prim_s_r.ttf

The quick brown fox jumps over the lazy dog

Ransom Normal — ranso__r.ttf

The quick brown fox jumps over the lazy dog

Shade Normal — shade__r.ttf

THE QUICK BROWN FOX JUMPS OVER THE LAZY DOG

Optional Fonts

Shadow Normal — shado__r.ttf

THE QUICK BROWN FOX JUMPS OVER THE LAZY DOG

Shalom Normal — shalo__r.ttf

THE QUICK BROWN FOX JUMPS OVER THE LAZY DOG

Signs Normal — signs__r.ttf

Slasher Normal — slash__r.ttf

The quick brown fox jumps over the lazy dog

Snow Caps Normal — snow___r.ttf

THE QUICK BROWN FOX JUMPS OVER THE LAZY DOG

Snow Caps-Condensed Normal — snow__cr.ttf

THE QUICK BROWN FOX JUMPS OVER THE LAZY DOG

Snow Caps-Extended Normal — snow__er.ttf

THE QUICK BROWN FOX JUMPS OVER THE LAZY DOG

Stars Normal — stars__r.ttf

the quick brown fox jumps over the lazy dog

Type Keys Normal — typek__r.ttf

THE QUICK BROWN FOX JUMPS OVER THE LAZY DOG

Typecase Normal — typec__r.ttf

The quick brown fox jumps over the lazy dog

Wampum Normal — wampu__r.ttf

THE QUICK BROWN FOX JUMPS OVER THE LAZY DOG

Wampum-Condensed Normal — wampu_cr.ttf

THE QUICK BROWN FOX JUMPS OVER THE LAZY DOG

Wampum-Extended — wampu_er.ttf

THE QUICK BROWN FOX JUMPS OVER THE LAZY DOG

Woodcut Normal — woodc__r.ttf

The quick brown fox jumps over the lazy dog

Woodcut-Condensed — woodc_cr.ttf

The quick brown fox jumps over the lazy dog

Woodcut-Cracked — woo_c__r.ttf

The quick brown fox jumps over the lazy dog

Woodcut-Extended — woodc_er.ttf

The quick brown fox jumps over the lazy dog

Notes

Notes

Notes

Notes

Notes

ISBN 978-1-906471-12-5